"The book grabs the reader by its clear straight writing, and moves along as a flowing narrative. A topic that could be dense and heavy becomes a page turner. Even sophisticated professionals can relate to the freshness of observations and the attempts to work through puzzles that change a life after brain injury."

—**Leonard Diller**, PhD, Professor of Rehabilitation Medicine, New York University School of Medicine and Director of Psychology, Rusk Institute of Rehabilitation Medicine

"'Mild Traumatic Brain Injury' is a pervasive, somewhat invisible, and grossly misunderstood disability that affects many, many members of the population who suffer for lack of credible information . . . *Remind Me* provides that information in a clear, entertaining and vital manner."

—**Sol Mogerman**, MSc Registered Clinical Counsellor, author of *Objects in Mirror Are Closer Than They Appear (Inside Brain Injury)*

"Diana Lund's book is an insightful, sensitive and very personal account of the effects of her 'mild' brain injury. She has an entertaining and witty writing style that takes the reader inside her altered cognitive abilities and personal relationships. Unlike many personal accounts that focus on the initial trauma and acute rehabilitation process, Diana relates a very different experience. Her traumatic brain injury was not initially diagnosed, she was not hospitalized, and treatment for her cognitive challenges was delayed and inadequate. As a single, independent, intellectually-gifted career woman, she was unprepared and confounded by the changes in her relationships and ability to work in the corporate environment. Her story highlights the importance of accurate diagnosis, workplace accommodations, cognitive remediation and emotional support. It is essential reading for clinicians, families, and counselors."

—**Marilyn Lash**, MSW, Partner, Lash and Associates Publishing/ Training, Inc.

Remind Me Why I'm Here

Remind Me Why I'm Here

✦

Sifting through Sudden Loss of
Memory and Judgment

Diana Lund

People with Disabilities Press Series
Stanley D. Klein, PhD, Series Editor

iUniverse, Inc.
New York Lincoln Shanghai

Remind Me Why I'm Here
Sifting through Sudden Loss of Memory and Judgment

iUniverse books may be ordered through booksellers or by contacting:

iUniverse
2021 Pine Lake Road, Suite 100
Lincoln, NE 68512
www.iuniverse.com
1-800-Authors (1-800-288-4677)

Photographer: David Watts
Front Cover Designers: Diana Lund and Heather Mair
Labyrinth created by: Lake Forest Garden Club
Permission to take cover photo: Courtesy of Lake Forest Hospital, Lake Forest, IL
(no event mentioned in this book took place at Lake Forest Hospital)

ISBN-13: 978-0-595-38351-1
ISBN-10: 0-595-38351-3

Printed in the United States of America

This book offers no individual advice on how to treat a brain injury and defers such decisions to your network of doctors and therapists. Unlike other injuries, each case is remarkably different and requires competent professional opinion. This book is only tailored to the author's individual case and may provide ideas to discuss with your curative team. Neither the author nor People with Disabilities Press Series nor iUniverse are liable or responsible for the results from the execution of ideas from this book.

To protect the privacy of others, some of the names have been changed.

Dedicated to all who live through the lens of brain injury

May the mysteries of brain injury clarify in plain view
and we shall know ourselves.

Contents

Part III   A Change of Season

Part IV   Just Deal

Part V   Death and Life

Foreword

A number of books have been published in recent years by survivors of traumatic brain injury. Because these books have been written by persons who are endowed with the talent for writing about their thoughts and experiences in an extraordinarily clear and articulate manner, such first-person narratives have significantly enriched the literature in our field. They provide us with a window into the inner, subjective world of persons with brain injury, chronicling their arduous personal journeys from dysfunction, perplexity, and despair, through compensation, and ultimately, to the voluntary acceptance (by these remarkable individuals) of the limitations that have been imposed by their head injuries, and to the finding of meaning in their life. One common element in these books is that the authors emerge without an embittered outlook on life even though one would expect that feelings of victimization are apt to engender the opposite attitude.

Readers can find two distinct types of such first-person accounts: those involving cognitive treatment and those without such intervention. An excellent example of the first type is the book written by Claudia Osborn (*Over My Head*: Andrews McMeel Publishing, 2000), which describes her experiences as a trainee in an intensive day program of neuropsychological rehabilitation. Then there are books of the second type—such as Sol Mogerman's *Objects in Mirror Are Closer Than They Appear* (People with Disabilities Press Series at iUniverse, Inc., 2001), or P. J. Long's *Gifts from the Broken Jar* (Equilibrium Press, 2004), and now Diana Lund's book. The astonishing thing about these second-type memoirs is that their authors provide us with lucid, step-by-step descriptions of their struggle toward a reconstituted sense of self, and that they have accomplished this remarkable psychological transformation without the benefit of help from professionals trained in specific remedial rehabilitation for the brain injury population. They "did it" with the help of wise, trusted and supportive people who were "there" for them to help guide them to self-examination.

Subjective accounts are not only moving, but, as in this case, they provide data which cannot be ignored by clinicians. They also provide clues for the scientific development of clinical intervention procedures from the ground up.

Ms. Lund's superbly written book offers us a number of questions worthy of contemplation: What combination of cognitive and personality characteristics will help one individual to emerge from the battle and regain one's personal identity? Could we identify the critical "moments" when persons (endowed with the desirable characteristics) turn away from despair and confusion to embark on the road toward self-acceptance? If we could identify these critical attributes, could we systematically intervene remedially to foster them and thereby ensure the ultimate success of such persons?

Remind Me Why I'm Here should be compulsory reading for students as well as experienced neuropsychologists, neurologists, psychiatrists, and other specialists who provide services to those who have sustained life-altering brain injuries—nurses, neuro-ophthalmologists, psychologists, physical therapists, occupational therapists, recreational therapists, case managers, social workers. Furthermore, survivors, and their families and friends will find edification and solace in this book.

Yehuda Ben-Yishay, PhD
Professor of Clinical Rehabilitation Medicine
New York University School of Medicine
Director, Brain Injury Day Treatment Program
Rusk Institute of Rehabilitation Medicine

New York, January 23, 2006

Preface

In between puffs on his pipe, he turns to look directly into my eyes, but I am not facing him. The person who plays my sister nudges me and points with her eyes and head toward him.

"Huh?" I mutter, then realize I am supposed to look at the person who plays my father, not into space. I focus my eyes on him. He asks, "And what, pray tell, do you intend to do with your life?"

"Oh, Mother," I start. "Uhm, Father," I correct. "Now is not the time for—" I have forgotten what time it is not and glance at my "sister" to see if she remembers the rest of my line.

"The time to decide," my sister whispers under her breath.

"The time to decide," I repeat as I lift the sides of my cumbersome hoop skirt and begin to walk stage left. Then, I flip-flop to walk stage right and trip, a little trip, on the lip of the area rug.

"Perhaps, my dear Winnie," my father pauses and I twirl around to face him, the hoop skirt orbiting around my legs, "I shall sign you up for the circus." He and my sister exit the faux living room stage. In the dead center of the set, I collapse into a heap, sitting with the back of my arm against my forehead and giggle. The lighting dims and fog envelops me. Stage hands rush in to swap out the set.

When the lights brighten and the fog dissipates, I am now wearing an acrobat's leotard, hanging upside down on a trapeze high above the stage. Unsteadily the bar is lowered, shifting me from side to side, and I fight to stay connected. People gasp. The bar levels. The audience hushes. How did I get here? Why am I here? What am I supposed to do? I start to swing back and forth since that seems a natural activity when you find yourself exposed in the spotlight, all eyes fixated on you.

For a rocky four-year period, from 1996 until 1999, I was like the actress who played the role of Winnie. I didn't remember my real life's lines or the motivation for my personality or where I was supposed to stand. When I was thirty-six years old, I was in a car accident which damaged my brain. I have mild traumatic brain injury.

While playing my part, I hadn't noticed much—neither the who, the where, the what, nor the physical detail. Confusion reigned. I repeatedly found myself in quirky situations, and in public, people snickered at my goofy or improper actions. While looking for a bookstore, I wound up in the wrong campus building on the backstage of a live college play. The script hadn't called for a woman bundled up in a down coat, hat, scarf, and gloves. At the end of many scenes, I was the last person on stage, chuckling inappropriately under muddy lighting and an ensuing fog. I saw only haze. When the fog settled, I awoke in a different scene trying again to get my bearings on a stage that seemed to pitch, roll and yaw.

My strange behavior was not due to the medication since I rarely took any. It was not caused by alcohol; after the accident, I stopped drinking (which only had amounted to a couple glasses of wine a month). My experience was purely a result of the brain injury.

Discovering that I was ill started slowly. In the first week I noticed unusual things happening to me. Instinctively, I wrote down the strange occurrences on loose pieces of paper. After a month had passed and my life continued to hoodwink me, I bought a notebook to record the events: misplacing items, walking into walls, mistaking a stranger for my mother. Months turned into a year, then two, then three. I recorded my life as a brain-injured woman and philosophized throughout the journey.

As I discovered, this subject is not well documented by actual patients since brain injury robs our memories, initiative, organization and vocabularies; and medications haze our already murky minds.

We have been at the mercy and the ignorance of those with well intentions who write about us. But they are not us and can only guess what goes on inside our heads. They guess because we have trouble communicating. They guess and don't even realize that they are conjecturing because their guess is a reflex; such a basic assumption about human nature, the premise is not even questioned. These guesses are usually filtered through how their own brains work. These guesses have sometimes steered them away from the truth about brain-injured people and ultimately, the truth about their own brains.

Having lived in both worlds, I transparently see the pitfalls. I am lucky to be able to describe them. My circumstance could have been frighteningly different.

I know people with brain injury who have gotten worse and those who are not capable of independent living. I know people with Alzheimer's disease and fibromyalgia who slip away more each day. They are witnesses to their own slow demise until, I imagine, they are so far gone that they no longer comprehend themselves. In contrast, after the first year, I had comfort in knowing that I had weathered the worst as long as I did not get a second brain injury. I held hope of improvement because I saw improvement. Eventually I figured out that my original purpose and identity no longer existed and began to work on disconnecting some of the wires configured to create the old me. Today I am remade.

Fortunately, I have recovered enough skills to write a book. I have clear-enough days now and am organized again. References abound: journal entries, doctors' records, legal testimony, witness accounts and some memories—particularly the emotionally-charged memories—remain. Most importantly, I have learned how to look through the opaqueness of brain injury to recover what most reliably happened.

Still, each day in front of my computer I struggle to factually relate the details of my story. Some memories are untrustworthy. From my office chair I type, "I felt sore" and the next day I correct, "I felt stiff and numb. Yet, I told others that I was sore because these were the words that came to mind to describe knowing I was hurt." During a detail-mining walk I have remembered that I felt like a spirit without a body in that time period and didn't feel much of anything. Another day while lying awake in bed I recount an event from memory and then discover that I can't "remember" any specific qualities beyond what are in my journal. My memory is not of the event, but from reading my journal many times. On a different day, while staring out a dining room window, unnervingly, my brain fabricates details. From pondering, I depict my cousin's stone house. But when I visit her afterward, I discover that her house is made of wood and its shape looks different from my image's structure.

All writers struggle with nebulous memories; brain injury guarantees that I consistently do so.

Accordingly, I've had to become a sleuth to find out what transpired during the months after the accident. When I don't recall a doctor's visit, I read the doctor's notes and find that he'd asked me thirty questions and recorded my answers. When my memory of a restaurant's location is obviously false—why did my brain fill in an erroneous detail?—I ask my friend where we had dined. When my journal informs me that a Christmas tree stood in my living room, I deduce that I must have shopped for a Christmas tree that year even though I can't recollect doing so. To write my story, I spend half of my time reconstructing the most likely specifics.

As uncertain as I am about the details, I exude confidence in my recollection of the emotional landscape. I alternated, sometimes like dyed hair and other times like colored disco lights, between white indifference, effervescent yellow happiness, howling blue sadness and bursting red anger all while inside a cloud of bewilderment. I know and remember clearly how the stages of brain injury feel. In fact, to recount some occasions, emotional memory is all I possess.

The injury's impacts on episode remembrance affect the act of writing as well. Half concentrating, I scribe, "her eyes were forward and slightly upward," when I meant to write, "her nose was forward and slightly upward." Or I pen, "I did not contact a disease" when I meant "contract a disease." Unable to hold onto information, I unlearn research I've once understood, I forget what I have already written, and I neglect to double-check a fact.

Besides my shaky short-term memory, my English skills have changed as well. My tongue used to curl when classmates wrote run-on sentences. More than any other indicator, I'd thought disorganized ideas and babble represented the measure of an uneducated man. Once thorough in conceptualization and impeccable in grammar and spelling, now I struggle with transitions, dangling participles, and that telling rambling text.

I've had to master how to get around my disabilities. To compensate for dim recall, I read references over and over again, trying to force something to stick. Because I don't multi-task well, to edit, I reread my piece several times, each time looking for a specific error or two. I rely on an editor to catch what I have missed. She doesn't complain, but she sure finds a lot of repeated words, misplaced apostrophes, and unrelated thoughts.

But those flubs are not as scary as the day a writing teacher returned one of my stories, a chapter from this book, with notes, "describe her," "any more details about him or description?" and "be more descriptive." Searching my memory for specifics, I found that I couldn't dig up any more information. This worried me. At that time I'd completed the first draft of my book. Rereading the sketchy pages, I realized, like my brain's recordings, the entire work lacked physical description. What author writes a whole book without any character descriptions? How was I going to get around this one? Just the other day I met up with a business acquaintance whom I'd met three times before. I'd thought she was white. But no, she was black.

On the other hand, my disabilities also help me. Editing does not feel repetitive, even on the twentieth time through the same story. Because I forget that I've already written a story, with ease I write it another way, hopefully a better way. Because the emotion of an event sticks out in my mind stronger than the details, vibrant metaphors pop out with regularity. I'll take the pluses where I can find them.

In weak moments, like retelling a dream unsure of its content, I find it difficult to believe that the first year of my brain-injured life actually occurred. But then I remind myself about my daily recordings, physicians' copious notes, eyewitness testimonials, reams of person-to-person accounts on the habits of brain-injured people and some dead-true memories. I've had to rely on all of these sources to make my words as valid as possible. However, my mind is tricky and may have left in some boners.

So why even attempt to write this book? Partly I write for personal reasons—to discover what really happened to me and who I became. My journal, written simply and one-dimensionally, does not answer many of my retrospective questions. Why wasn't more done for me medically? Why didn't people take me more seriously? Why did I fail in so many previously successful areas of life?

Another part of me writes for the brain-injured community. My motivation is best explained via a dream I had, which, that morning, I wrote on a slip of paper.

> I am on a college campus, some college campus I've never been to before, with towering trees and crisscrossing walkways and stately buildings. Perhaps it is an Ivy League school. I am purposefully walking to a campus building, but not to go to class.
>
> In the lobby the walls have dark wood paneling with large rectangular cutouts. I sit in a red leather tall-backed armchair at a round dark wood table. A tiered crystal chandelier hangs overhead. Some students are seated with me at the table and others are just passing through.
>
> Suddenly, the doors close and lock. The chandelier shakes and the walls recede. The prisoners of the room shriek chaotically; however, I feel calm. Brain injury has taught me to expect the unexpected and to remain open in the realm of the bizarre.
>
> A disembodied voice from above speaks to us: "You have all had a debilitating illness and rebounded toward health. You are light. Go back into the world and do good."

Since I was allowed to return to this universe, despite a car crash that damaged my brain and ruined who I'd been, I feel a driving purpose to explain my journey. I must help others because I have known their confusion, their helplessness, their despair, and have burst through it and into the clear. What kind of person would I be if I didn't attempt to share the lessons from my suffering? With all that I have learned, what use is it kept inside of me? One thing I know for sure: brain-injured people are smart when it comes to understanding other brain-injured people.

My desire is that the brain injured and their families can pick up what to expect from this injury sooner than I did. Comprehending the beast is no small undertaking. Mild traumatic brain injury hides in the recesses and controls the show. At times the raucous invader masquerades as a cordial invited guest. It has many layers that combine in a factorial of ways, and this makes it hard to locate the culprits. It is a master of illusion and elusiveness. But once you nail its schema to the wall, some degree of management becomes possible which in turn alleviates some of the suffering.

But I write my story too for even grander reasons. Most everyone at some point in their life will face abrupt change, or experience a loss of control or torment in some profound way.

As I came out of the haze, I began to see farther than brain injury. I discovered holes in my belief system and how wrong I was about understanding others' capabilities and motives—erroneous thinking created by my healthy brain. That thinking was a result of experiencing life through only one type of brain. I want people to understand and care more about their brains than they currently do. Then maybe they will understand more about each other, such as what it means to be human, and love and compassion will blossom.

I offer a glimpse into the first year of my journey (the upcoming sequel will condense eight years of brain injury and learning). My former brain would not have believed my own story just as other uninjured brains have been skeptical. All I ask is that you read with an open mind. This is my memoir, based loosely on memory. This story is bigger than me.

Acknowledgments

This book would not have been possible without my loyal and eagle-eyed editor Mary Lewis. Writing guru Michael McColly taught me how to weave emotion into a story and Sandra Wisenberg improved my grammar.

Many thanks to my writing group: John Sweeney, Linda Gartz, Diane Nititham and Roberta Dillon, whose advice and ideas have guided my stories toward blossom. And thanks to those friends—Tina, Heather and Dave—who took a peek at the first draft and pointed me toward the professionals.

My gratitude to the writers before me whose books inspired and became shining lanterns on my path: first and foremost—Floyd Skloot, Elizabeth Cohen, Beverley Bryant, Claudia Osborn, Nancy Mairs and Caroline Knapp.

Marilyn Lash and Stan Klein, you took a chance on a new author and showed me the way. I'm indebted. Phil Whitmarsh, you were always professional and efficient with my project. Barrie Fromme, always the courteous host.

To my relatives who have experienced brain injury—Tony, Boots, Lil, Tom, and Gary—I now understand some of what you are going through. Keep fighting, and give in some and let others help you.

Joanne, Rick, Tina, Steve and Mark kept me going no matter how big the physical or emotional hurdles. Without them, I would not be in this place in my heart today.

Mom and Dad, thank you for doing your best to raise me.

Dave, you're a true partner who keeps it interesting every day. Your patience with my deficits and support for this project have meant the world to me.

Grateful acknowledgment is made to the following for permission to reprint previously published material:

Hansard Reporting and Interpretation Services: Excerpt from "Standing Committee on Justice and Social Policy," Legislative Assembly of Ontario, by Hansard Reporting and Interpretation Services on June 4, 2002 (http://www.ontla.on.ca/hansard/committee_debates/37-parl/Session3/justice/J001.htm). Reprinted by permission of Hansard Reporting and Interpretation Services.

Chapter Layout

Each chapter has a title, a time frame, a feeling and a quote in its heading. The time frame refers to how much time has elapsed since the accident. For example, "first week" means the events in the chapter take place during the first week after the accident. The feeling in the heading indicates the general mood of the chapter as does the quote. All opening quotes not in italics are the author's.

PART I
An Odd Discovery

1

Sandwiched

DAY ONE
HYSTERICAL

For every action there is an equal and opposite reaction.
—Newton's Third Law of Motion

My plummet from grace was like being sucked into a tunnel of light at the speed of light, disintegrating my clothes, my skin, my matter. Just as fast, the source spat me out through another hole of pure shine, shuffling atoms and patting me back together. I landed on my butt and wondered, *Hey, what just happened here?* I'd plunged out of favor with the universe.

The Preceding Years

I lived an ordinary life with a bright mind. Ranked in the top echelon of my salary level at a computer software company, my brain was always working—solving problems, mulling over others' statements, rethinking decisions while engaged in the moment. While I was asking someone if her baby was still teething, I was wondering why John, normally talkative, had remained so quiet in the meeting. Or, I was figuring out the simplest and most efficient way to track subcontractor issues. My brain, nanoseconds-fast, sped steps ahead of most others' and steps ahead of my tongue. I would slur my speech, skip words, or talk rapidly in chase of my ticker tape of thoughts. My pace exhausted some of my listeners. Occasionally they requested that I slow down or repeat myself. Slowing the tempo was hard to do because the thoughts would "get away." Except on the difficult questions, like determining if a new field should be added to the problem tracking form. Then, I paused to quickly run through the options—Did we already collect

3

this information? How had other divisions within the company solved this problem? Could the problem tracking tool be customized in this fashion? What effect would this change have on the tens of other software tools? to the existing company processes? "No," I'd say, "the impact to the company outweighs the need. This is how you can get around that problem." People said that they could see the wheels turning in my head during these brief pauses.

Outside of work, I played sports nearly every day and had a full and satisfying social calendar. Near day's end, to shut down the internal voice, I exercised, watched mindless TV, or wrote down my thoughts so I could stop thinking them. In sleep, my brain processed in double time, ten-hut to multiple dreams a night, sometimes solving the day's remaining problems. Each morning, my day dawned with a dream review to pick out revelations for the day ahead. To learn, to think, to grow. That was what I lived for. That was how I lived the first life.

The Switch-Over

Transformation would occur in an instant; injected into my soul, an imposter would slip quietly and insidiously into me and associate my face to uncharacteristic clumsy, dim-witted, and emotional acts. From one body I would live two lives, one right after the other, and my recollection of having lived these lives would be clearer than others' murky memories of past incarnations. Once I knew, really knew two me's, I could unravel and then reconstruct my beliefs about illness, intelligence, God, friendship, perception, judgment, prejudice and alcohol. I'd be able to write about my changed views well before I could discuss them clearly.

Anybody's day can include driving to work, to the store, to a movie—nothing seemingly unsafe, until BAM, the driver is reissued a life of struggle. A car accident which results in brain injury happens to somebody in the US every 42 seconds.

What befell in an instant would take years to disentangle.

Smashed in an Instant

In my head I've replayed this chilly spring day many times. A frozen icicle of a memory that doesn't melt or grow, as fresh as yesterday, I always begin the sequence with the missed alarm.

Two days after Daylight Saving Time (DST) began, I slept right through the 5:30 A.M. DST alarm. It wasn't until 6:30 A.M. DST, 5:30 A.M. in the old time, when I shot out of bed. While I sprinted through my morning routine, the uncommon setback irked me. Leaving late would put me in the heart of rush hour traffic and arriving late would impact my crammed schedule.

On the run, I grabbed my purse, briefcase and keys, flew out my back door and locked it. While I bounded down my back steps, I clicked my remote to unlock the doors to my car. Without missing a beat, I flung open the car door, jumped into the driver's seat, and tossed my armload onto the seat next to me. Every move I made was the most efficient.

As I backed out of the last driveway on a dead-end street in a western Chicago suburb, I turned on the heat and the radio. The DJ announced that it was 7:00 A.M. After I put my car in drive, I buckled my seat belt, flipped my mirror from night vision to day vision, and moved my purse and briefcase from the front seat to the floor behind me.

On a three-lane local road north of my hometown, I found myself in a new traffic pattern. Vehicles clogged the roadway, backed up for a mile due to a freight train which had recently chugged through the intersection. Because of a stop light on the other side of the tracks, traffic pulsed stop-and-go.

An omniscient driver, I usually watched the motorists around me for anything untoward. I gave aggressive and weaving drivers extra berth and did not proceed on green until I was certain the cross traffic had stopped. During the first stop of the stop-and-go pattern, I watched in my rear view mirror to check that the driver behind me noticed we were stopping. He did. I repeated the same routine on the next stop. *Okay*, I thought, *he gets the stop-and-go rhythm.* Lulled into calmness about being in an unforeseeable stop scenario, I no longer looked in my mirror.

Once more the traffic sped forward. This time there was a longer stretch of "go" where the cars reached the 35 m.p.h. speed limit and beyond in a rush to be on their way. Again, a line of cars stopped ahead of me. At the bottom of a small hill I eased my car to a stop, a car length behind the car ahead, and waited to go.

WWWWHHHHAAAAAMMMMMMMMM***! It was the loudest noise I'd ever heard: metal hitting metal, metal crushing, glass smashing, plastic cracking. It seemed to blare continuously for minutes. The only visual I had during the accident was one snapshot inside the cab of my car when the seat belt clicked and caught me from hitting the windshield and steering wheel: both hands on the steering wheel, feet off the floor, one shoulder held back by the seat belt, and hips bent forward. Snapshots, even action photos, do not show motion. My visual recall of the crash does not include movement of me, my car, or anything inside of my car.

My next moment of recall was a dazed feeling, like waking up from a deep sleep, my mind straddling two worlds. Information came in slowly: debris scattered across the road, oncoming traffic at a standstill, the car behind me nearly sideways to the road. *Oh, right, I've been in a car accident.*

As the news sank in, my concern grew that I was blocking traffic. I looked to my right and spotted a dead-end side street. I turned to look at the driver behind me and asked him, via hand signals, if we should move the cars to the side street. I interpreted his return signals to mean that he agreed. Then, we drove our damaged cars to the designated area.

Once at a point of safety, I glanced at the front of my body. No blood. I pronounced myself fit and then broke out into uncontrollable crying. My whole body shook. My chest heaved in and out as I wailed in short breaths. Strange. I didn't know why I was crying.

I was not prone to cry and did not rattle easily. Twenty years ago I had remained cool when I was driving my mother's car 40 m.p.h. over a four-lane bridge and the hood flew up. There were cars in front of me, on my side and behind me. The bridge did not have a shoulder. Inside the car, my mother and sister frantically shouted. Instead of stopping on the bridge, I decided that it was safer to keep driving until the shoulder reappeared. I could see just enough through a slit of light at the bottom of the windshield and could look out the side windows to judge how close I was to the edge of the bridge and side traffic. I had steely composure for a teenager with only a driver's permit.

My mom, the poet, trained me well. Her nose forward and slightly upward, she once said of her devotion to the artistic life, "I don't have a practical bone in my body." Her lack of practical bones created a dependence on me to be the practical one. I rescued her from situations that she wasn't aware she was in. Simple situations, like overcharges for merchandise. And complicated situations, like when the policeman in a Mexican border town wanted a sexual favor from her in exchange for removing the Denver Boot from the wheel of our rental car. And life-threatening situations, like when I discovered a problem with the brakes on her car. Later, the mechanic confirmed, one week more, and the brakes would have completely gone out. I always looked out to protect her and in the process, learned to protect and problem solve for myself. Under duress, she got emotional and I got rational.

I had turned remaining-the-sane-one-amid-crisis into a profession. As a project manager, I managed risk. People contacted me daily to solve problems that got big. Because of my experience in getting the unknown under control in a non-emotional way and in bringing a stabilizing influence to a mediation, my reaction to the accident baffled me. The accident was minor, I had not been hurt, but, I was crying. My observant/problem solving mind kicked in, as was my custom: I first attacked a problem by reframing it. Instead of asking, *Why was I crying?*, the only question I could settle on, and one I couldn't quite answer, was, *Could this be me?*

I don't know how long I cried or how long I pondered my emotional reaction. Time took on an eerie quality of not being what it seemed. In the next flash of awareness, my car door was open and someone was stooped next to me, asking me if I was all right. My social grace kicked in. I stopped sobbing, and put on the face that I was together and none worse from the experience. My answer sufficient for him, he got into his car and left. Calmer, I noticed a third car parked on the side street. The two other drivers were out of their cars, and I joined them.

"How are you?"

"Okay," I guardedly responded. "How are you?"

"Okay." While a tumble of words fell from his mouth, I noticed his glassy eyes. At some point he gave, "I was adjusting my mirror," as the reason for the crash.

Someone spit out a surprising fact: the accident had involved *four* cars. A Jeep Cherokee rear ended an Infiniti G20 which rear ended a Buick Regal which rear ended a fourth car. A straight-line collision. To my horror, I learned that I, in the G20, had hit the car ahead of me. That would explain why my front end was smashed, but, for some reason, I wasn't even curious about the damage.

The driver who caused the chain reaction, construction-worker muscular, talked about his company car. He said he wanted the company to take care of his injured vehicle and to give him a new one. Then, he wouldn't have to deal with this mess. Later, his irresponsibility and callousness would gnaw on me. He would be able to walk away from an event that he had caused while my life would change, become difficult, with no option to walk away, and no choice over having been put in this predicament in the first place. This day, however, I felt no tempest—only irritation. I thought I was in a fender-bender, notwithstanding the evidence. The Cherokee had bled out its electric-green antifreeze guts which pooled underneath the SUV. The smashed headlights and taillights of three cars littered the road. And there were serious car dents and creases that would take thousands of dollars to fix.

In our circle of the shaken, neither I nor the balding third driver had a cell phone to call the police. Reluctantly, the muscle man volunteered to make the call and then slunk off to his own vehicle.

"You know the man who spoke to you at your car?" the third driver asked.

"Yes," I responded.

"Well, he was driving the car that I hit."

He was? I thought my mystery man was an innocent witness who rushed in to help me, not a victim himself.

He continued, "He is a teacher and had to leave to teach a class. The damage to his car was minimal."

"How do you know all this?"

"I spoke with him before he spoke with you."

You did? I thought that my mystery man had spoken *only* to me. Yet, the third driver seemed to know what he was talking about, so I believed him.

As we waited, another vehicle drove up. This man had been in a car accident where the other driver drove off. Over the phone the police told him that our accident had priority over his, which was when he decided to meet the police at our accident site.

At one point, I retrieved my briefcase from my car, took out a pen, paper and my car insurance card, and then set my briefcase on top of my car's trunk. As I walked back to the group, the other accident victim reminded, "Don't forget to put your briefcase in your car."

"I won't."

We exchanged names, addresses, phone numbers and insurance data. The wait seemed interminable. The longer I stood, the colder and stiffer I became. I continued talking, having less to say, putting up appearances, covering over the state of shock that I did not know I was in.

By the time the police arrived, what must have been forty-five minutes later, I was cold to the core. The police asked if I needed an ambulance. I declined for several reasons. First, an ambulance seemed unnecessary for someone who wasn't bleeding. I wasn't even sure if my sore and stiff neck and shoulder warranted professional medical care, so certainly I didn't need immediate paramedic care. Secondly, I feared hospital tests, shots and lethal mistakes; my second-hand experiences taught me that hospital procedures were potentially uncomfortable, potentially painful, and in some cases, when a nurse administers the wrong drug, potentially deadly. If I had a choice, I wasn't about to be a patient in a hospital without a familiar hand to hold and someone on my side to oversee my care. Lastly, I felt guilty about being absent from work for what I perceived to be minor injuries. Taking an ambulance would unduly delay my return to the office. I added to my statement to the officer, "I have a sore and stiff neck and shoulder."

Next, the officer wanted minimal information on the accident, which took about five minutes to explain. He thoroughly examined each vehicle for damage and then took each of our licenses and registration cards. We retreated to our respective cars while the policeman wrote up the accident. I turned on the heat full blast.

The policeman, who must have thought I had the worst injuries, gave me the accident report first and sent me on my way with an instruction to go to a doctor. This solved my internal debate: *I should do what the policeman said. I shouldn't go to work until after I have gone to a doctor.* I headed home first so that I could use my phone to make arrangements.

While I drove off, I heard a tap on the window. It was the other accident victim. He retrieved my briefcase that I had left on the trunk of my car and scolded, "I told you not to forget this." I drove the three miles home in a banged-up car—smashed headlights, smashed taillights, trunk frozen part way open, crumpled accordion back end, dented front end, creased cab—with no recollection of how I got there.

Once home, I called work to let them know what had happened and that I would need the day off. Then, I called my best friend Tina, my biggest emotional supporter. I felt fine, I told her, my car was damaged but I was not concerned about replacing it, and my biggest upsets were the arrogance of the man who'd hit me and the accident's impact on my busy work schedule.

Clearly, I was a work-focused individual. This trait would soon fade away.

An hour later I hung up with Tina and called my boyfriend Rick. He listened to my whiplash symptoms, which, by this time, included a massively swollen neck. He instructed me to ice my neck since I had not thought to do so. The best doctor to handle my case, he said, would be his neurologist, whom he later found out was unavailable. Alternatively, Rick made an appointment for me with a pain care specialist at the same office and rearranged his work schedule so that he could drive me to the clinic in the afternoon.

Rick must have arrived at my house with a worried face, and he must have hugged me and told me that he loved me. He must have tried to make me comfortable. That was his nature. We had been dating exclusively for over a year and were considering marriage and having kids, building an extended family with his two sons from a previous marriage. We were both athletic, socially active, optimistic and a bit too strong-willed. All I can remember after talking to Rick on the phone is sitting in the doctor's waiting room with him.

The receptionist handed me a stack of "new patient" forms to fill out before I could be seen by the doctor. Unable to read or respond to the forms, I asked Rick to fill them out for me. Instead of reacting with alarm to sudden illiteracy, I logged it as too-much-happened-today, unable-to-concentrate.

When Rick got to the part requiring a signature, he began to recite, "I understand and agree that health and accident policies are an arrangement between an insurance carrier and myself. Furthermore, I understand that—"

"Stop," I snapped, "Just give me the forms and I'll sign them." I could not understand what he was reading to me.

"Sign here."

I signed.

"And here."

I signed.

"And here."

I signed.

The signed papers would later allow the medical group to put a lien on my house when I failed to pay my bill in a timely fashion.

The doctor diagnosed me with whiplash, gave me a foam neck brace and wrote a prescription for a non-steroidal anti-inflammatory drug and a muscle relaxant. She also wrote a note to excuse me from work for a week.

Back at my house, Rick examined my car. On my rear bumper he spotted an imprint—the reverse image of the Jeep Cherokee's license number. Unable to move my neck, because it was swollen in place and wouldn't budge in its brace, I moved my eyes to the pointed spot.

License number on rear bumper.

His lanky body folded in a squat, he pointed out that the sharp edge at the bottom of the wheel well was slanted up, dangerously close to the tire.

Don't drive unsafe car.

Then he tried to open my trunk, but it was frozen in place.

Trunk stuck.

Sometime early in the night, I fell asleep.

This is where my memory for detail completely fails me and only my memory of residual feelings remains. From my imagination I conjure an emotionally true account about the dreams I had that night.

There she lies soundly sleeping, alone, on her queen bed. What she values most in her life is gone. Now it is time to tell her. Tonight will be our last chance, for she is slipping away fast. We need to make it stick. Make this be the last idea that sticks in her head; she won't know its full meaning for a long time.

I take a triple braided rope, methodically wrap the right end around the right hand and the left end around the left hand, and then pull tight. The rope vibrates from my tug. My accomplice slides on black gloves, draws a whip out of his holster and cracks its tail in the air. Another of my thugs plugs his electrical prod into a twenty-foot extension cord. There is no off switch. The Menace needs no props. He will use his bare hands. We huddle close. Grimaces and snarling faces illuminate crimson from the light of the hot cattle prod.

I, the overbearing Strangler, along with Whipping Dog, uncoiled, the luminescent Electri-Fryer and the maniacal Menace are here to work over the sleeping Queen. Quickly we infiltrate her mind's barrier and deliberately terrorize her beyond repair.

"It's time to wake up, my Pret-tee," the Strangler taunts. "Say hello to your worst Nightmares. Ever."

My eyelids sprang wide open. Revealed: I had been in a *serious* car accident. Over and over and over again, I imagined the ferocity of the crash's force and the insignificance of my strength while in its grip. The sense of touch eluded me. I rocketed in air like a rag doll hurled forward and then jerked back by her apron strings. I shuddered: had I not been belted, I might have died.

Strangely, I also felt like the luckiest girl around. I had escaped with my life.

2

Dazed

I'd always thought that shock was measured in hours; my body shock would last days and I would not discover that I was in shock until I was out of shock.

Two days after the accident, I was getting ready for bed, putting toothpaste on my toothbrush when I foggily noticed I was fumbling. I wondered why and then realized I was only using my left hand. Confused, I looked down at my usually dominant right arm to find it snug against my body, sling-like, my hand curled in a fist. I was temporarily startled. *This is my arm? It's hog-tied! I guess that I've been scrunched like this for the last couple of days. Hey, I must have been left-handed for the last couple of days!*

That first week there were other clues that I was in a fugue.

Clue 2: I found an empty laundry basket in a strange spot (I do not recall where, only that the basket wasn't where I'd usually kept it), which prompted me to go to my laundry room and open my washing machine. Inside, I discovered wet, rotting clothes. I must have started a load and then forgotten about it.

Clue 3: Rick called me at home. He was surprised, but relieved, to find me there. I couldn't understand his confusion because he knew I was stationed at home resting my injured body. He told me I had paged him, which I had not remembered doing, and that I had left my work phone number, not my home number, on his pager. My telephone number error, novel for me, had confused Rick into thinking that I had gone to work against doctor's orders.

Clue 4: Remembering to take my prescription pills was accidental with the sight of the pill bottle my reminder. My ritual started by reading the doctor's directions: *Take this medicine with a snack or a small meal.* I ate, and when finished, I wondered why I had eaten when I had not felt hungry. The link of food to the pills was forgotten.

Clue 5: When I picked up my phone handset to make a call, my line was dead. A search of my house uncovered another phone on the same line with its handset laying belly-up, the electronic leash broken. I must have forgotten to hang up the phone at the end of my last call. Friends later asked me why they couldn't contact me.

Clue 6: My own cleanliness was suspect. After some showers, my hair was still grimy, like I had forgotten to wash it.

These strange happenstances amused me, and I did what came natural. A list maker by habit—daily adding new items, crossing off completed items, and reprioritizing—I spontaneously recorded the oddities on a list:

Clue 7: Filling out checks wrong and even from wrong checkbook.

Clue 8: Putting cats on front porch and forgetting.

Clue 9: Hard to ride in car (things coming at me)—exhausts me.

What seems bizarre to me now is not the absentmindedness or the disorientation, but the self-observational content of the Forgetfulness list. Before, I had listed my top twenty to thirty ideas and to-dos, like these:

- Computer programming solution: use recursion.

- Process documents' key: build a hierarchy of documents from general to specific and interlock.

- Add hook in subcontractor quality plan for configuration management naming convention.

- Fix car: squeaky brakes, sun roof leaks during a hard rain, cruise control broke.

My quirky behavior matched my quirky perceptions. When food was flaming while I sat on a couch in the living room, I could not discern the burning smell. Only after a smoke alarm screeched or smoke streamed into the room, did I rush into the kitchen and find that I'd been cooking dinner. A black hardened substance in a red hot pan remained. Dinner would be a banana and yogurt. If I had been steaming a vegetable, dinner would have become charcoal-flavored broccoli. It really didn't matter. I could barely taste my food anyway.

I lost my sense that I was touching something and felt little pain. More than anything else, I felt stiff and numb. Yet, I told others that I was sore because these were the words that came to mind to describe knowing I was hurt. I should have been in a heap of pain; my neck looked enormous.

The lack of pain was more than numbness. I did not control my body. Indeed, my arm and hand moved to brush my teeth and I signaled my body to make this action. It felt, though, like my body moved on its own, separate from me. I hovered above at various distances and watched once in a while.

My eyes watered excessively and were sensitive to light and motion. My focus drifted in and out, and I could not tell how far away an object was. I walked directly into walls, not that I noticed, bumping my shoulder while trying to thread myself through the doorway. I walked into bushes, eyes wide open, a branch poking my eyeball with not even a precursive blink. The more my brain tired, the worse my vision became.

With my corrupted senses, I perceived the world perversely.

Stepping outside was like stepping off a plane that had landed in Tahiti—so lush, so tropical, so different from anything I'd known before. Yet, my "Northern tip of Tahiti" had mutated. Broken off from the original island, "Tahiti North" floated through the Bermuda Triangle and picked up my group, the Lost People, who christened the land The Tip of Madness and Confusion. I opened my back door to exceedingly bright sunlight, vibrant colors (as if switched from shades of gray to Technicolor), and exotic birds. All of the birds' songs blended into one muffled yet loud sound. I stood on the back porch landing, stunned by sensory overload, unsure if I wanted to venture forth.

Eventually, I tried to sit outside because it was a nice-weather day, the fresh air would be good for me, and I had time off from work. But the cacophony, the harsh light, the darting insects, squirrels and birds, the swaying willow branches and telephone wires, and the flapping leaves overwhelmed me. I swore my squinted eyes saw known stationary objects waving. My brain could not process the multiple incoming data streams and in an all-circuits-blown panic, my flight response kicked in. As if running for cover from a B-2 bomber, except I couldn't run, I retreated with urgency. More of a mental scamper than a physical one, I leaned against the side of my house for balance, inched along the perimeter, up the stairs, and then inside for silence, darkness, stillness and rest.

Inside wasn't exactly peaceful, only toned down from the outdoors. Each room stimulated me with its varied rich textures, its lighting and color play, its noises and its slight movements of objects. I lived inside a moving, breathing, vocal beast.

I can only think to describe my surreal perceptions with an equally surreal metaphor.

In my kitchen I was inside Daisy Duck and in my living room I was in Goofy. Daisy had see-through breasts and looking out of them, I could tell that she appeared much larger than other birds. Inside, her organs floated on tufts of feathers and her inner skin glistened bright white with pockets of high intensity. Perhaps she was gleaming clean because she drank a lot of water. I heard her muffled gulp and then, approaching water from a distant pipe. Suddenly, water gushed and splashed into her stomach. In the background, a constant buzz told me that her organs were always running. She didn't talk much. I cringed in Daisy; she was too bright and loud. Goofy, on the other hand, looked somber and brooding. If Goofy took off his gloves, you would know what I know from the inside. He has deep crevasses, cracks and pock marks, and yellowed skin. His hands are old. If Goofy took off his shirt, you'd see a sunken chest. And inside his chest he is a mass of red veins going every which way. Unexpectedly, Goofy's organs shook, just briefly, and then rested until the next eruption. Similarly, he spoke in spurts and stops. When he hushed up, though, the living room was womb-like and I felt coddled.

It could take me up to an hour to settle down in there. I sat and stared, and when I wasn't checked out, I was amused. I didn't hallucinate; everything I saw existed albeit with wacky qualities. Sometimes my calico cats, my only roommates, melted into black, orange and white streaks when they raced past. Slowly I came out of my trance, wondered how I got there, and then was ready to do something.

That something did not involve professionally-produced sound or moving pictures. TV and radio were intolerable, especially the commercials, which sparkled and dazzled at the highest intensity. In this age TV flips rapidly between images and frankly, my brain could not keep up—too much information in too little time. Like an African bushman plopped down into a fast-paced indecipherable world, my internal cadence could not align and the external would not wait for me. So, I stepped off the spinning globe and cocooned under the covers of my bed or the blanket on my couch, weaving myself an insular shell with no TV and no radio and no CDs, shades drawn.

When I wasn't bewildered about what I was supposed to be doing, I petted a cat, folded clothes, jotted a quick note, or dusted the room. I came alive in these moments of activity; the sun radiated out from my body and brightened the room's ambience. During other illnesses, a serious infection after wisdom tooth surgery, a bad sprain that required crutches or a bout with pneumonia, I had felt wounded and down. Only when I'd recovered did my dad remark that it was good to see me smile again. In relation to these illnesses, my car-accident after-glow appeared incongruent. But this detail escaped my laissez-faire mind.

During that first week, sensory distortion and deadening compromised the first stage of my memory—registration. Consequently, I never stored the unregistered events in short-term or long-term memory nor could I retrieve them later. Instead of memory, mostly I rely on others' accounts and deduction that repetitive post-accident experiences, like banging my side on doorjambs and finding smelly, wet clothes in my washer, must have occurred during those first seven days.

Despite my sensory impairments, I am amazed I didn't notice that I couldn't run until several weeks after the accident. A previously competent athlete, I used to run every day to play sports or to do simple tasks, such as to get from my house to my garage (a half block). Also, I had stamina. On game day in soccer, I ran for thirty-five minutes straight, took a ten-minute break, and then ran another thirty-five minute half. For more than a year, I wouldn't be capable of running.

From a clearer frame of mind, I can say that taking medicine haphazardly was ineffective; it messed with the pills' timing and limited my intake. A year or two after the accident, I found the pill bottle, my first prescription from the accident—nearly full! At least, that is my faint recollection of the pill discovery. I concluded that I had been too sick to comply with my treatment regimen.

From research, I now know that a figure-ground disturbance, the inability to put one item in the foreground and the rest in the background, is the term to describe the single, blended sound I'd heard. Every bird's tweet carried equal importance, and my brain couldn't dissect the combined melody. Besides hearing, I had also lost my ability to discriminate when seeing, tasting and smelling.

This first week I did not tell my parents about my accident because I didn't want to add unnecessarily to their troubles. My mom was a recently-released patient from a locked ward at a psychiatric hospital. My dad, a Korean War veteran, used alcohol to cope with post traumatic stress and loneliness. I am unclear about why I did not call my only sibling, my sister in Colorado. We talked every month and visited each other two to four times a year. I'm not sure that calling her even crossed my mind. But if it did, I may not have called her because I was the older sister and did not feel comfortable asking her for help.

In my family I was the one who spent the least amount of money, who ate the least amount of food, and, besides my dad, who asked for the least amount of help. While growing up, I clearly understood that spending money was putting my dad in the poorhouse, and asking for help was not appreciated when others were busy or needed more help than I did. In an unconscious way, I learned to expend as few resources as possible. Enlisting my family's help did not feel appropriate or right.

Rick phoned me all week long and would have been with me if the logistics of his life had been different. First and foremost, he was a father with custody of two sons: one nine years old and the other twelve. The kids lived with Rick on school days and every other weekend. Mainly, we had honored Rick's divorce agreement which stipulated that no girlfriend could stay overnight when the kids were there. The one exceptional violation was when I had sprained my ankle and hobbled on crutches. Immediately afterward, Rick's lawyer had warned us that any more breaches of conduct would put winning permanent custody of his kids at risk. So even though Rick wanted to settle me into his guest bedroom again, he wasn't going to disobey the judge and his own lawyer a second time. The other stickler to spending time together was the forty-minute to an hour drive, depending on traffic, between Rick's home and my home, between Rick's office and my home, and between Rick's office and Rick's home—a perfect equilateral triangle, a perfect equilateral headache.

On Friday, the fourth day of injury and the beginning of a child-free weekend, Rick scooped me up and brought me to his house. My blue-eyed nearly six-feet tall rescue man was concerned and expended much effort caring for me both physically and spiritually. Knowing how much I liked to read, about a book a week, he checked out a pile of books I might be interested in. He did a great job on selection—as if I had chosen the books myself. Feeling a little more alert, I tried to read each book. But my vision was blurred, the words moved across the page, and when I could read the words, I found the sentences befuddling. These books I put in the rejected pile; I told Rick, "You can return these to the library. I'm not interested in them." Finally, Faye Resnick's second book about the Nicole Brown Simpson murder, *Shattered: In the Eye of the Storm*, was fittingly the one book I could basically understand in small doses at a time. Simply written, *Shattered* read like her first book, *Nicole Brown Simpson: The Private Diary of a Life Interrupted*, which I'd already read. The media blitz over-familiarized me with the case, so the subject matter was easy to understand.

Rick entertained me further with the card game Cribbage. I rarely played cards because card games did not challenge me; however, Cribbage was a little more challenging and a little more fun than most. On previous occasions, I had counted points without error and merited points from my opponent when he made card counting mistakes. Usually, Rick took too long to make a move and I became bored, anxious or annoyed. These were the reasons he did not enjoy playing Cribbage with me. But in illness, he saw playing a game that I would most likely win as a way to buoy my spirits.

During the game, I found myself playing off of my long-term memory. If I was dealt a standard hand (I had those memorized), with some effort, I recognized it and knew how to play the cards and count the points. If the hand was non-standard, I got confused to the point of tears. Rick jumped to my aid, explained the strategy or point counting, and gave me back points that I had missed instead of claiming them for himself. In frustration, I exposed my cards for more help, completely ruining the round. As the game wore on, my mood plummeted. I quit. The game was above my abilities.

Rick realized that I didn't seem to be myself. However, he did not connect my game playing to a deeper medical problem. Perhaps he thought that I would return to normal when my fatigue and whiplash pain lifted.

Near the end of the day, on Sunday, Rick took me to the grocery store. Once inside we parted ways—he to shop for himself and his kids, and me to fulfill my one-person household needs.

The food on the shelves bamboozled me. Every item screamed at me, "Pick me. Pick me." I could not go straight to the brand that I liked since I couldn't find it. My visual figure-ground disturbance turned the aisle into one of those scribble pictures (or stereograms) where if you stare long enough and at the right spot in a repetitive pattern, a 3-D picture eventually emerges. Staring at the scene didn't help me. I had to narrow my field of vision to only one item to see it properly.

So, I looked at each product on the top shelf, starting at the left and working across, then down a shelf, sometimes taking a box down and trying to read it, sometimes getting so involved with the advertising that I had to own it. I put it in the cart, my brand forgotten, no longer able to choose according to price, need or rational want. At the time, though, I had no idea I was experiencing such inabilities. For lucidity: Here's an encounter I've created based on Rick's pattern of reaction to my irrational selections later on.

Rick finds me in the cereal aisle, his cart fuller than mine, and asks, "Hey, how are we doing?"

"Uh, just looking for cereal," I say.

"Here's your cereal," he remarks as he finds it with ease and puts it into my cart. As his monkey-like arms are in the cart, possibly, he picks up an odd looking box of cereal. "What's this?"

"Oh, uh, I thought I would try something new," I reply. I have put the cereal in my cart because the box has attention-grabbing visuals and wild claims. But I don't know this about myself yet.

"It has too much sugar. You wouldn't eat this."

"Oookay. Uh, put it back then."

"Where did you get it?"

"Uh, I don't know."

Rick puts my selection back on the shelf. I still want to have it.

I needed Rick to find my brands for me. I needed Rick to help me figure out what I needed. I needed Rick to get me in and out of the store in quick measure. I needed. I needed. I needed.

I thought that I needed help because I felt heavy with exhaustion. I used my shopping cart as a brace for my wobbly body and similarly, I could have used toothpicks to prop open my droopy eyelids.

From the store, Rick drove me to my alien-feeling house, unloaded my groceries, and set me up for the night. Shortly after that, he left to take care of his own matters and to be home when his kids returned.

By this time I had figured out three things about myself. My right arm wasn't very useful, my vision was blurry, and I was forgetful. I did not tell anyone about these incapacities because they didn't concern me. I did not think of them as problems.

At home, I spent most of my time resting or sleeping. Lying flat on my back became mandatory after an hour or two of sitting or standing. My body required it. My body required much more sleep too. The first night I slept hours longer than normal, but not until many months later could I sleep straight through the night again. To meet my body's needs, I took on the life of a cat—napping as long as I could, whenever I could.

More than body shock, the problem resided inside of my head where thousands of electrical impulses flashed simultaneously. It felt like my connections were broken; they snaked within my skull like downed wires after a fierce storm. I laid in bed, sparking, with absolutely no thoughts, unable to sleep, no electric company to call to reconnect the lines. Later on I would meet another woman who experienced this electrical brain phenomenon. She labeled it the "vibration," which refers to an electrical vibration or tingling rather than a physical movement. According to dated notes about my symptoms, my brain tingled for at least two months. Since I never wrote down when the tingling stopped, I can only rely on my memory which whispers to me that my brain continued to vibrate for a full year.

In bed by 9 P.M., I sparked until I fell asleep at 1 A.M., woke up at 5 A.M., sparked until I fell asleep at 6 A.M., woke up at 8 A.M. and rolled out of bed at 9 A.M. I alternated between blank wakefulness and mediocre slumber. Dreams no longer visited me. Instead, limbo replaced what had once occupied my nocturnal mind.

3

Beyond Reason

DAY SEVEN
CONFIDENT

People who lose their minds are the last to find out.

Prior to the car accident, I'd possessed many characteristics that an employer likes to have in an employee: punctual—usually early—qualified, efficient, initiatory, organized and thorough. I'd only missed work under the most adverse circumstances; six years was my longest streak without a sick day. Every year I rated in the top percentile range and received good raises. So when a week's absence had passed since the accident, I sensed that I had been gone an eternity.

Over the next several years, this would be the second to last time that I would feel time pressing down on me. Quickly, I was losing the fourth dimension and traveling toward the timeless zone where only "now" held palpable meaning. Blind to my condition, I deemed myself more than ready to return to my job.

The twenty-two mile drive to work in my other car felt like a virtual-reality driving game with the scenery whizzing past. It appeared as if the road signs, the trees, and the buildings were going to bombard my car. The white lines on the road sped at me with velocity and I found it difficult to stay in the center of my lane. Still an icon of safety, I was strapped in tight for my white-knuckled "Indy 22" ride.

I used to drive to work in a specific pattern, switching lanes at about the same points, taking the most efficient way there. My best guess is that I stuck to my habit and took the same route I'd always taken. However, I was unable to adhere to my driving pattern. Switching lanes was not manageable because my head would not turn and I was unable to keep track of the other vehicles. Cars mysteriously appeared in my field of vision and then popped out like magician David

Copperfield and his assistants. So much was happening around me that I had no time to check my mirrors. My new objective was survival. I became a slow-lane driver, attempting to change lanes only if absolutely necessary. Judging from my later recognition that I drove like a grandmother, that first day back I must have been the slowest driver puttering along the eight-lane divided expressway.

I motored to a four-story building in a high tech corridor close to the express-way, parked in the front lot, and headed to my second-floor office in the middle of the building. The walk from the front door of the building to my office normally took me about seven minutes, but this day I must have taken longer. Usually speedy, I plodded and uncharacteristically rode the elevator up one floor.

A typical work day was packed from beginning to end. As a project manager of a multi-country, multi-company computer software development, I was responsible for overseeing the execution of select contracts, worth millions. Daily, I attended three to five hours of meetings; led one-third of those meetings; read from thirty to one hundred e-mails; returned ten to twenty phone calls; talked to the stream of people who showed up at my cubicle; wrote proposals, plans and process documents; and created some computer programs on the side. With my finger on the pulse of the projects, I reacted quickly to issues and motivated others to fix the problems. I had a core set of friends, about fifteen people, whom I visited in my spare moments or over lunch. In the last month or so, I had spent little time with my work friends because I was too busy as a key player in an upcoming quality audit by an outside firm. The division was looking at our team to pull off a high rating and the pressure was intense. In particular, my promotion hung on the results.

I liked my job, my coworkers, and the fast pace. I didn't like company politics, the results of company politics, or those endlessly repeated company phrases that homogenized employees. After five years with the corporation, I felt more positively about the company than negatively and envisioned myself working there for many more years.

On Monday mornings, my boss expected me to send out a series of reports to a hundred or so people. I had automated the bulk of the work, boiling my part down to updating a couple of files, running one computer command (to create the reports), printing the reports, and sending out e-mail to an alias. My tight schedule demanded that I give myself fifteen minutes to complete this simple task. But the first Monday back, I toiled over the reports for half a day. Other work seemed harder and took longer to produce. I spent an hour writing this e-mail about my absence:

Safety tips coming from a recent car accident victim:

1. Wear your seat belt with the shoulder strap over your shoulder. . . . A better design would be to have both shoulders held back.

2. The postion of the headrest in your car will play a part in the extent of damage to your spine. . . . I had arranged my headrest to the proper postiion prior to the accident. . . .

3. Buy a car that is designed to withstand a collision.

4. If you see in your rear view mirror that you will inevitably be rear-ended, the best thing to do is to brace yourself against the back of your seat. This advice came from my doctor who sees a lot of car accident injuries. . . .

On me, I have been improving with each day and expect to recover fully. . . . I am still groggy and not fully functioning so I will only be focusing on high priority items.

Obviously, I could still compose a coherent letter. Yet, a few items alarm me now. *Position* is mistyped, twice, and obviously wrong. In the past I was an impeccable speller/typist and spent the extra effort to send out information with no misspellings. I proofread the letter several times more than usual and missed the error with each read. Secondly, I announced to my hundred-person alias that I could not do my job. The pre-accident, more politically astute me would have focused their attention on what I *could* do for them. I used to choose my words carefully because I had witnessed how such slip-ups resulted in lowered standings and demotions. In response to my flub, my best work friend at the Austin, Texas site eloquently wrote, "If you're not 'fully functioning' yet, may be best to stay away from those high priority items." I quizzically reread that statement a couple times, not fully comprehending the implication.

Absent for a week, a contact point for every section leader on a complicated and time-strapped project, my electronic mailbox was jammed. I tried to read my e-mail, but I couldn't squeeze sense out of the bulk of it. Ingeniously, I created a pile I labeled *Items I Will Get to Later*. I tried working on assignments, but instead, I also sent these to *Items I Will Get to Later*.

All day long my body urged me to lie down, but there was nowhere to do so without causing stares and potential reprimand. Why didn't the company have a nap room or Japanese "cat carrier" beds stacked to the ceiling? At least my only meeting for the day, which was an unusually light schedule, was cancelled.

Adding to my discomfort were the turtleneck and pullover that I wore. The combination was too hot for indoor work that baffled me, sweating from concentration alone, and the turtleneck constricted my swollen neck. When people showed up at my office, my neck, like one fused piece, couldn't pivot to look at them. I had to turn my full body and then turn my full body again to look at the computer screen.

As a Popsicle stick doll with a painted red face, I talked to these people, but I could not remember what they wanted me to do. While I was talking to regular-visitor Mike, the only person I remember seeing that day, he had a strange look on his face: mouth open and a little cock-eyed, a wrinkled brow, and asymmetrical eyes. His face had not resembled a Picasso drawing before, but I kept on talking.

Mike was not my only visitant. Jeff, a dear friend of mine with the spark of life in his eyes, has told me that he also stopped by my cubicle that day. Well-read on matters of the brain, he recounted his visit in an e-mail: "Your description of the accident primed me to look for symptoms, and I noticed aberrations in your attention, concentration, and recall, which suggested concussion. You were receptive to the diagnosis and said that you would follow my suggestion to see a neurologist." As far as I can recall, we never had the conversation.

Weeks later I would notice that my speech was not as coherent as it once had been. I spoke in short sentences, wandered off the point, or missed the point of the conversation altogether. Short questions/comments I could handle; longer questions/comments I would get lost. In contrast, my writing fared better. I could hold thoughts down on paper, make the thoughts bigger and the sentences longer than my spoken words.

Did Rick stop by to see me? We worked at the same company in the same building on the same floor, my office around a couple corners from his. But only once had our work intersected. Both busy people frequently not in our offices or even in our offices' building, we rarely encountered each other on company property. In fact, our very first acquaintance occurred at a purely social lunch in a restaurant with mutual friends—my work friends and his college friends—before we ever worked in the same building. At that time, he was married and I had a boyfriend. The group lunched occasionally. A year later I switched jobs and by coincidence, landed in the same department as Rick. We were both surprised to discover our offices close together, him divorced and me back in the dating pool. Soon after, we started meeting after work and then began dating. So, because of his nonstop, location-frenzied schedule, I'm not sure that Rick had opportunity to check in on me that day.

After six hours at work and pushed well beyond my limits, I called my boss to let him know I was leaving early and that I'd had a great day. I was convinced that I had done a good job—got the reports out, sent out my "I'm back" letter, and moved many work items from pile A to pile B. I couldn't see at the time that pile B was simply another name for pile A. The work was not done. It still sat in my pile. At best, my productivity was a mirage.

That evening I had a monthly appointment with a psychologist to work on my relationship issues. Mainly I relied on her advice to help me progress toward marriage and kids; I had spent way too much time focusing on career. My sessions concentrated on being laser-sharp about what I wanted and what I could overlook, and opening my schedule to activities where I could potentially meet men. Once in a relationship, the psychologist helped me through the inevitable male/female power struggles and other weighty issues, such as "I think he might be gay but he is under family and societal pressure to be heterosexual," "He's turning ultra-religious and going to church every day," or "My boyfriend and his ex-wife argue frequently and it is affecting my relationship with him." She also was teaching me how to respond to a mother who had mentally ill episodes and a father who drank almost every day, and how to handle working in a company where being a woman in my occupation was a rarity.

For one full year I'd attended project-specific meetings where I was the only woman in the room. I had the typical male/female work problems: some males interrupted me, some males repeated my opinions as if I had never said them, and some males treated me like I was their secretary. My therapist and I talked about how a woman can address these issues and she recommended authors Deborah Tannen and Pat Heim.

Lately, we were exploring whether Rick and I had what it took to be married and have kids. She and I delved into the usual questions a priest would ask a couple before he marries them—about money, religion and communication.

Too drained to drive to her office, I took the appointment over the phone. I described the accident to her and recited my great return to work stories. Spontaneously I blurted out, "A friend at work told me he thought I had a concussion." I felt as if some medium had entered my body and was saying things of which I, myself, had no knowledge. Once said, the news seemed about as important as saying I needed a haircut.

"A concussion!" Her emphasis startled me. "Who said that he thought you had a concussion?"

Clueless, I responded, "Uh, I don't remember who."

"Why did he think that you had a concussion?" she inquired.

"Uh, I don't know."

"A concussion is a serious problem that requires a doctor immediately."

"Serious? Oh no, I don't have any *serious* problems."

"Diana, I need you to listen to me. I've had clients with concussions and the list of potential symptoms is endless: from memory loss to raging anger to incoordination. Damaging the brain can affect mental, emotional and physical functioning. This is not something you should take lightly."

"But, but, you're wrong about me." I found her claim hard to believe. Wouldn't I be the first to know that I had such problems? Wouldn't my medical doctor have mentioned a concussion? Wouldn't I be a zombie? I didn't actually say these words or even think them as words. They were sentiments as strong as knowing that the sun would rise every day. Without stating the obvious, I resisted her preposterous assertion as if my life hinged on my being right. As I floated in and out of the conversation, "No," and "You're wrong," were about all that I stubbornly uttered. What I couldn't realize was that I lacked the ability to reason and hadn't the memory to understand and recognize the extent of my illness.

In response to our deadlock of opinion, my therapist switched tactics. She tested me. "I want you to remember these three words: Texas, yellow, pencil." Later, she asked, "What were the three words?"

"Uhm, Texas, uhm, yel-low, uhm . . . uh . . . " Finally I had to admit, "I don't remember the third word."

"Scary. You had an excellent memory. Now you can recall only two items in a list of three. I think you should see a neurologist tomorrow."

Yet, I was not bothered by her results. "I have to work tomorrow," I told her, "and, and, I don't need to see a doctor. I am not brain sick." Inside I felt like the same person as I was the week before; smart, logical and practical were still in the top ten characteristics of my identity. How would you reason with someone who could not recognize her own shifting shadow?

We volleyed back and forth, the ball mostly in my therapist's court. By the end of the session and worn down from the long argument, I agreed to call in sick to work so that I could see a neurologist the next day. I only agreed to do this because I trusted my therapist and I had never heard her speak this strongly about anything before. In no way did I believe that she was accurate. I fully expected the neurologist to realign *her* thinking.

4

Diagnosed

Every 21 seconds, one person in the U.S. sustains a traumatic brain injury.[1]
—fact from Brain Injury Association of Illinois

"Who is the president of the United States?" the doctor asked me.

I paused a few seconds, then answered, "Clinton."

"Red. Amarillo. Thread. Repeat those words."

". . . Red. Amarillo. Thread."

"Subtract 7 from 100 and keep going."

"100, uhm, 93, uh . . . " To compute 93 minus 7, I decreased 9 by 1 to get 8, my tens digit. *93 minus 7, the answer is eighty what?* I'd forgotten the answer to 13 minus 7, which would have given me my ones digit, so I broke 7 into 4 plus 3 and took 4 from 10 to get 6. ". . . 86." The next one was easier because 6 was only 1 off from 7. "Uhmm, 79 . . . "

"Spell world."

"W—O—R—L—D."

"Spell world backwards."

". . . D . . . " *Uh-oh. What is the next letter?* I spelled *world* forward in my head and when I got to L, I said, ". . . L." Again I spelled world forward to get the next answer ". . . R." Then I completed the answer, ". . . O . . . W."

"What were the three words?"

"Uh, Red. Uhm, Amarillo." *Huh? What was that third word?* My mind drew a blank and I conceded, "I don't recall the third one."

These questions were the extent of empirical testing to determine if I had a concussion. The neurologist seemed to think I was normal until my boyfriend spoke about how I would have answered the questions before the accident, rapidly and with no error. My answers contrasted with my background and talent; I had been an A student in the mathematics doctorate program at a Top Ten university and my computational abilities resembled my dad's. Dubbed "the human calculator," my dad could add long columns of numbers in his head and pop out an answer quicker than using a calculator. Subtracting seven from any number should have been instantaneous. Recalling three items should have been a "no-brainer."

The doctor probed about any mental changes since the accident. I would have answered that there were none, but Rick jumped in and listed many. Ten minutes later, the neurologist diagnosed me with a cerebral concussion with memory difficulty (later I learned that he could have also called it a traumatic brain injury) and he told me that, in a week or two, I should be back to normal. To be certain, he prescribed a brain SPECT scan to get color pictures of my brain and its functionality. The more pressing problem was the pain in my neck and shoulder, medically known as cervical and dorsal strain/sprain with myofascial pain. For this problem, the doctor prescribed a week or two of rest. Lastly, he scribbled a note to keep me away from work.

With this doctor I accepted the concussion diagnosis as calmly and flatly as if he'd said that I'd come down with a cold. His lack of worry confirmed my position of the transitory and light nature of my condition, though I didn't really see that I had a memory problem at all. As instructed, I scheduled an appointment for two weeks later, and the receptionist told me to schedule the brain SPECT scan at the hospital of my choice.

To my Forgetfulness list, I added half-jokingly, *I have amnesia and I don't know it, or maybe I know it and don't remember it.*

The MD's concern about my whiplash symptoms and recommendation of up to two weeks off from work, the longest amount of time I'd ever called in sick, did not rattle me. Unlike most patients diagnosed with health problems, I felt unbounded, unceasing, unilateral joy. The genesis of this joy is blurry. But by the time of the doctor's diagnosis, jig-dancing joy was in full swing. Effervescent, I shined from the inside out.

I remember being exceptionally happy the day I graduated from college, the first in my lineage to do so. Another stand-out day was getting hired with a salary that would lift me out of poverty. And I can't leave out those first ecstatic months of being in love. However, these event-driven moments of happiness were always tempered by somberness tucked away in the folds of my brain. Alongside sat the party snub, the auto repair overcharge, and my fallibility. I could never get away fully until brain injury.

Inner gloom had vanished. I could not access anger, resentments, grudges, nor sadness. Everyone became angels as pure as virgin snow capable only of love. I had reached utopia, a neonate out of touch with the world, basking in bliss and most likely, a massive dose of endorphins—proteins released to battle my physical trauma. Subsequent research makes me speculate that I'd damaged a section of brain close to the temples, the inferior temporal gyrus, or the section near the forehead, the supplementary motor area in the left frontal lobe. When electrically probed during the awake-portion of brain surgery, stimulating these sections can send the patient into an exuberant state.

If I am lucky, I will never experience false, constant happiness like that again. But as far as picking a single state to be, happiness would be my top choice.

My pure, rapturous state lasted approximately a couple of weeks before it started to slowly wear off. During that time many visitors came to check up on their sick friend. They saw me happy and giggling and thought that I was not in need of more support. If they would have looked deeper, they would have sensed an inappropriateness to all that happiness. I laughed when I showed people my cracked up car in the driveway. I joked that if I'd been in a hit and run I would have been able to catch the abandoner by reading his flipped license plate number stamped on my rear bumper. I would have laughed if my house burned down, which I would be at risk of doing for the next year.

I would have smiled at a funeral, like the Texan Darlie Routier did. News broadcasts showed her "celebrating" at the graves of her two sons—spraying silly string and singing "Happy Birthday" one week after her boys died. All three of them were stabbed, but only Darlie, slit across the neck and upper torso, survived. The investigators said that her statements about the crime did not match the evidence. The police arrested her. Subsequently, jurors, who were capable of having many feelings and of controlling them, must have found her grave site demeanor as damning evidence, like the rest of the country's reaction, and convicted her of murder.

For political reasons, I'd rather not publicly identify myself with a prisoner on death row, but perhaps she was hit on the head, acquired a traumatic brain injury, and neither her nor her doctors diagnosed it. The brain injured can act quite happy when deep sorrow is the natural human response. My injured endorphin-rich brain could produce only one sustaining emotion. It was a powerful concoction.

Jeff, my brilliant friend who properly diagnosed my condition, stopped by to take me and my funny bone out to lunch. My memory is of a Mexican restaurant close to my home in a location where a commercial building has never stood. My mind required a location in order to store a memory of the event and since it didn't have one, it made one up. I'm not sure why it picked something clearly erroneous.

We were seated in the middle of the restaurant—maybe. Throughout the meal I uproariously laughed, nearly falling off my chair a few times, whenever a busboy put a paper tablecloth on an adjacent table. I heard him unrolling the paper, tearing it, SSSSHHHT, and then I heard it crinkling as he carried the giant white paper rectangle between tables. His forward motion made the paper stick to the front of his body. He was a walking, crinkling sheet of paper with a head, eight fingers and two feet. At the destination table, he flicked the paper up and it floated down to its resting spot.

When the paper was crinkling, I heard nothing else—not Jeff talking, not the other diners, not silverware clanging on plates. These other sounds became facets of crinkling. One busboy looked at me, head tilted sideways, as if to ask, "What is so funny?" Jeff kept trying to quiet me down, and at the end of the meal, he hurried me, practically rolling in the aisles, out of the restaurant. To me, eating out was a bit frantic, but a riot nonetheless.

In my happy state I added to the Forgetfulness list:

- I have ringing in my ears. I just didn't hear it. [I assumed that the tinnitus started at the time of the accident and that I hadn't noticed it until a week later.]

- My job is daunting—now I have appreciation of what I did.

- Perfect choice for an assessment team—I can say, "It never happened," with a straight face. [I felt two conflicting pressures from my involvement in the quality audit at work. The first pressure was from management who expected good results. The second pressure was internal to remain honest. Projecting that I couldn't remember the past, I was joking that these two pressures were no longer in conflict.]

I am fortunate not to have been forever-stuck-in-happiness like some of the brain injured. On a talk show and at a brain injury conference, I've spotted a couple of people in a place that for me was temporary. I identified immediately with their fate—no longer free to choose their own attitude. One woman on Oprah preferred her brain-injured husband's suspended rapture since she knew he was happy and he lodged no complaints about her. Her main benefit was that she remained in control, no questions asked, and she got to feel good about it. On the downside, because many of his reactions were inappropriate, this relationship failed in part to stimulate her personal growth—failed in part to bubble up those deep issues a spouse usually unearths.

At some point during the second week, I think, I drove back to the accident site in my other car. There was a steady rain and my windshield wipers were barely adequate at clearing my view. Yet I was able to see, as I drove slowly through the site, that the road was completely clean—as if the accident had not even happened. *No car-part litter? No skid marks?* And then it hit me. I had not heard skidding or hard braking or horn honking before being struck. The driver who hit me was unaware that he was about to rear end me.

Why would someone be unaware? I questioned, ignorant of the self-reflective irony.

I had two contradictory answers: he was adjusting a mirror (his story immediately following the accident), or he was reaching for a tissue in his glove compartment (his insurance agent's story). I did not know what to believe.

My memory of my return to the site is blotchy, and I do not remember feeling any emotion in particular while there. Possibly I was happy.

With week three came the onset of pain, particularly to my head, neck, shoulder and lower back. An all-consuming energy-draining muscle-wrenching eye-watering nausea-inducing pain, it signaled the commencement of my descent out of shock, the departure of pure bliss (although I was still quite happy), and my first longish look at my inner world.

That week I noticed that I was dizzy. My surroundings continually moved, I couldn't focus my eyes steadily on one spot, and I fought for my balance. The world had turned floppy. Every day I spilled drinks and dropped food, usually on myself, staining my previously immaculate wardrobe. When I tried to turn on a light, I missed the switch and jammed my fingers. When I walked, the ground was not where I thought it would be. I'd trip, stub my toes, or raise my leg too high and plunk down hard. My stride still had a normal look to it, but with a spice of klutzy moves. In particular, uneven sidewalks, area rugs, table corners, walls and cat toys messed with my rhythm.

Far worse, I periodically fell down the stairs. Mostly, I stumbled down two or three steps at a time. Yet, sometimes I tumbled down the entire flight, sometimes thrown suddenly to my knees or bumping down on my butt. Jerking, clutching, sliding, careening. Twisting an ankle or landing on bent toes. I crawled the rest of the way, each time surprised by singular events.

Several years later . . .

"Look, that plane is barely moving!" I exclaim.

My passenger Dave, who reads scientific magazines, looks up at the plane and says, "That's parallax."

"Huh?"

"We're moving and the plane is moving in a similar direction, which makes it appear from our viewpoint as if the plane is crawling."

"But it's hanging in the air like a UFO. I think it's going to crash!"

"It's not going to crash. This is the same problem that early astronomers had to solve. Originally, people thought that the earth was stationary because we couldn't sense any movement. Yet from observation of the positions of the sun, astronomers theorized that the earth revolved on an axis and orbited around the sun. What they saw could not be explained unless the earth was moving. The speed and direction of our car is distorting our perception of the speed and direction of that plane."

Parallax: "the apparent displacement or the difference in apparent direction of an object as seen from two different points not on a straight line with the object . . . "[2]

"I still think the plane is going to crash. Watch for smoke."

Ever since the accident, my life had become a string of strange self-contained events.

I am on a walk.

Where am I going? I don't know. Maybe I should walk home.

I am out on a walk and meet a woman going in the other direction. She remarks, "So we meet again."

Odd. She thinks we have met before. I don't know her.

I have a brochure in my hand. Minutes later, I do not have the brochure in my hand. I look for the brochure, but cannot find it. I want to retrace my steps, but find I have no recollection of the steps I have taken.

That's weird. I don't know what I did in the last fifteen minutes.

I am undressing for bed, and as I am pulling down my pants, my eyes spot a large purple bruise on my thigh. I can't tie my bruise to any event. Upon closer inspection of my body, I uncover more bruises, scratches and bumps, none of which I can account for.

Whoa! I'm more battered than I know. I've always been close to my body and known the story of my scrapes. I have something seriously wrong with my memory!

I knew that I had a memory problem and I repeated the doctor's diagnosis to anyone who asked about my health. Yet, my experience up to the accident was that I had a photographic memory and after the accident, my long-term memories of facts, figures and experiences were still transparently clear, a-hundred-foot-view-of-the-ocean-bottom clear. I could still provide a detailed account of a girl-friend's wedding ten years ago. I could still remember that John Bradshaw described the personality traits of the first-born, second-born, nth-born in *The Family*, a book I'd read six years before. I could still recall that I looked pretty in my sister's blue-purple floral dress. My memory felt superb. I just couldn't separate out the long-term ocean from the murky short-term inlets.

Not recognizing people, losing things, forgetting what happened ten minutes ago, all seemed like minor inconveniences. After five, ten, fifteen minutes, or a distraction, experiences disappeared from my mind's grasp. Memory loss didn't register as a real problem. I couldn't remember that I couldn't remember, at least not while I was in action.

I have come to realize that in my new brain organization, I had memory up until the accident, scattered memories after the accident of traumatic or unusual events, and then, some awareness of what was happening at the moment. I wasn't aware and would continue to be globally unaware for months that there was all this unaccounted time. How would you know if you had unaccounted time in between your memories and now? How would you know to look for something that you don't know is gone? How would you identify your own memory parallax?

Just as earlier people had used the stationary earth as their reference when looking out into the universe, my reference point in life had always been my strong memory. The reference worked for awhile until a dramatic observation—the sun's positions, my body's unaccounted bruises—no longer fit the mold. Memory parallax.

Only after my bruise discovery, did I understand, at least for one circumstance, the heavier impact of memory loss. My colorful body shifted an esoteric concept to something concrete and meaningful and serious. Furthermore, having taken this ideological jump once, I would find it easier to tag other events as memory-loss occurrences and learn to be frightened of my condition.

But then, unable to track the speeding jet, my discovery slipped out of my consciousness and I retreated to my baseline stupor. The only ideas I had were in reaction to what was happening at the moment. Passers-through, those elusive airliners never stayed long.

My self-image, unwavering despite the accident, suddenly shifted from realism to optimism. My intelligence now doomed me to repeated failures.

5

Mildly Sick

Sometimes a doctor's words are only opinions.

I worked in what I called an "extended office." The company was global and during five years on the job I'd developed close phone relationships with others in Texas, England and Ireland. Ed Bradly, who always went out of his way to help others, had a soothing voice. He knew something about everything and was the top engineer at the Texas site. He was also a rancher who delivered baby calves, fixed broken wells, and repaired barbed wire fences. When I mentioned I'd always wanted goats but my suburban town had an ordinance against owning farm animals, he gave me an 800 number to call for the purchase of pygmy goats. He thought that a miniature version might elude the ordinance's nose.

Michael Bristol, English, was a formal chap with perfect diction who instituted aviation's phonetic alphabet for communicating problem identifiers. Instead of saying "problem 1234ZBEF," we said, "problem 1234 zulu bravo echo fox-trot." He studied Shakespeare and occasionally weaved in, "Brevity is the soul of wit," or "We know what we are, but know not what we may be," during our conversations.

Shane O'Reily, high-strung and proactive, chased down and extinguished political and project-related fires. People were always running around trying to get stuff done for him. On one conference call we were talking about a high risk to the project when he said in his Irish brogue, "It's just not going to happen!" If this were on a musical scale, it would look like:

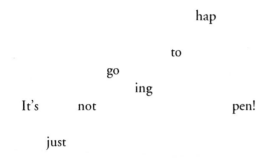

Everyone in the U.S. conference room froze. We, and especially Shane, were all about making it happen. Then tiny smiles cracked through the shock—we had a new catch phrase. From then on, when the Chicago-based project managers encountered the project's daily risks, we couldn't resist singing in our best Irish accents, "It's just not going to happen!"

A year or two of talking to these voices, sight unseen, I finally met (before my accident) the Wizards of Oz. When face to face, I discovered I'd formed mental images of them. In person, Ed had a full beard and mustache with a face under there somewhere. His hair was gray. He was a grandfather. I had expected a clean-shaven Ed, as clean as his solutions, and a young guy, as quick as his wit. Michael Bristol was black. I had never seen a black Englishman before. Of course the English would have diversity in their population. What was I thinking? And Shane. He was a slight man, no more than 130 pounds, much smaller than the powerful stature I'd presumed from his speech.

With brain injury, new acquaintances were like these colleagues and their voices. I didn't picture them when I thought of them, and in person, at a second, third, fourth or fifth encounter, if I remembered who they were, my mental images were nothing like their appearances. So when I tell you that my neurologist, Dr. O., was of medium height, dark-skinned, with dark hair and bushy eyebrows, and he wore a knee-length white coat with powder-blue embroidered chest-high lettering and a big pocket on each hip, and he hung a stethoscope around his neck, I know that most likely, I describe fantasy.

Back to the Neurologist

Two weeks from my last appointment, I returned to the neurologist's office. Unfortunately, my physician, Dr. A., had left the practice and I was transferred to a less experienced specialist, Dr. O. His nurse brought me to the examining room and I walked right into the doorjamb, backed up a step, moved a little to my right, walked through the door, and found a seat. Must have. I smacked my shoulders on doorjambs with regularity.

The new doctor asked me if I had taken the brain SPECT scan, which I had not. I had called a hospital at my boyfriend's prodding, but the radiologist there told me that the doctor's order was unusual for an auto accident concussion. He said that the test was usually executed for Alzheimer's disease. I adopted the radiologist's opinion, as I was now prone to do, and did not make the appointment.

Besides, after the radiologist told me that the test involved a radioactive-dye injection, I felt tremendous fear about being radioactive for life. From my mathematical background, I knew that radioactivity only lessened across time. It never died. Of course, I still thought and spoke in mathematical terms: the exponential radioactive decay graph is asymptotic to the time axis, or at the very least, pictured the concave graph approaching, but never touching the horizontal time axis.

My fear did not match reality. Years later I read that a common injection for SPECT, radiopharmaceutical technetium-99m, is FDA-approved (at least for heart imaging) and has a half-life (the time for half of the substance to decay or be eliminated from the body) of six hours. I had imagined the half-life to equal hundreds of years.

In response to the new neurologist's question, I only told him that I did not get the brain SPECT scan. I failed to mention my talk with the radiologist and my fears about the test. These ideas did not come to mind.

My mind was otherwise occupied. Doctor O. spoke with a thick Eastern European accent, and it took my total concentration to understand him. He had asked a yes or no question and that was as far as my mind went. I felt good about figuring out the question and responding correctly.

Appearing frustrated with my answer, Dr. O. wrinkled his brow while he looked down at a stack of papers attached to his clipboard. He read and flipped a page, read and flipped a page, and then became furious in his flipping, back and forth, back and forth, seemingly awash in confusion about what to do next. The ruffling of paper consumed my attention. Eventually he settled on a page and began testing me.

"Ball. Flag. Tree. Repeat those words."

". . . Ball. Flag. Tree."

"Subtract 7 from 100 and keep going."

"100, uhm, 93, uh . . . 86, uhmm, 79 . . . "

"Spell world backwards."

". . . D . . . . L . . . . R . . . O . . . W"

"What were the three words?"

"Uh, Ball. Uhm, Flag. A-a-a-n-n-d Tree."

"What is this (pointing to a watch, testing for agnosia, the inability to recognize objects)?"

"A watch."

"What is this (pointing to a pencil)?"

"A pencil."

He asked me more questions and recorded my answers on his sheet of paper.

Because I passed his thirty questions, he could not tell that anything was wrong with me. He could only depend on my reports of memory loss, slowness to respond, disorientation and dizziness—still a problem even though the first doctor indicated I should have been normal by now.

Unconvincingly he recommended, "Dr. A. wanted you to get a brain SPECT scan. So, I guess you should go ahead and get one." He added, "I also want you to get a neuropsych evaluation to flesh out cognitive problems, but I don't know yet who to recommend. Soon, I will call you with the name of a neuropsychologist." Then he was gone.

Driving home, I remembered the doctor asking me to repeat three words. Without him around to observe, I could only recall "ball" and "flag."

Four days later, Dr. O. called. On a slip of paper I wrote: *Dr. O. does not recommend brain spec scan. (Dr. A. did because of memory loss)*. In his notes, obtained years later after I paid for copies of my medical transcripts, Dr. O. wrote: *She won't go for SPECT*. Our divergent interpretations make me wonder what happened during that phone conversation. Was it the accent, even more garbled over the phone line? Was it my fear of the test or his lack of conviction in another doctor's test choice that colored the discussion? Was it a miscommunication, a misunderstanding or a combination of all of these possibilities?

Even though I did not schedule the brain SPECT scan, I did understand the doctor's other message and made an appointment with his recommended neuropsychologist.

For the neuropsych testing, I drove myself through bumper-to-bumper traffic, entering and exiting two expressways and crossing a multitude of intersections with stoplights. The hospital, where my sister used to be a candy striper, and the route, the same route as to my parents' house, were in my long-term memory, so I was able to drive to the hospital parking lot without getting lost. In the lot I was pleased to have an hour before my appointment for a well-needed rest from the harrowing rush hour drive.

My pleasure was short-lived. I spent the next half hour looking for a place to park. Several parking lots surrounded the hospital. Each lot had a sign at its entrance which explained who could park there and it wasn't me. I drove from lot to lot, doubling back, getting snagged in loops, until I found a spot a mile away from the hospital entrance. Then, within the hospital, I hurried from sign to sign, doubling back, getting snagged in loops, until I found the neuropsych testing area. Fatigued from the labyrinth, I arrived just in time for my full-day appointment. I had passed test one.

Immediately, we got down to business and the administrator verbally presented instructions for the first test. She ended her blurb, "You must try your hardest. I don't want half effort." I had found this a strange and insulting direction. In college, one of the reasons my name had appeared consistently on the dean's list was because I'd always approached exam-taking seriously. "Half efforts" had never crossed my mind. Yet, repeatedly throughout the day I would hear this border-line scolding.

Employing my full suite of smarts, as usual, I proceeded through their tests. Like university entrance exams, I had an allotted amount of time to complete each categorized exam. The neuropsych test categories included memory, physical dexterity, vocabulary and math. More basic than the SAT's, the neuropsych math section, for instance, had no question beyond a fifth grade level.

Horrifyingly, I, who had taught college mathematics for seven years, struggled on many easy math questions and was sluggish throughout. I could not recall most items on a recited grocery list, nor could I get the details right on a narrated story a paragraph long. Something was definitely fishy. If there was one life skill I'd mastered, it was test taking.

Taking an exam, especially a math exam, had been exhilarating. I'd aimed for two goals: turn in a perfect score and be the first one done. The night before a school exam, I'd created one sheet of paper with all of the important information, cramming it on the page, writing in small print. One day my college roommate saw one of my small print pages and thought I was nuts. But it had been important to me that it all fit on one page because I took mental photographs. I hadn't wanted to flip mental pages while taking the exam because doing so had seemed too inefficient.

Five minutes before a school exam, I'd taken one last look at my page summary, stored it in my backpack, got out my pen, and then anxiously waited for the teacher to hand out the test. Shaking my pen and my leg back and forth, my heart had sped in anticipation. I was a racehorse, ready to spring out of the gate.

I'd worked an exam in order, darting from one question to the next. If I hadn't known an answer or I'd thought I was taking too long on a question, I skipped ahead. In the background, my mind had worked on the answer to the skipped question. Sometimes in the middle of answering one question, the solution to the nagging question would pop in. As one differential equations' professor said to me when I'd turned in his first exam after fifteen minutes, "You either have no clue in this class or you are very bright."

Afterwards, my mind had consciously and unconsciously processed the exam. While firing a tennis ball into the corner of my opponent's court or vigorously pumping the pedals of my bike, I'd have realized that I'd made the wrong variable substitution, which probably cost me four points. By the end of the day, I'd have figured out my errors, if any, and my grade.

When I was teaching calculus, the students I'd struggled to help were those with test anxiety. I could not identify with them and their fright nor could I understand their difficulties. In contrast, I'd viewed tests as great devices to speed up learning, not cripple it.

During neuropsych testing, however, I experienced the origin of test anxiety. I had never felt more helpless with a test in front of me. I ran out of time, I drew blanks, and I answered some questions with pure guesswork. My brain was utterly slow to respond. I felt defeated, stranded in the desert of barren thoughts. The question I had, the question I had not asked before was, How bad did I do?

At the end of the day, the test administrator gave me a test of a different sort—the MMPI-2 (Minnesota Multiphasic Personality Inventory), a questionnaire of approximately 400 true/false questions. Because I had studied this exam in abnormal psychology class to meet the requirements of my other major—psychology—I knew the neuropsychologist was testing for mental illness. Each answer I gave would score me closer to or farther from depression, schizophrenia, mania or some other mental madness. I moaned about not wanting to take the test, but the administrator objectively instructed, "Answer each question as true if it describes you and false if it does not. These should be first impression answers. Do not think too long to answer each question." Pressured to proceed, I opened the booklet and began, well aware that my answers to similar questions must be consistent.

I enjoy music and dancing.

Before injury I'd listened to music and danced weekly, but after injury I couldn't tolerate the clatter of music and I didn't have the physical coordination to dance. I hoped that eventually music would sound melodic to me and eventually I would regain coordination. So, which person was I—the one who liked to dance to music or the one who wasn't physically capable? My personality was split right down the middle. I left the question blank for the time being.

I am a very sociable person.

I had considered myself sociable. But since the accident I was tired all the time and didn't have the energy to socialize. When I did talk to people, I couldn't follow what they were saying. Did this mean that I was no longer sociable? I still wanted to be sociable. I left this blank and moved on to the next question.

I am in just as good physical health as most of my friends.

Finally, a question that doesn't start a debate in my head. This one was obviously false. My friends were not in screaming pain every day like I was.

I struggled mightily on this, the hardest test of the day, to determine who I was. I ended up writing notes to myself as I went along, like, *I do not like physical activity,* and *I am an outgoing person.* I wasn't sure if this was true or false, but this was the story I gave to describe my mythical self.

Scattered Pieces

Across time, my unusual observations accumulated like jigsaw puzzle pieces in short stacks throughout the house. To keep the ideas all in one place, I bought a notebook and in it, I recorded my entries by date. The first day, car accident day, covers two and a half pages and is quite verbose. The story flows. The next twenty pages or so are mainly blank, with exception of the first weekend with Rick, the first day back to work, a letter to Rick, and week summaries—a copying of loose pieces of paper of the week's events. One or two sentence/phrase entries, each event is unconnected to the next, which mirrored the thoughts in my head. Not until the one-month date and beyond are the pages filled. Around two months, paragraphs make an appearance and the thoughts become fuller. I frequently wrote about driving a car. (I have cleaned up the English from my rough notes.)

> **Start of third week**: I was the first car in the left hand turn lane and completely missed the green arrow. I waited another round while cars honked behind me.

Middle of third week: Turning left, I did not see an oncoming car that was behind a turning van until the last second. I had mistakenly thought all cars in the van lane were turning left.

End of third week: In a right hand turn lane, before turning right on red, I forgot to look for cross traffic. I knew I had to look for something, so, I looked for left hand turners who were facing me. They were waiting at a red light.

Middle of sixth week: When I adjusted a mirror, I forgot that I was driving and darted into a shallow ditch. I narrowly missed a row of mailboxes.

All of this was happening; no alarm sounded in my head. I was unable to deduce the conclusion that shouted, I SHOULD NOT BE DRIVING!

Plain, vanilla driving addled my brain. More complicated, locating unfamiliar places while driving frazzled me. I traced circular paths as I zeroed in on a location, or, I forgot where I was headed and drove past my destination, or, I stopped the car to reread the next direction. My tires took extra turns, my transmission shifted forward and back, and my odometer racked up useless miles. Vacated were the days of acute direction, of driving to my best friend's dad's home from memory although I'd only driven there and to that area once before, years before.

I lost my sense of direction whether in a car or by foot. When I walked out of a store in a mall, I asked myself, *Should I turn left or should I turn right?* The relationship of the shops to each other was missing from my head. I didn't even know which shops I had already visited. Consequently, some salesclerks saw me several times on the same day as I traversed a meandering path. Eventually I tired and repeated the same wanderings in the parking lot. When I reached my car, I questioned, *Who parked here?* then answered, *It must have been me.*

My cooking attempts were no more successful. Many days I was too tired to figure out what to eat and how to get it into a state of ready to eat. Some days, though, I tried. I'd put a chicken breast without lemon in the oven or rice without butter on the stove and promptly forget about it until it became blackened chicken or black rice. I doused them with water that sizzled and then steamed. Then, having forgotten to turn off the burner or the oven, I sometimes discovered my hot kitchen hours later or a fitful night's sleep later. Kitchen fires coincided with my cooking days.

Because I was unable to adequately prepare my own meals, I mainly snacked. With no coordinated foods in the house, lunch was a granola bar and cheese, or applesauce and walnuts. I went hungry a lot.

My cats didn't seem to mind my bungling episodes. In fact, they seemed to like me better. My white-pawed cat, Mitts, had always been a lap cat. For longer periods of time, she cuddled with me on the couch and in my bed. Majesty had always been above showing that she needed me and never hung out in the same room as her sister. During my illness, though, Maj took to my lap. There were even times when both of them nuzzled on top of me. Perhaps they sensed I was in trouble and offered up their love, a double dose, to help heal my wounds.

The Letter

Around this time, the caretaker honeymoon was over and Rick wanted our relationship to pick up where it left off—back to relationship growth. We'd been considering marriage, discussing what our life would look like. In particular, we explored where we would live, how finances and religious tradition would work, and if we would add our own children into the mix.

I definitely wanted to have a baby and prior to meeting me, Rick had thought his siring days were over. Yet my strong mothering desire and my excitement about the possibility began to arouse something within him, and he was starting to envision a third child.

Other areas weren't as easily negotiated. Although he had not set foot in a church during the year of our courtship, Rick wanted to begin attending Sunday service, like he'd done while a youth. He asked me to join him. I wasn't the church-going type, nor had I been brought up that way. But after a long argument, I made an effort and accompanied him to the church of his choosing for a Christmas mass. After parking the car in a lot the size of a shopping mall's, we followed a stream of others to the main auditorium. Already full, ushers herded the flock to a cafeteria. The room filled to capacity and the crowd controllers sent the next arrivals to another satellite room. When the preacher appeared on a big movie screen, I didn't connect with his telecast words, said too literally. Moreover, some of the ideology upset me, although I don't remember precisely why. At the end of the service, slides of starving children engulfed the screen. Their protruding bones and emaciated looks disturbed me deeply, nightmarishly, like shown larger-than-life shot-up bodies of a real crime scene. While my gut wrenched, several ushers passed around collection plates and I felt manipulated into giving a large donation. In that church, I didn't perceive room for independent thinking or metaphysical interpretation and rejected the notion that I would ever attend a service there again. After much debate, we sampled a church with a small congregation. But neither of us liked that one much. That's about how far we'd gotten.

On the issue of money, we arrived at an impasse. Rick wanted one joint checking account, like in his first marriage when he was the only one working outside of the home. In his eyes, a true marriage meant a union of money (and heart and goal). But I reasoned differently. I was acutely aware that I would not be his first wife and our biological kid(s) would not be his firsts either. From that view, I found it unfair to expect me to dump my savings from twenty years of working into a joint account which would include uses for: his alimony, his custody lawyer, or his kids' guardian ad litem. At best, I could only agree to separate accounts and to a third joint account for agreed upon purposes.

We also hadn't figured out where we would live. My house was definitely too small for him and his sons. Rick quickly jumped to the conclusion that we should live in his house. But the topic required deeper introspection. I foresaw that his sons would consider me an intruder, occupying territory that belonged to their mom. Furthermore, several aspects of Rick's house bothered me—its inner darkness from a scarcity of windows, its plain architectural style, its brown color scheme. Even Rick admitted that his first wife had picked the house and he'd agreed to purchase it to make her happy. Yet, he viewed the place as a constant in his children's life. To meet me partway, he promised to give me carte blanche to redecorate—which didn't address enough of the issues.

Because Rick trusted we would arrive at a joint decision, he'd felt ready to marry me. But I wasn't ready to commit until I saw how we negotiated our way through these difficult tests. He interpreted my stance as a "lack of faith" in our relationship, which weakened his drive to wed me. Then I became brain-injured.

At first, Rick didn't see my injury as an impediment. Like the religion, money and living arrangement issues, he believed that time would heal all. So, after the first month passed and he dutifully and lovingly took care of my extended needs, he began to get antsy. He wanted resolution on our open disagreements so that we could get married or I suppose, break up.

In opposition, my therapist felt strongly that I was not up to the task. She suggested that I write down my symptoms to show Rick why I was not well enough to work on our relationship. With her help, I defined my illness in the following letter which took me several hours across several days to write.

> I've been trying to act as if I could think as before (and only until recently was just becoming aware that I could not). Similarly you have been treating me as if I had those same reasoning abilities. This has lead to disastrous results.
>
> Let me give you the gist of my mind. I am entirely living in the present. I forget what happened five minutes before unless my environment or someone else gives me a clue and then I may remember foggily. All events in my life

since the accident are blurred and inaccurate. The closer to the car accident, the blurrier they are. My long term memory is in tact and I live off of that, mimicing my former self and remember things as they were rather than as they are. I can only think of one thing at a time. My conversations are slow and I find myself starring and with blank thought. In an unknown environment I go into sensory overload (new physical environment, new thoughts, new people, . . .).

And this illness keeps fooling me. I think I am ok when in fact I am not. I have less trust in my own perceptions. I am not the person I once was and find myself mourning the old me and half having faith that I can build a better me.

Because of my current state, I ask that we not talk issues until I am well. We've tried to do this, but have not been successful.

P.S. I've been using this time off to do a lot of irrational thinking.

Composing this letter was like trying to explain a 3-D concept from a 2-D world. In my head thoughts came into view one at a time—a picture on a puzzle piece of a lock of hair, and later, another middle piece of a half eye. Separately, they did not make sense. On paper, though, I could move thoughts close to one another and make connections. I could make the words flow. More than individual parts, I could see the summation, a section of a woman's shaded face. Amazingly, writing broke through my single-file thought barrier.

Writing, as well as the guidance of my therapist, saved me. The scribed thought captured moments of clarity, and rereading what I had drafted increased the chance of remembrance. My verbalizations were curt, tongue-tied and short-sighted, but my writing came out clear by the tenth edit. I was thankful for being left with an avenue to respond intelligently.

Now, I am surprised about how accurately this letter described me then. It even shows a sense of humor at the end. Yet some of the misspellings drive me insane. Not correcting them is like not scratching an itch. So I have to tell you *tryed* should be *tried*, *lead* should be *led* and *starring* should be *staring*. Other misspellings, *long term* should be *long-term*, *in tact* should be *intact* and *mimicing* should be *mimicking*, don't bother me at all.

Neuropsych Test Results

Half a month after the neuropsych testing, my neurologist gave me my results. The test interpreter, neuropsychologist Dr. U., diagnosed me with a mild traumatic brain injury (MTBI) with an IQ of 108. My problem-solving ability appeared somewhat deficient and my memory functioning appeared mildly problematic, but my overall intellectual functioning was solidly average, my comprehension appeared appropriate, and my attentional functioning was very strong. The result from the Personality Inventory, valid because I had answered questions with the same meaning consistently, was that I had a tendency toward hypochondria.

Doctor O. presented the information to me as a good news scenario, like I should rejoice that I was normal and stop focusing my attention on the injury.

His diagnosis didn't seem right to me, but I couldn't quite put my finger on the problem. I told him, "I feel, uhm, disappointed. . . . How can I be average when I was a top student?" In fact, when I was a senior in college, the mathematics professors presented me with an award equivalent to valedictorian of the mathematics majors.

Sometime later I added, "I don't feel normal—the pain, the dizziness—I'm forgetful." Normally, my brain captured information like a fine-knit net snares anything that swims.

Further along in our conversation about the test results, when he said he wanted to send me back to work, I remarked, "Uh, it seems too soon for me to go back to work. I'm not sure I could do my work as before."

He agreed that I had a brain injury, had lost range of motion in my right arm (could not raise it higher than my shoulder) and had pinched nerves. For these reasons, he recommended physical therapy and an extended leave from work. He didn't find it necessary, but said that he would write a prescription for rehabilitation to improve my concentration and memory. At the end of our short session, he handed me a copy of the ten-page neuropsych report.

When I arrived home, I read through the findings line by line.

> The clinical scale configuration was suggestive of a tendency to develop physical complaints in response to stress. This raises the possibility that some of her experience of symptomatology subsequent to her injury may be heightened by this proclivity.

After a dozen readings, I interpreted this paragraph to mean that I tended to complain to people about ailments I didn't have. This wasn't true; the life I'd lived exhibited a proclivity to hiding physical maladies. I worked when sick without complaint. I played sports with blistered feet, sore muscles and asthma, without letting opponents or teammates know about my weaknesses. And I only visited doctors when absolutely necessary. The last time I'd seen a doctor for a physical exam was about seven years before the accident to meet a work requirement, and for a specific problem, about a year before to examine my ankle after a carton of ice cream fell off a grocery store shelf and hammered it. I viewed physical ailments as personal information, only spoken about on a need-to-know basis.

The next item on the report that stuck out like an ace-bandaged ankle was:

> Her attentional functioning is very strong. Her comprehension appears appropriate.

Hours before I received my neuropsych test results, I wrote in my journal:

> I spilled an item in the refrigerator. To clean I took out a couple items. I got so involved in the cleaning that I forgot to put items back in refrigerator. When I came back into kitchen five minutes later I noticed them sitting out.
>
> I was stung by a wasp on my bare shoulder—oblivious to the event until a minute later when pain registered in my brain. It took another minute to decipher the pang and shoo the circling wasp away. My already stiff and sore and swollen neck and shoulder became stiffer and sorer and more swollen. [rewrote entry to make it understandable]

My journal entry the day before I received my results was:

> difficulty concentrating (had to reread lines of book a number of times to understand)

The last fallacious report item, according to my journal, was:

> She has a recent medical history significant for an apparent mild traumatic brain injury sustained in a motor vehicle accident.
>
> I did not have information regarding her injury, however, by her report, it was relatively mild.

From the act of listing my problems in a letter to Rick as well as the experience of failing at test taking, I came to understand, at last, that "mild" was not the proper description of my problems. I concluded that the diagnosis of mild traumatic brain injury had to be erroneous.

In my journal I highlighted these report errors as only "points of disagreement." Worry, anger and sadness were absent, then, as they were when I described to the neuropsychologist, at his request, my list of symptoms. On the "Background" section of his report, after my long list of physical complaints—disorganized, inefficient, dulled senses, light and motion sensitivity, and difficulty concentrating, comprehending, reasoning and making a decision—his last statement reads, "Interestingly, she feels more worry-free than she previously did."

Where the medical profession failed me, my therapist filled in. Upon her request, I had Dr. O. send her a copy of the neuropsych report. She reckoned my IQ had dropped about thirty points and reinforced my notion that my personality had changed. I was slow to respond and spoke vapidly. I used to take the initiative and now I was lethargic. I used to get upset if there was a hint that I had a bad memory, but now I was ambivalent.

She thought the hypochondria result was invalid because the Personality Inventory assumes that the test taker is not physically ill. In opposition to the hypochondria label, her frustration was my *lack of concern* about my condition.

Seven years later I verified that she was right to disregard the hypochondriac result. The MMPI-2 has thirty-three somatic-concern questions to assess hypochondria. On somatic-concern questions, "My sleep is fitful and disturbed," "I have numbness in one or more regions of my skin," and "I feel weak all over much of the time," I confidently answered true. On somatic-concern questions, "I wake up fresh and rested most mornings," "I hardly ever feel pain in the back of the neck," and "I have very few headaches," I confidently answered false. My sleep was fitful from the brain injury. My right arm and leg were numb from pinched nerves. I was continually tired and felt weak, and my head and neck uninterruptedly throbbed.

The test designer or interpreter assumed that the more I marked a physical complaint, the higher my tendency toward hypochondria. Because my valid physical complaints made up for 70% of the hypochondriasis portion of the test, my test result was positive for hypochondria. These complaints were not manufactured by my mind; however, my brain did interpret my body so that I could make these complaints in the first place. Yet, I wasn't really making a complaint to anybody. They were asking me to comment on this topic. I complied.

Lastly, my therapist was worried for me because I seemed to have lost my ability to worry. She recommended that I get a second opinion. By this stage Dr. O. should have ordered more medical tests. He had not located the physical cause of my shocking symptoms. More importantly, he and the neuropsychologist, the "vowel doctors," didn't seem to believe that I was brain-injured.

6

The Evacuation Upstairs

FIRST THREE MONTHS
PERPLEXED

I have a good memory, but mine is very short . . . [1]
—Mr. Toby Barrett, Chair of Standing Committee on Justice and
Social Policy, Legislative Assembly of Ontario

Doctor:	"Will a month from now, Monday, May 29, at 6:00 work for you?"
Brainy Me:	"Sure, I could do that." I have mentally checked my work and social calendar to determine that I am available.
Doctor:	"Here's a card for your next appointment."
Brainy Me:	"Keep it. It's in my head and that is good enough."

Sometime later, when I have my datebook out, I will pencil in the appointment as an unnecessary precaution.

Doctor:	"Will a week from now, Monday, May 29, at 6:00 work for you?"
Brain-Injured Me:	"May 29th is a week from now? Hmmm. Uh, what was the question?"
Doctor:	"Can you come in for an appointment on Monday, May 29, at 6:00?"
Brain-Injured Me:	"Uh, I can't find my datebook. I'll call you later to schedule an appointment."
Doctor:	"Here's my card. Don't forget to call."

The brain-injured me writes a note on the card: Call For Next Appointment. I put the card in my handbag so that the next time I am digging around in my purse, I will see the card and make the appointment. Left to my own devices, I will not remember to call when I get home.

Instead of work, I went to doctors' appointments—anywhere from three to seven appointments a week. I saw the neurologist, the psychologist, the neuropsychologist, the chiropractor, the medical tester, the physical therapist and the masseuse. Getting me to these appointments on time was another matter altogether.

During the first three months after the accident, each morning I consulted my datebook for the day's doctors' appointments by looking for the first date not crossed off. On some days, I called a cab to take me to my appointment. This insured that I'd get to the appointment on time. Other days I wrote a note to myself, Leave For Physical Therapist At 1:00, and placed it in a prominent place in my house. Sometime close to 1:00, I would need to pass that note to know to leave for my appointment.

At 1:15 I might get that terrible phone call. "We have you down for an appointment with Dr. So-and-So at 1:00. Can you still come?" After some of these calls, I made a precautionary arrangement with the receptionist to call me an hour before my next appointments, even though she was reluctant to do this for me.

At my first physical therapy (PT) session, my body was so starched-clothes stiff that my physical therapist banned me from exercise and sent me exclusively to massage for awhile. During these kneading sessions I winced and sweated from the pain of movement and pressure, but emerged a little looser each time. By the fourth week of PT, an exercise portion was added to my regimen to strengthen my muscles on the right side of my body and to improve coordination and balance. For home, my physical therapist provided color-coded five-foot-long rubber bands (black rubber bands were tauter than yellow ones or vice versa) as part of my personal exercise equipment. She also gave me pictures of exercises with instructions on number of repetitions and frequency, and advised daily walks.

After one particular workout at the PT gym, I had a great idea on how to meet my walking requirement. Instead of taking a cab back home, I would walk. Of the two routes I could take, I opted for the shorter trek over the more scenic jaunt because I did not want to overdo. When I stepped out of the PT Sport Center, I felt the bright and strong midday sun on my body and in my eyes. It was much hotter and brighter than I remembered from when I arrived for my workout. *Sun won't stop me.* I was determined to walk home and make my physical therapist proud.

The first four blocks before the main intersection, I kept a moderate pace on the sidewalk, looking ahead for the next shaded spot. When I reached the stoplight, I felt good about achieving a stepping-stone goal. But peering across the street, I noticed that instead of a sidewalk, gravel shoulders flanked the road. I switched sides to walk against traffic, a heavier traffic than previously. There was no shade in sight, and cars whizzed past at fifty m.p.h., kicking up dust and sometimes gravel. The dust stuck to my moistened skin, the gravel dinged me once in a while, and the sun drained my energy. I'd walked a grueling mile under these conditions when a group of young Mexican men shot by, hanging out of car windows and whistling at me, a svelte brown-haired Caucasian woman of medium height. I picked up my pace even though it hurt. I tried to ignore them because engaging them might put me at risk. I was not able to run under any circumstance.

Powdered, roasted and thirsty, I pressed on, slowly, for another mile of that eternal stretch. In the last couple of blocks of that road, a sidewalk appeared and some shade trees. I rested there, a dusty red from overheating and sunburn. Astoundingly, I was only halfway home. I'd underestimated the distance and overestimated my abilities—a wicked combination. Only a few months before, walking a flat five miles would not have fazed me.

For the last half, my surroundings were more hospitable—sidewalk, shade and slow, occasional, residential traffic. Every section of my body ached and particularly pained were my whiplash areas: neck, shoulder and lower back. I walked with a definite limp and moved uneasily. I tripped more. The objects around me became wavy and I saw mirages of water in waves of heat over the pavement. *Was I a droplet shy of dehydration?* I pictured my faucet at home, turned on, with water gushing forth, and I daydreamed of my bed, the corner of the blankets turned over, inviting me to sleep. *How could a simple walk have turned out disastrously?* Not soon enough, my fading steps carried me inside my home, to the kitchen faucet, and then to my bed.

In the first few months, my environment, as seen through an altered brain, triggered a bombardment of world improvement ideas. I'd be at a stop sign unsure of who was required to stop and who was not. Then I would think, *Wouldn't it be great if the stop sign facing me could indicate which cars at the other corners also had a stop sign? If the top edge of my stop sign represented the car facing me, the right edge represented the car to my right and the left edge the car to my left, wouldn't it be an accident-preventer if the edges of my stop sign were painted bright yellow when the representative corner also has a stop sign?* Actually, I only had a vision of a stop sign with yellow edges and white edges commensurate with my stated theory above. Once beyond the stop sign, the idea would vaporize. When I heard a rumor a year later that a person with a brain injury invented fluorescent colors, I had no trouble believing that, in a flash, the idea was born. The environment was as alive and stimulating to me as Willy Wonka's chocolate factory is to kids.

When my brain wasn't interacting with the environment or my brain was tired, my neurons would shut down and seamlessly, I would stare into space. I'd think that a few minutes had passed, but in actuality, a vacuous hour had swept by; five minutes is five minutes is an hour. I think of this state of mind as my black hole.

When I slipped down the black hole, I had no thoughts. I sensed nothing. Even if my eyes were open, there was no light. The mood was as quiet as snow falling on a mountain slope. Zero happened. My mind escaped to complete, utter oblivion. I wasn't turned into ashes, but into nothingness. I was annulled; I never existed. I didn't have control over my mind. With the force of a river, I floated where the current took me and if nature was forgiving, it wouldn't send me over a waterfall.

When I awoke, I wasn't sprawled on the floor, but sitting in a chair. I didn't necessarily know where I was, how I'd gotten there, or what was happening. The accumulation of how much time I spent each day in this obliterative state was substantial. That first half year, I slipped down the black hole about every fifteen minutes of consciousness unless I was engaged, say, with driving.

To stay alert, I needed to focus on a project. In the past, I'd usually kept up several projects simultaneously since I didn't like the down time when one endeavor ran into a snag. But since I was trying to recuperate and was low on physical stamina, I settled on one undertaking. I would sew something to wear.

I drove to the store to pick up supplies, and chose material and a simple four-piece shorts pattern. At home I discovered that I did not buy matching thread and returned to the store to make another purchase.

Now, I had sewn shorts, shirts, complicated dresses and blazers, and had designed and sewn all of the drapes and shades in my home. However, I was unable to complete the mindless shorts project. After reading the first couple of sewing instructions, I stared at the pieces of cloth. What was I was supposed to do? Back and forth I went, unable to figure out the next step. Out of frustration, I tried another approach. I folded the instruction sheet so that exactly one direction was visible. As I read the words, I did what it told me to do. Still, I messed up by sewing the wrong panels together or an outside edge to an inside edge. After I used a seam ripper to disconnect the pieces, I sewed it up again, wrong. Ugh. Who wears bright purple and teal green plaid, flannel shorts anyway?

I tossed the soft fabric sections aside. Instead, I would paint the outside of my house. I never did like its dark brown color.

With loss of balance, I would not be able to paint the second story; I decided to paint only the first floor. At the paint store, unclear on what color family I wanted to search, I selected every paint chip that I thought would match the ugly brown—which was most of the paint chips. Sorting through these chips and picking one color was mind boggling, especially when I kept setting down the samples and losing them. After a long selection process, I chose Jackson Tan.

I'd painted a small section with the new color when my mother stopped by and commented on the poor color selection. Now when my mom, a premier decorator, says that the colors are discordant, then the colors most certainly clash. I'd inherited her color coordination talent and was astounded we were in disagreement. But looking at the house, I could see the incongruity. She *was* right. I went back to the color selection phase and picked another light tan. Had I not learned the lesson?

There were many days when I could not paint because my shoulder and arm were in red-hot pain or it was raining or the sun glowed too bright. (These factors would elongate the project, leaving my tiny house "under construction" and displaying a patchwork of colors for a year.) I began to hope for clouds as I was happiest then. I recall a string of cloudy days that sunk most everyone's mood. Aligned with darkness, I must have been one of the few bursting out in glee.

Thinking back on my decision to paint my house, I sounded so logical and made so little sense. Who paints a house because they want an activity that is not physical? I shake my head in disbelief when I think of all the months of self-inflicted pain, writhing in my bed from over-exertion. At least I got it half-right and didn't attempt the second story.

After a month and a half, I was able to watch TV again, but only in short intervals. My favorite find was the infomercial. I watched the same shows each week: Victoria Principal skin products, hair removal products, and later, orthotics and the Ron Popeil rotisserie. The sellers were as excited about their wares as I was. I could age without wrinkles, stop growing hair in culturally unacceptable places, walk in comfort, and cook a fabulous healthy meal with minimal work and easy cleanup. This was the life I wanted, if only I could increase my attention span and rouse my initiative to get the products to my house. After multiple viewings, I collected myself, and the creams and other wonder products began to arrive.

I liked the Principal program of joining the club and receiving three products a month. With one phone call, the exciting products kept arriving at my doorstep. Many months later, I'd made enough brain progress to stop the flow. By that time, however, I had amassed a seven-year supply of beauty.

I was no longer the goal-oriented frugal shopper of the past. For example, filling a prescription was supposed to be a simple trip that ended with the purchase of pills and maybe a couple other essentials. I really didn't like drug stores and used to make a quick trip through them. This new brain, though, walked into the store and saw dozens of things neatly stacked on shelves in brightly colored boxes with interesting designs. They were there for the taking. The sight alone unleashed a wanderlust in me. I remember dropping off a prescription and with fifteen minutes to wait for the pharmacist to fill it, I spent that time and more luxuriating in the merchandise. I swept each aisle, reading each label, trying to decide if I wanted to buy something. If I couldn't make up my mind between two products, my solution was to buy both. Then I got to the Garden Claw, a gardener's must-have. I'd seen the ad on TV many times and remembered the exciting description of the product. I took down the colorful, three-feet tall box and read, *Cultivates! Loosens! Aerates! Weeds!*

I thought, *My god, it can do four jobs in one tool.*

Vinyl comfort-grip handles. Electro-coated.

Ah, soft on my hands.

Unique spiral action.

I don't own a garden tool with spiral action.

Your garden and back will love it!

I have backaches. Perfect!

My heart raced as I relived the commercial's fervor. Yes, I had to have one. Never mind the fact that I had searing neck and back pain which made it unlikely that I would be able to cultivate, loosen, aerate or weed. Never mind that I was barely a gardener. About one hundred dollars and two hours later, I returned home with the Claw, other prizes and oh, my pills (which I never took) to combat dizziness.

Filled with exhilaration, I telephoned my boyfriend, an avid gardener. Instead of acting impressed with my purchase, he explained, "I don't believe in turning over soil except when creating a new garden bed." Then, he tried changing the subject, but I wound my way back to the marvels of the Claw. When he came over, I took out the blue twisty jewel from its package and continued to talk lyrically about it for the next half hour. Even if the Claw did not live up to expectation, the tool was worth it for the amount of joy it brought me that day. I still have it. I still occasionally use it. I still cherish it more than most gardeners who own one.

My uncontrollable shopping opened my mind to the gambler psyche I'd seen in my sister. After her divorce, six years before my car accident, I flew out to Denver to be with her. She was down to her last sixty dollars in her bank account and, needing more, saw gambling as a way to increase her cash. I argued from the mathematical viewpoint that, more likely, she would lose her money. But the lure of the possibility of having more drew her to the casino, with me, an unwilling participant in tow. I couldn't bear to watch her falter and spent a couple of hours trying to find a place in town that was not a casino. While I browsed in some shops, she gambled her money away. I could not understand what had driven her to such depths.

That is, until my brain functioning turned me into an emotional shopper. No matter how many times I was burned with products that did not live up to the hype, my emotions continued to rule my spending habits. Advertisers sing alluring melodies to our emotional brains and those without the logical stops have no defense to resist. Had it been me, I am not sure that I would have done differently than my sister, vulnerable after divorce, down to my last dollars with a strongly emotional brain.

One day I drove to the rehab center recommended by my neurologist (per my request for an endorsement) for a tour of the facilities. I arrived exhausted and nauseated from the twenty-minute trip through rush-hour traffic. After a short wait, the owner showed me the facilities and then brought me to a conference room for a one-on-one discussion. She shut the door, closed the blinds to half-light and turned off the overhead lights. We talked about brain injury in general and their holistic, cutting-edge program. Then, she switched her attention to me. "Just by watching and talking to you, I can see how the brain injury has affected you. For example, you can talk with one person, but add a third person into the conversation and your comprehension decreases dramatically."

Yes, your description fits me perfectly, I realized. *Thank you for figuring this out for me.*

"Our program can teach you how to compensate for this." She went on, "But, there is something else more troublesome—" and suggested, "I think you should stop driving."

How did you arrive at that conclusion? I wondered. Because she seemed way off the mark, I immediately dismissed her advice. "My driving is fine."

"I don't think you understand that your judgment is compromised. Please get this checked out by asking your neurologist for his opinion."

I don't need to ask my neurologist. My driving is fine, I told myself.

At the end of the session, I got in my car without a thought and drove home to my daily struggles.

Grocery shopping had a wily accoutrement: the shopping cart. At the deli counter I waited my turn, ordered, received my goods and then put the lunch meat and cheese in a cart. As I wheeled the food away, a customer hunted me down. I had taken her cart. Other times, I left my cart in the middle of the store while I went to look for one last item. After I picked up tomato sauce, I couldn't locate my cart and switched to a methodical sweep, walking down each aisle of the store. Not shopping in superstores cut down my search time.

In the checkout line I sometimes failed to unload the entire contents of my metal basket. While the cashier was busy ringing up my items, I'd slide the cart past her nose.

"You mean to buy those, don't you," she would say disapprovingly.

Embarrassed with my oversight and shrinking from guilt, I'd reply, "Oops. I overlooked that package of chicken," or "Oops. The cat litter was too heavy for me to lift."

An honest mistake, I hoped that she saw it as such. Not once did store management prosecute me. Besides, I was an extravagant shopper with a big bill having bought unnecessary items that caught my fancy.

Some trips, I didn't always make it to the checkout line. I stayed too long, got too tired and then panicked, leaving my shopping cart, full to the brim, in the middle of some aisle. Barreling out of the store, I sought safety and peace.

Did I tell you about the Claw? It looks like a blue three-foot fork with four sharp tines in four directions. At the top there is a yellow horizontal bar to grab the tool. The gardener plunges the tines into the soil and then rotates the bar. It's a manual Rototiller. My heart soared while looking at the Claw, displayed in my living room on top of my Florentine wool rug.

That spring I did use the Claw, minimally, to sow a garden: a glory of peas, beans, broccoli, carrots and onions. These living vegetables brought me my greatest pleasure of the year: watching plants grow. On a cloudy day I could watch the garden for an hour at a time and swear I saw a bean sprout. Like hastened motion photography where a month was packed into several minutes, I saw moisture bubbles form and pop at the soil's surface, earth moving one atom at a time and bugs crawling over dirt boulders. Each day the soil burst alive with miracles; my hope was for myself, that someday my retrograded brain would have enough nutrients and sunlight to grow again.

One spring night, a strong storm blew in and snapped off massive tree limbs from my seventy-five-year-old willow tree. The debris covered half my backyard and stuck out of the ground, two stories tall in places. My garden, surrounded by towering branches, survived.

Like I was experiencing a storm's aftermath for the first time, like young children are said to do, the next morning I was startled anew with its destructiveness. I required environmental cues, even in cases where one would think that an image is seared forever on one's brain.

In that time period before the two-month mark, one vision successfully branded itself onto my gray matter. While my boyfriend was driving, we passed an accident—a rear ending that looked as horrific as my accident was. Upset and queasy, I prayed for the victims. They could not possibly know how different, pained and hassled their life would become. I still did not know that the full force of impact was yet to come.

7

Gray Matter

SEVEN YEARS
CONCENTRATING

Studying the brain takes a brain.
—pining for my old brain to decipher medical and scientific verbiage

"Tissue-Specific Expression of a Type I Adenylyl Cyclase Rescues the *rutabega* Mutant Memory Defect: In Search of the Engram," an article in the journal *Learning and Memory*, is about a research project on the memory of a fruit fly.

"Help!" I whimper, "What does this mean? Is it important to me? Is this true today and if so, do we know more? What could a fly brain imply about a human brain? There must be some implication. Otherwise, why would *Learning and Memory* contain multiple articles on fly brains?"

Over the course of four years of wading through scientific verbiage for professionals, watered-down science for lay people and science made easy for kids, of rereading, rechecking, correcting, and napping—Were those myelin jackets around the neuron? No, they are only on the arm of the axon. Am I sure that gender assignment is coded in the hippocampus? No, I've mixed that up with the hypothalamus—I have settled on my words. As simply and as clearly as I can explain, for your readability as well as my own, I describe the brain on a cellular level.

The brain is composed of two types of brain cells: neurons and glia. A neuron looks like an ink splatter with webbed tentacles. The tentacles that send electrochemical signals are called axons; the tentacles that receive electrochemical signals are called dendrites. A neuron has one axon, a smooth fibrous arm up to three feet long, capped with a few to a thousand fingers, each with a knobbed tip. The rough-surfaced dendrites of a neuron, at most several millimeters in length, branch out like a tree. Axons connect to dendrites, but the finger tips don't quite touch the tree branches, which leaves a gap called the synapse or the synaptic gap.

The average, three-pound brain has about 100 billion neurons, and each neuron has approximately 10 to 50 glial cells which support it. Glia deliver nutrients to the neurons, eat parts of dead neurons, and insulate the neuron's axon, sheathing the axon's arm with a string of white, fatty, myelin beads. The gaps between the beads, the nodes of Ranvier, are where electrical potential can switch from a negative polarity to a positive one as the axon takes in sodium ions and releases potassium ions.

This electrical impulse jumps from node to node in a chain reaction, traveling down the axon until the finger tips release neurotransmitters, such as serotonin or dopamine, into the synapse. Some neurotransmitters bind to the connecting dendrite, like lock and key, while others might ooze to other neurons and connect. From the combination of the specific neurotransmitter and the specific receptor, the receiving neuron interprets a message: "Fire" or "Don't fire." Continuously, hundreds or thousands of these messages barrage a neuron which will only fire when the excitatory messages exceed the neuron's electrical threshold. The signal is brief; enzymes degrade the neurotransmitters or the sending axon sucks back the neurotransmitters.

Of the more than 200 neurotransmitters, scientists have studied only a handful. Neurotransmitter acetylcholine assists memory, norepinephrine affects mood and general brain arousal, dopamine aids smooth movement and enhances reward while learning, serotonin affects sleep, perception, higher order thinking and emotional arousal, GABA controls seizures, and endorphins regulate pain. Norepinephrine, dopamine and serotonin are manufactured in the brain stem and then distributed across the brain to other neurons.

Establishing a network among 100 billion neurons is dizzying, but we hitch and unhitch daily in parallel patterns, in exponentially growing and declining patterns and in patterns where the paths reverberate back on themselves. Forever honing our brain to our environment and shedding excess neurons, we change, we remember, we forget, we adapt.

Blood keeps the networked neurons alive and supplies the neurons with glucose and the other nutrients needed to fire or secrete neurotransmitters. Take away the blood supply, say a blood clot in the brain or a hemorrhage in the brain, and the oxygen-deprived brain cells die within minutes and healthy, neighboring brain cells can die for weeks. Damage the cells by disconnecting them, say by shaking the head or by hitting the head, and the brain cells can no longer function. The damage cascades to what the brain controls—physical, mental and emotional functioning.

Looking back on that first year of electrical fireworks in my head and of frequent forays down the black hole, I imagine my remaining live neurons were firing wildly into the synaptic gap and my dendrites were not picking up the signal. Either my dendrites were too far from the axons, or my glial cells no longer fulfilled their role of facilitating the signal to the dendrite, or my neurotransmitters were flooding my neurons or drying up in my brain, or my axons were sheared, twisted or torn, or my receiving neuron was dead. Among the carnage, my glial cells worked at clearing away the neuronal debris while my neurons attempted to rewire.

Struggling to cope with a nightmarish, possibly epileptic, condition, I swam in the electrical darkness of the aqueous gap. When I came up for air and before I shorted out and plummeted down the black hole again, my working neuronal paths tried to process my environment and respond to it. I peeked at each scene in disjointed windows. Lips moving. Blink. A phrase. Blink. A teacup on the table. Blink. Smoke filling the room and I don't know why. In the background, my neurons zapped me, the electrical current's intensity ebbing and flowing with the usage of my brain.

To outsiders, an invisible Post-it note on my forehead read: "This site is under construction. Expected completion: to be determined." My family, my friends, and I waited to see how much my brain would rebound and ultimately, who I could or would become.

8

Brain Images and Waves

MONTHS TWO TO THREE
TORTURED

Doc, give it to me straight up.
—me, several years later, expressing frustration I should
have felt in trying to understand my injury

New Doctor

I hooked up with Dr. S., a reputable neurologist in Chicago who asked during a line of questioning about my accident's specifics, "Did you hit your head?"

"Oh, no," I replied.

Not willing to let my answer stand, he inquired further. "Are you sure?"

"Oh, yes. I am certain." This question didn't even merit a second thought.

But the doctor wanted to grasp more. "How do you know?"

I felt surprised by the question. "How do I know? Uhm, well, I don't remember hitting my head." Because I recalled numerous details about the day of the accident, I assumed the trauma had branded the important particulars onto my brain. I wouldn't forget a head wallop. A fact like that would not have slipped through.

Yet, my answer only bolstered the doctor's point. "Diana, many people who suffer a concussion aren't aware of hitting their heads. Let me ask you this. After the car accident, did you feel a bump under your hair or on your forehead?"

"Uhm, n-o-o, I didn't think to check."

"Objectively speaking, from the physics of the accident and your congruent brain injury symptoms, I suspect that you hit your head and also that the collision knocked you unconscious, maybe only for seconds."

The suggestion that one of my certitudes might be wrong jolted me. *I hit my head? I was unconscious?* Sitting on top of a paper sheet on an examining table, confusion swirled in my head. *Could this version of events be possible? No, can't be. I know what happened. Don't I? Of course I do.* "Oh no, I wasn't unconscious."

"But you can't tell me what happened during the accident. I think that you were unconscious."

The doctor talks confidently. Yet, the doctor wasn't there. I just wouldn't forget this. I don't know. Maybe the doctor's scenario is plausible. Then and there, my version began to crumble.

The neurologist ordered a slew of tests: EEG to determine if my brain had seizures, MRI to determine if I had gross brain damage, and ENG to determine if the cause of my dizziness was an inner ear problem. To my question, "Is it safe to drive?" he responded that I could drive on a limited local basis (unintentionally I omitted any driving difficulties and because I hadn't realized yet that I was having blackouts, I didn't mention those either). He did not recommend a cognitive rehabilitation program since he personally believed that the brain heals itself in time. However, he was willing to prescribe rehabilitation, the MD-accepted neurological life raft, if I wanted to go. Giving his professional opinion, Dr. S. told me, "You should not return to work yet."

That evening in a restaurant, two months post accident, as suddenly as I'd partially lost my hearing, my hearing returned. When the hostess seated Rick and I in the middle of the noisy establishment, all sound was muted as if I was wearing ear muffs. Then, over appetizers, across a minute of time, I gradually began to hear more clearly and loudly the sweet deafening din of others conversing. The return of sound came back that suddenly. And miraculously. My brain intoxication was wearing off.

I still had the constant buzzing in my ears, and over the next months its volume would fluctuate. By month four, I would awake each morning and instantly ask myself the same question: "Are my ears still buzzing?" I wanted that racket gone. I had the notion: If the buzzing disappeared (it did), then my brain would work flawlessly and my other symptoms would disappear (they didn't). Other days I had the opinion: If I could get more sleep (I did), then my brain-injury-induced behavior would vanish (it didn't). Still other days I felt: If my dizziness would stop (it did), then I would act normal (I didn't). Unlike a drunk who knows that if he could just stop drinking, then his head would clear, I couldn't uncover the switch to turn off the madness.

Scheduling

Rick phones. "I got your message that you booked your hospital tests at the same time as my MRI. I'm very upset that you did this."

I feel upset with him. From the quiet environment of my home, I spit back. "Hey, I left you a nice message about my upcoming hospital tests. If our test dates clash, then you can reschedule your MRI."

"I don't want to reschedule my MRI. I need my shoulder looked at as soon as possible. I've had this appointment for a couple weeks."

"I'm not rescheduling my hospital tests," I respond stubbornly, aware of the tremendous effort it took me to schedule these tests.

"You should reschedule."

"I'm not. So-o-o, uhm, we will each keep our appointments?"

Rick softens, "I want to be there with you when you get your tests and vice versa."

I'm still upset with him. "Then cancel your MRI."

"Why should I when you made the mistake?"

"What? No-o-o, I didn't make any mistake."

"You scheduled your appointment right on top of mine."

"Well, it's not like I knew that I was doing this."

"But you did. I told you when my MRI appointment was, and you told me that you would schedule your appointment on a different day."

I counter, "What? You never told me about your MRI appointment."

"Yes, I did."

"No, you didn't."

From out of a hat in left field he says, "I called you on Monday afternoon after my group meeting and told you."

"Are you sure?" I can't attach days to events anymore so saying that something happened on Monday is not helpful.

Rick backs down. "Oh, you don't remember a thing. I'll reschedule my appointment."

I had no recollection of our initial scheduling conversation, but on my wall calendar in my handwriting was Rick's MRI appointment and my hospital test appointment. They were scheduled an hour apart on the same day at different hospitals. Time and events, missing from my brain, stunned me. I did not build arguments on faulty premises, yet that described precisely what I had done. This evidence proved that Rick was right. Furthermore, I knew, briefly, that if I carried on like this, my relationships might break under the strain. I was no longer true to my words.

Medical Testing

On the day of the EEG and ENG, I woke up crying; I was scared that I didn't have enough courage to withstand the ENG. By the time Rick arrived to take me to the hospital, I was frayed nerves. I talked about not going. But Rick, who had taken the day off from work, would not accept backing out of the appointment. Because I had stayed up most of the night and not eaten since dinner, as per the tests' instructions, I begrudgingly conceded. Besides, my mom had planned to meet us at the hospital and my two supporters would get me through the day.

As Rick and I approached the high-profile medical facility, we saw a mob of reporters, TV crews, and multitudes of others. We wondered aloud, Why the crowd? until bystanders filled us in: they were waiting to glimpse Princess Diana. Regardless of my desire to join the onlookers, Rick and I pushed and squeezed and cajoled our way through the horde. Right before the hospital was cordoned off for the grand arrival, we entered the high-rise. On the lift, two hospital staff, looking exceptionally spiffy, talked about the princess.

"She's going to arrive any minute."

"We're probably the last ones to ride this elevator before she does."

"Are you going to get to see the princess?"

"Oh yes. I'm coordinating some of the arrangements."

"I will too. I work on the cancer ward."

I looked at the elevator buttons. I had pressed floor seven; the other lit button was floor eight. Suddenly, I wanted my tests done on the eighth floor. Even better, I wished for the princess to stop by to see how I was doing.

My mom was seated in the waiting area for the neurological patients. Once I'd registered, my entourage left, partly due to my encouragement, for a glance at Princess Diana. Shortly after their departure, the receptionist called my name.

I was nervous during the EEG because the test, although painless, was unfamiliar and the nurse was rough. She pressed hard with her red drawing pencil when she marked my scalp with the spots to put the electrodes. After she had worn her pencil down to dull, my head was a football play diagram with X's and O's. Next, she squirted gobs of jelly on the marked spots and then attached the wires to my head. Voilà, behold the human experiment. *I'm ready for that knowledge transfer. Please be careful not to electrocute me.*

At one point during the test, the nurse asked me to sleep for twenty minutes. Even though I'd slept only a few hours at night, I could not drift off in the EEG lab. The electricity over the princess had me wired. She was one floor above, and in my imagination, directly overhead. All I required was a periscope between the floors.

At the end of the test, the nurse plucked off the electrodes. To clean my scalp, she shoved my head from side to side, aggravating my whiplash. Furthermore, her rubber gloves stuck in my hair. Each time she pulled away, clumps of my mane uprooted from my head and clung to her gloves.

At the end of the cleansing, my mom and Rick returned for their princess with tousled locks of goop. To maintain my dignity, Rick handed me a baseball hat for my head. I capped my tangles and from behind the brim, my jealousy spilled out over their real princess sighting.

Immediately, one of the hospital staff whisked my group off to the next stop on the tour—the ENG lab. Mike, the friendly technician administering the tests, tried to make me feel as comfortable as possible. A welcome change. First, he sat me in a chair in the middle of the cylindrical room and asked me to wear funky electronic glasses. The peculiar eyewear could have been big or heavy or wired; I don't recall its look. He explained that the glasses would record my eye movements. After I was situated, Mike turned out the lights and closed the door, leaving me alone in darkness. Moments later, a red laser dot appeared on the black concave wall ahead and Mike's voice came over the speakers, "Diana, are you doing okay?"

"I'm doing fine."

"Good. For this first test, I want you to follow the red dot with your eyes." When the dot swayed to and fro, I felt like I was on a boat in high sea, getting dizzy and nauseated on top of the dizziness that started my day.

In the next test, Mike operated the dial which spun the rotary chair in circles at varying speeds while I followed the dot. I felt disoriented at the slow speeds and light-headed and queasy at the medium speeds. This test reminded me of a county fair ride, The Parachute, which I'd taken with a girlfriend. For longer than normal, the operator had rotated us round and round in a tilted circle. Then he reversed direction. Despite our screams that we, the only two riders, had wanted off, the malicious carnie delighted in speeding up the ride. We'd spun faster than approved safe. The blood drained from our faces. When we looked sick enough, the greasy-haired worker stopped the ride and released us from our chutes. Ten paces later, we'd puked in the field. Mike was nice, though. He piped in reassurance, "Hang in there," and "Only a minute more," and "You can do it."

After twirling me around in the chamber, Mike moved me to the "dentist's" chair. When he operated a lever, my tall-backed seat tilted. From various positions of head-lower-than-feet, he checked dizziness using the special eyeglasses that he had me wear. The worst position was full tilt with my left side slightly worse than my right. I actually felt okay during that test.

But after that, the real horror began. Next, Mike turned on a machine which blew out air of different temperatures through a plastic pipe. This tube he then directed at my ear. Warm air flowed into my ear canal for about five minutes, which doesn't sound like a long time. But when someone is causing intense uneasiness, five minutes is a very long period indeed. My ear didn't hurt. Instead, the warm air made me squeamish and more squeamish and even more squeamish still. When sitting up, nausea tries to make its way up. For this test, practically hung by my toes, the natural flow direction reversed—down was from stomach to mouth. Nearly twenty-four hours since I'd ingested food or drink helped me at this point.

After enduring warm wind in one ear, I took a long break to regrow my land legs. Bored with the wait, Mike, Rick and my mom spurred me to continue. So, I gathered my courage and toughed out another round on my other ear.

During my next break, Rick received a page from his lawyer. "I'm going to step out and take this," he told me.

"Don't go," I pleaded. "Stay with me for the last test."

"I can't. I've been trying to reach Lyle for the past two days. If I wait, he might become unavailable again."

"But I need you."

"But, Diana, your mom is here. You can hold her hand."

"Yes, but I want to hold yours too." The long day of testing had gotten to me and I cracked, "Why can't you be here for me?"

"I can't. My kids are important to me too."

Rick walked into the hallway to make his call. Five minutes passed, then ten. The technician, not willing to delay any longer, coaxed me back into the chair for the "cold wind" test. My mother's frigid hand held mine while dizziness overrode nausea. I begged for Mike to conclude the test and later appealed that we not freeze out the other ear. Nearly at my breaking point, out of stall tactics, I resisted disappearing and instead acquiesced to group pressure to finish the exam. When the winds stopped blowing, I felt wretched and emotionally abandoned.

At the end of an afternoon of congenial torture, the technician gave me a flyer on the causes of vertigo. Three were related to the ear: ear infections, ear membrane rupture and ear rocks. Of these three, ear rocks fit my case best—breaking off on impacts as minimal as high-impact aerobics. The next potential cause, eye problems, described me. But the description of the dizziness, unsteady on thick carpeting, did not match my flavor. I also discarded dizziness from medication since I no longer took any prescription drugs. That left the most probable causes of my vertigo—neck injury (cervical vertigo), brain stem damage or nerve damage (of the nerves that connect the vestibular system to the brain). For cervical vertigo, treatment includes physical therapy and medication. For the other two causes, the treatment description was fuzzy: "the goal of treatment is to prevent further injury."[1]

A 1996 poster from the Brain Injury Association of America similarly recognized, "The only known cure for brain injury is prevention," and consequently excluded treatment from its mission, "to create a better future through brain injury prevention, research, education and advocacy."[2] That poster crushed me. I interpreted: *now that I am injured, no one can help me heal.*

Yet, doctors do prescribe drugs for brain-injured patients. These pills are not treatments, but symptom controllers for anxiety, spasticity, sleep disturbance. Except for seizure medications, as of 2003, all brain-injury medications are off-label. In other words, the physician prescribes the drug for a purpose or in a manner other than what is described in the drug's labeling. Possibly the FDA approved the drug for another disease or another population. Still, for many brain injury symptoms, such as memory loss, doctors don't know of an effective off-label drug to offer.

At the hospital cafeteria, baseball cap on head, I nibbled. Then Rick packed up my leftovers or threw them out, and we said good-bye to my mom. Not ready to get into anything that moved, I ambled around the city to settle my dizziness, my arm holding onto Rick's. After a few short blocks, Rick directed, "We should be heading back to the car."

Still woozy, I countered, "Oh, it's too soon. I can't even think about riding in a vehicle."

"But rush hour is approaching. If we don't leave now, we'll be stuck in traffic."

"But I'm still dizzy."

"I'll drive slow. Come on, we should go."

"Uh, I don't know about this."

Rick turned us around. We walked back to the parking garage, found his car, and I hesitantly stepped inside. Fifteen minutes into the ride, I shouted, "I'm going to vomit." Instantly, Rick pulled off to the side of the highway and the urge backed up a degree. At my demand, Rick exited the highway prematurely. We got out of the car, with me stepping carefully, and headed slowly to a restaurant. Not until an hour's meal had passed did I get back into his car again.

I spent the next day in bed, swimmy and queasy. A landlubber clinging to the ground to stop the internal sway, I crawled with a wobble to the bathroom when I needed to pee.

A week later I met Rick at another hospital for another test—the MRI. As per Rick's instructions, I'd scheduled a double appointment: a brain MRI for me and a spine MRI for Rick (to diagnose his shoulder problem). Because of Rick's claustrophobia, he'd asked me to book his MRI first. But at the hospital, the nurse had already set up for my brain scan, and Rick got angry at me for the mix-up. Of course, I couldn't remember any prior conversation about who should go first.

The nurse sent me into a locker room and I changed clothes and then slipped the video cassette she'd given me into the tape player. Because I'd had a good experience years before when having an MRI taken of my hairline-fractured ankle, I felt calm about the upcoming test. But the video changed my outlook. From the recording, I learned that halfway through the procedure the nurse would inject me with a contrast medium. My ankle MRI procedure had not required an injection. Afraid of shots and radiation, I immediately stiffened. (I falsely assumed that the contrast agent was radioactive, when, in fact, it was gadolinium, a non-radioactive dye.)

When I entered the test area in a hospital gown, unnerved, I informed Rick and the nurse, "I can't go through with this test."

"What? Why not?" Rick asked.

"They're going to give me a shot. No one told me about a shot." Tears flooded my eyes and I began to breathe out in short bursts.

"Oh, you can handle a shot."

"No, I can't." I cried harder.

Rick put his arms around me. "Now, calm down." Then he looked me in the eyes. "You need to get these pictures taken so that they can see what is wrong with your brain."

"I can't do it," I whined.

Unfazed by me, the nurse stepped in. "Okay. This has gone on long enough. We have a tight schedule here and must get moving. Rick, I need you to leave so we can get started."

"Can't I stay here with her?"

"No."

"But she needs me."

"Sir, I'll ask you one more time. Now, go find a seat in the waiting area."

I couldn't believe she was sending my supporter away. I reached out for Rick. "Don't leave me."

"But I have to go. You'll make it through, Diana. Be strong."

"I'm not going to make it."

Despite my reservations, the nurse sternly ordered, "Lie down on the table." Her demeanor startled me. I hesitated. "You've already put us behind schedule. I need you to lie down. Now."

I quieted down and got up on the sliding table. Within minutes, I was inside a long, narrow tube. The nurse's hollow voice, piped in from the microphone in her control room, bounced around inside the cylinder, "Remain still for the next thirty minutes." Then she coldly warned me, "If you move, you will need to take this test again."

During the MRI, drums thumped loudly. The sonic waves, aimed at my head, felt like cruelty to me, a noise-sensitive person. My heart raced and leapt outside of my body. Involuntarily active, I fought to hinder movement. My mind screamed to get me out of the tube, yet the nurse with a long needle waited for me at the exit. Mentally, I writhed terrified through and through.

Amazingly, the first set of brain pictures was clear enough and the table mechanically rolled out of the tube. I closed my eyes and trembled while the nurse slowly injected me with the ice-cold dye. The icy liquid traced up my arm and into my system, and the feeling of "radioactivity" infiltrating me spooked me. Yet, when the needle lifted out of my vein, my panic layer of fear lifted. Back inside the tube, I settled down to tense.

Like booming speakers can move bread crumbs across a paper, the vibrations of the MRI rearranged my jaw bits (my meniscus disc at the jaw hinge is crumbled and for reasons unknown, has been in pieces since I was a kid). By the end of the test, my jaw shook uncontrollably. The contrast medium gave me side effects: dizziness, nauseousness, headache. Later that night, on the verge of retching, my head in excruciating pain, I could not sleep. For the next year, the jaw pain would stay with me and my jaw would quiver involuntarily when my muscles got tight—from cold or from stress. Later, I spotted an advertisement for the open MRI and wondered whether that option had existed for me in 1996 and if so, whether that version of the test would have affected my jaw.

A week after the MRI, I wrote in my journal about my incapacity to understand a scientific TV show aimed at kids:

I feel like my brain has been ruined. For the first time in my life, I feel stupid. I sure hope I don't have to live the rest of my life this way. My brilliance is gone.

On the same day I also wrote:

I feel disconnected from my emotions. There are many instances where I should have, would have had an emotional reaction, but I don't. The next day or a couple of days later a cue in the environment reminds me of the incident and I think, I should have been angry or sad, but I wasn't and I don't feel that way now. When I see someone emote anger or sadness for me, then I can imitate that and relearn reattachment of emotions to events. The most graphic illustration of a time I felt emotion since the accident was when my therapist felt bad for me because of my injuries. It wasn't until she felt upset and continued the point for an hour that I felt upset. Sometimes I say that I feel bad because intellectually I know I should, but, I do not feel that way. This will and has caused me trouble across the board, especially with decision making and problem solving.

According to neuroscientist Antonio Damasio in. *Looking for Spinoza*, the ventromedial prefrontal region in the frontal lobe detects emotional importance of situations. Possibly this area of my brain wasn't functioning properly.

Test Results

At the two-and-a-half-month mark, the test results arrived and all were normal. This was good news, but I was perplexed as to why nothing showed up on the EEG, ENG or MRI when so much was wrong with me. My best days felt comparable to my drunkest hours. Everything—EVERYTHING—about my internal landscape had changed. Dr. S. explained that the EEG and MRI might not have come back normal if I'd been tested closer to when the accident happened. He further elucidated that the MRI finds gross structural damage and misses damage the size of a pin head. On the brain, damage at the cellular level may cause significant brain malfunction. The ENG results indicated that my dizziness was not caused by an inner ear problem. To investigate my balance and vision issues further, the doctor suggested I see a neuro-ophthalmologist to examine my eyes.

Years later, I learned that my neurologist followed standard protocol. Typically with patients with mild traumatic brain injury (MTBI), a neurologist prescribes the CAT scan or MRI. However, these tests only show tissue damage and commonly come back negative. More likely, the patient has axonal damage which shows in the newest tests like the brain SPECT scan, the PET scan, the PET/CT fusion or the MRS, that measure the brain's blood flow and chemical levels. If I'd known I should have requested one of these tests or if I could have followed through on the first neurologist's brain SPECT scan instruction, I am convinced the results would have exposed the culprits.

At my seven year mark, after hearing a talk by a neurologist on epilepsy, I deduced that my head injury caused a form of epilepsy where my mind blanked out suddenly. Because my mind went somewhere else when I was seizing, I didn't know that I was having seizures. Because I looked like I was in a long stare while seizing in front of others, my friends didn't recognize my behavior as a seizure. Because my EEG medical test results were negative, my doctor didn't detect that I had acquired epilepsy, like 17 percent of patients with MTBI do. Yet, I lost consciousness off and on throughout each day of the first half year of brain injury, particularly when my environment did not require my attention, such as, when no one was around or the objects around me remained stationary. Even though I believe that driving a car kept my brain engaged enough so that it didn't seize, I clearheadedly believe that I should not have been driving. In fact, the possibility of a loss of consciousness is grounds for cancellation of a person's driver's license under Illinois State Law. Had Dr. S. known, I'm sure he would have set in motion the revocation of my driving privilege.

Dr. S. did rule out gross tissue damage, and I feel grateful for his expertise. But I also think that he should have kept looking for the specific physical explanation of my many, unexplained symptoms. Had I known the areas of brain damage, my doctor could have deduced and then my psychologist could have addressed a fuller list of expected problems, a psychopharmacologist possibly could have developed an individualized drug therapy to correct or alleviate any chemical imbalance I might have had, and I could have shown physical proof to my employer, to insurance, to other doctors, attesting that I was not crazy, deceitful or hypochondriacal.

With this neurologist I felt a mutual trust. He gave me encouraging words. The inconsistency I exhibited on the memory test indicated to him that my memory would return. He wanted me to take another neuropsych test with his recommended doctor at my six-month mark because the first neuropsychologist's report showed no numbers. He called my brain sensitive and referred to it as a higher-level engineered product. These brains have a greater response to BI than lower-level ones, he said. There is more to go wrong. Then, he drew a brain function return curve that had a smooth, steep, positive slope with most functionality returned in the first year and minimal improvements thereafter. The curve approached one hundred percent improved, but never reached it. He indicated that he expected my recovery to follow that curve. Lastly, he wrote me a note to return to work on a part-time basis three months after the accident.

Speak to people with MTBI about functionality return and a somewhat different story unfolds. Most talk of the three-year mark as the point when they start to feel normal (but not necessarily act normal), as happened in my case. Rather than a smooth improvement curve, they talk of progress as leap-aheads, backslides and lulls—a volatile stock market graph with an upward trend, barring a second BI. A year, instead of representing my "normal point," equated to how long it took me to internally identify and understand approximately ninety percent of my MTBI symptoms. That substantial improvement ends after a year is another doctor-propagated myth. I have met people with BI who report improvements as far as fifteen years after the accident. For me, progress slowed after my five-year anniversary, but I did experience one major improvement in year six and had a growth spurt in year seven (see Appendix A: Faculties Returned Timeline).

Another Test

For my neuro-ophthalmologist's visit I put together a two-fold plan, a new level of sophistication for me. First I would see the eye doctor and then I would call my friend Jeff, who worked nearby, to meet for lunch. In preparation for the adventure in the heart of downtown Chicago, I wrote down the address of the doctor and Jeff's phone number.

Typically, mornings were when my eyes worked best, and the morning of my eye exam began similarly. In fact, my vision seemed exceptionally crisp and clear. While pleasing in and of itself, I felt oppositely—disappointed. My ophthalmologist wouldn't examine me during a more regular, more decrepit state, and surely, I thought, my doctor would be unable to locate my problems.

In the neuro-ophthalmologist's office the technician took my history and noted that I poked my eyes frequently, usually walking into branches. Once the technician filled out many forms on me, he left the room. Ten minutes later the ophthalmologist entered. The doctor had no test for light sensitivity (photophobia), but he did administer several other eye tests. For the last test, the only one I remember, he put in a special type of eye drop, dilation drops, which enlarged my pupils. Light flooded in and within minutes, all I could see were basic forms with soft, undefined edges. The doctor then peered into my eyes through some type of scope. After the doctor completed the exam, he summarized the morning's results: my vision checked out 20/20, my periphery vision was normal, and my eyes were not damaged—even with all those eye pokes. Relieved, in a flip-flop of opinion I translated the good news to mean that my rare clear eyesight in the morning did not tamper with the results, and that my dizziness and vision problems emanated from my brain, not my eyes. (I had forgotten that neck injury may also have contributed to my vertigo.)

The visual cortex, an area in the back of the brain, controls vision according to a medical book that I read a couple years later. Since then, I have supplemented my reading with V. S. Ramachandran's *Phantoms in the Brain*. Ramachandran, one of America's top brain scientists, says that the relationship of vision and the brain is more complex than people realize. Two pathways travel from each eye to the brain. The "old" pathway traverses to the superior colliculus in the brain stem and controls more of our primitive reflexes. The "new" pathway traverses to the visual cortex, and then the signal disperses to approximately thirty areas in the brain. Each of these areas processes a certain facet of vision, such as the middle temporal area for seeing an object's smooth, continuous motion or an area in the temporal lobe called V4 for seeing in color. Because of this brain organization, brain damage limited to a specific area may damage one facet of vision while the others remain intact. For example, some blind people can detect an object's presence, position and orientation.

I definitely had some strange vision problems. In a restaurant, I had difficulty recognizing the sight of my own mother! I was meeting my mom at a local eatery and had arrived first. Watching the door for her entrance, a woman walked in whom I thought was my mom. But when I looked at her, she showed no recognition of me and sat down in the lobby to wait for her party. I kept staring at her to ascertain that she wasn't my mom; she kept glancing back at me and squirming in her seat. When my real mom came through the door, I had the same uneasiness and uncertainty until my mom acknowledged me. Unnerving experiences such as these solidified to me that my brain, probably my temporal lobes where person recognition takes place, was dysfunctional. (Technically, I had a mild form of prosopagnosia.)

Light sensitivity, another of my vision issues, is common among the brain injured and the autistic. I accepted BI as the explanation here. Bad depth perception explained walking into walls and bushes, words moving across the page, and my inability to connect my hand with another's and shake. It also indicated parietal lobe brain damage. All my vision symptoms consistently worsened when my brain was over-stimulated. Without stretching logic, I concluded that BI had changed my vision. Luckily, the inconsistency of my vision problems was a harbinger that my sight should improve over time, and it has. I now have fairly good depth perception, clear vision for most of the day, and somewhat less sensitivity to light than the first years of BI.

After the appointment, I was legally blind due to the dilation drops and my photophobia. Although I could only see amorphous shapes, I still committed myself to the second part of my plan to meet Jeff for lunch. From my pocket I pulled out a slip of paper with Jeff's work number. My writing looked like a gray blob! Thinking on my feet, I flagged down a stranger, a moving form, in the lobby.

"Excuse me," I started. Unclear if this person was a man or woman, I left off the sir or ma'am title. "Do you know where I can find a pay phone?"

"There is a bank of phones around that corner to your right," the male voice answered.

"Thank you. I have one more question. I'm having difficulty reading this writing. Will you read me the phone number?" I handed him my slip of paper.

"Let's see. 713-1218." He put the paper back in my hand and headed off to his busy downtown life.

"713-1218, 713-1218, 713-1218," I repeated to myself while I walked forward, turned right at the corner and walked straight to the wall with the fuzzy phones. "713-1218, 713-1218, 713-1218," I repeated to myself while I tried to read the numbers on the phone's keypad, but they, too, were blurred. On my own, I pictured a four row by three column key pad, found each key by touch and dialed, while repeating the number. The most difficult real-world mental calculation I'd attempted since the accident, alternating between two simple tasks, I applied everything I had to the chore. Amazingly, I connected with Jeff and told him I'd meet him at the Madison and Michigan Bennigan's, a restaurant I'd eaten at many times before, a restaurant with no *paper* tablecloths to provoke another noisy disruption of our meal.

Outside the doctor's building, my partial blindness and disorientation from the BI made it impossible to tell which way to go. I asked a passerby to point me toward Michigan Avenue and she told me to head to my right. I stumbled that way, tripping on uneven sidewalks, curbs and litter, until the sound of fast cars ahead tipped me off that ahead lay Lake Shore Drive. The stranger had directed me the wrong way.

I eventually fumbled my way to Bennigan's, an essentially blind woman without a cane, a seeing eye dog or experience, plunked down in the most trying of conditions: the epicenter of one of the world's largest metropolises during the lunch hour. I crossed busy streets only when others filled the crosswalks and arrived beyond fashionably late. As per usual, I had screwed up the arrangements.

I'd told Jeff that Bennigan's was on Madison and instead it was on Adams, as he'd said it was. Unfortunately, he listened to me and went to Madison first. At the restaurant he waited on the inside while I waited on the outside—too blind to recognize anyone. Ultimately, he spotted me and came out to retrieve me. We had not experienced this level of bad information and miscommunication prior to my accident.

In two short weeks, my doctor's note had me returning to work. In two weeks, I expected to pick up where I'd left off: managing huge software projects with hundreds of details and a plethora of contacts.

9

No Savant Idiot

Like a bird flying into a window, shaking off the surprise, then flying into the window again, an invisible assailant kept slamming me down.

Leading up to work

Thinking ahead about my return to work, July 8, when looking at that date entered in my scheduler, I had some hope that my brain would recover fully. A partial recovery might appear acceptable to the outside world, but to me, the state of my wits was the segregating factor for performing at the apex or not. I likened myself to an injured athlete who could contribute to the team, but not win a medal. Onlookers still "ooh"ed and "aah"ed at my talent; however, the injury was the difference between having marketability and not having it. The "nots" were mounting in my mind, struggling opposite hope on the other side.

In my last week of R&R, I raised my activity level as preparation for a more strenuous routine. On the first day of this final work-free week, I met friends Ken, his wife Jill, and a couple others at a pizza joint. We ordered dinner and during the wait, jabbered about our lives. After an hour had passed, the manager came to our table.

He explained, "You requested a specialty pizza with thin crust, but the chef cannot guarantee that your thin crust pizza will turn out. He recommends either regular crust or deep dish. Which do you want?"

"Why won't the chef make a thin crust pizza?" and "Why did it take an hour to inform us?" are the usual questions to ask. Instead, I asked (in response to what we wanted), "Could you bring us a pitcher of water?"

The manager ignored me and Ken picked up with the manager. "Let me get this straight. You make three types of pizza's here: thin crust, regular crust and deep dish. But you can't make us a thin crust pizza?"

"It's not that we can't make you a thin crust pizza, sir, but that it wouldn't taste right with the toppings you selected."

"I really don't see how the crust's thickness can adversely affect the taste of the pizza. No, we don't want to change our order."

They argued back and forth until the manager conceded to our request. "Sir, I need you to sign a waiver, then, stating that you will pay for the pizza even if it does not taste good."

"That's ridiculous," Ken responded, but then gave in a little himself. "But if that is what we have to do to get our pizza, then okay."

After the manager left, everyone at the table discussed what had just happened.

"Do you believe it?" Jill began. "They offer thin crust pizza on the menu, but can't make one for us."

"Yeah, what's up with that?"

"Then," Jill rehashes, "the manager is going to make us sign a waiver."

"Wait a second," I interrupt. "Did you just say we have to sign a waiver?"

"Yes."

"A waiver for what?"

"That we'll pay for the pizza whether we like it or not."

"You've got to be kidding."

"No, didn't you hear him tell us that?"

"I must have missed that part."

A sunset later our special specialty pizza materialized along with the bill—with no deductions. Nonplussed by the situation, I said nothing. Again, Ken argued with the manager over the poor service and the lack of compensation until the manager reduced our total. I used to defend myself and others, and my sharp verbal arguments had withstood counterattacks quite well. Brain-injured, my friends now protected me.

As we left the restaurant, I eyed the pitch-black sky and panicked. Car headlights at night blinded me and on the darker streets, I could barely make out the road. Incapable of driving myself ten miles to home, Ken and Jill calmed me down with a solution. In my car, Ken chauffeured me, and in the family car, his wife trailed behind us.

A couple days later, adhering to my deliberately busy agenda, I spectated a triple A baseball game. Stimuli filled the stadium: the bright sun, the loudspeakers, nearby conversations, and moving people—arm wavers, foot stampers, head turners—not to mention the baseball game. I had difficulty focusing on any one event. During the national anthem, from "O-o say can you see" to "the home of the brave" I searched the stadium for the flag. During the game, I felt just as discombobulated. Unable to follow the announcer, the game and the scoreboard, I couldn't track the strikes, the balls, the outs or the score. Baseball progressed too fast. In between innings, the fans participated in activities organized from the ball field: t-shirt tosses into the audience, baseball trivia quizzes, and a fake horse race with nominal prizes to lucky ticket holders. In the pandemonium, unable to spot the horses, my brain hit overload and my vision blurred. To escape, I excused myself for a bathroom break.

People crowded the stadium's pathways, and the movement of the walkers and noise from multiple conversations distracted me. Squashed between mobile baseball fans, I traipsed back and forth, squinting my eyes in search of a rest room. Eventually I spotted a door with women streaming out, and ducked inside and joined the shortest of two lines. Immediately I felt the glare of the ladies in the room. I smiled back weakly, oblivious to any error on my part. But upon further inspection, I traced the other line of women back to another door. The bathroom had two doors! I gasped upon the realization that I'd entered through the exit. The ladies who had come in through the proper ingress civilly waited their turn; whereas I appeared like a low-life line cheater artful at beating the system. I couldn't wait to go home.

On another day at another outing, the restaurant's halogen bulbs bothered me as did the ceiling light/fan combination that created an annoying, strobe light effect over our table. After appetizers, I got up to "powder my nose." Wandering the area in a circuitous fashion, lost among tables of diners, I knew my chances of locating the rest room increased as I covered more ground. About five minutes into my search, without having to ask the question, a waiter pointed me in the general direction. Ecstatic to finally find the powder room, I rushed in through the door, only to be stopped in mid step at the sight of urinals and a man peeing. *Damn. I'm in the men's washroom again.* I scurried out, hoping he did not see my face, and slipped into the correct, women's bathroom. This was different from getting caught up in college chicanery of swapped signs where the men's room door read *WOMEN* and vice versa. I'd wanted that explanation back.

Eventually I would learn to read the door's sign before entering; however, interpreting it wasn't necessarily a simple matter. Places followed themes. Instead of Men and Women, the entryway placards might read *Señors* and *Señoras*, or *Guys* and *Dolls*, or *Goombas* and *Femininas*. I would stand in the hall pondering if

I was a goomba or not, or a doll or not. Sometimes a woman came through one of the doors and then I knew which door to choose. Other times I impulsively guessed, ready to quickly determine if I should continue in or run out. Luckily I'd retained enough of my language skills, which got me through the proper entrance each time.

Back at the table, I continued on as if nothing of note had happened. Our food came, we ate, and when finished, I stood up to leave. No one else got up.

"Aren't you ready to go?" I asked.

"Aren't you forgetting something?"

"What do you mean?"

"To pay the bill."

"Oh." I immediately sat down. To myself I wondered, *How can I forget to pay the bill?* The question frightened me and my next thought scared me even more. *Yikes, brain injury can lead to criminal behavior and possible arrest.*

When we stepped out of the restaurant, the sky loomed dark, again. I managed to drive the mile home, close to legal blindness, relying heavily on rote memory of the roads.

On the Fourth of July, Steve, a good friend and former golf buddy, took me to see the Western Open. My lack of depth perception was apparent when I kept walking into tree limbs on the course and getting poked in the eyes. "Ughhh," I grunted while jerking my head back, startled by the branches' surprise attacks. The stabs made my orbs water and my sight cloud. Instead of watching golfers Phil Mickelson, Tom Lehman and Steve Stricker, I parked myself at the sidelines of life behind the ropes with my eyes closed.

Later that evening I wanted to see the fireworks, a couple blocks from my house. I'd forgotten to make arrangements with friends or family (Rick was on a week-long vacation with his kids at this time) and walked to the fireworks solo alongside a community of groups. I arrived at the start of the flying lights in bloom and was taken aback with how bright and how loud they were. The lights left psychedelic trails on my brain long after they'd disappeared in the sky. The boomers sounded like bombs dropped feet away. I crouched, fingers in ears like two guns to my head, flinching at the cracks and kabooms and activated car alarms. I thanked God for the shortness of the show that year and returned home to discover I'd left my indoor skittish cat, with a five-minute-a-day outdoor habit, outside, suffering from a secondary trauma (of my primary BI).

I topped off the week with an early birthday celebration, my thirty-seventh, with my parents at a horse racetrack. My dad purchased a program containing descriptions of the horses and the jockeys. Theatrically, Mom read aloud each horse's portrait for the upcoming race so that we could decide our bets. Because I couldn't concentrate long enough through the paragraph descriptions to recall which horses I liked and their corresponding numbers, I asked my mom to stop the recital and doused her jolly good fun. To place a bet, I made up numbers—4 to win, 6 to show and 3 to place—and then gave the clerk my money, anxious to lock in my bet before the race began. When the horses breathlessly stampeded around the track, I hadn't a clue as to which one to root for. An hour at the track and my eyes were watering, my vision blurring, my brain was scrambling—the daily pattern was repeating—and I longed for home.

With one day left before my big return to work, I'd made plans to spend it with my boyfriend at his house. However, after my week of disasters and exhaustion, I opted for the prudent choice—to stay at home. In stasis, my emotions circled around the week, weaving themselves into a tight ball. I could not handle extra activity. I depended heavily on others. I was not ready to return to work. By midday, I was in tears. My fantasy perceptions had unraveled and left a heap of haywire string. *Work colleagues are going to cannibalize me.*

The Nightmares returned and visited me each night of the last week. The theme was always memory loss, disorganization and disorder. The most vivid dream took place in France, a place where I hadn't traveled in real life with a language I had never studied. In the dream, I was trying to get home to the States. Every time I went to the airport, my papers weren't in order for getting out of the country. I'd take notes on what I was supposed to do, only to lose the notes and forget the steps to freedom. I never escaped the country.

Work

The preparatory week included a conversation with my boss Chris. He'd taken away my pet project, given it to a coworker, and assigned me to act as a consultant to the coworker. While on the phone, I didn't comprehend what was happening and felt ambivalent about the change. The next day, though, I felt ousted. My return would mark a new era where I was not trusted, I was not golden, I was not perceived as the same employee I'd been before my absence.

A drastically different work life on the horizon, my therapist and I wrote up a list of my job-impacting deficits. For balance, we added some quick remedies to a few of the deficits.

> **Short-term memory**—I forget names, dates, information, whole conversations, where I put things. If I don't write something down, I may not know it ever happened.

concentration—Keep conversations short and to the point. Make me repeat what was said. If you have something important to say, tell me to concentrate first.

parallel processing—I can do only one item at a time, including interacting with only one person at a time.

decision making/arguing—I have difficulty constructing an argument or responding with a good decision on the spot.

concept of time—I don't know if some event happened two days or two weeks ago.

lack of planning—I am impulsive. I generally decide to do something right before I do it with little foresight.

pain level—My pain level is high and I fatigue easily.

environment—I am sensitive to light and sound, necessitating a telecommuting life-style part of the time.

Once I returned to work, no matter how hard I tried, my lack-ofs would prevent me from performing my people-intensive, planning-intensive, issue-intensive duties done under the gun. If my boss had reassigned the role of project manager to me, unwittingly, I would have funneled the ventures down the crapper.

The first day back, as soon as I entered the corporate building, the lighting dazzled me. Momentarily, I stopped in the foyer and stood, stunned and blinking. *They've put in whiter lights*, I thought. Bravely, I proceeded up to the second floor and for five minutes, walked past row after row of fluorescent lights, shielding my eyes from the illumination. When I arrived at my work space—with the same five-foot burlap walls as all the other cubicles, my nameplate attached with Velcro to its outside—the overhead beams mixed with the brilliance of the computer screen. The combined glare flooded my pupils as if I was on an open tanning bed. I squinted and internally mumbled, *Huh, I don't remember my office being this bright. O-o-oh, my office hasn't changed, I have.* Knowing I would not endure in this niche, I searched for knowledgeable people to help me reduce the glow. A couple offices over, I found someone who assisted me in writing a light turn-off request to maintenance. I don't think anyone responded to my e-mail on how to temper the energetic colors on my Vivitron 21 computer monitor.

On my break, because I was overfamiliar with the layout of the work buildings, I routinely found the women's bathroom. But there was another problem.

While I was in the stall, my brain erased the path I had taken to get to the rest room. When I tried to get my bearings, the sameness of appearance of all the work bathrooms disoriented me. My thoughts began to spin. I didn't know which bathroom clone I was in, which floor, which building. A mild panic took hold while I dried my hands. I hadn't a clue as to where I should go nor how to get there. Slowly, I stepped out the door and looked around to see if anyone noticed my disorientation. Thankfully, no one was in sight, so I lingered by the water fountain while I scoured my surroundings for something identifiable. When I recognized a name on an office wall's nameplate, I exclaimed to myself, *Oh, this is the floor my office is on! I must be returning to my office.*

In the hallway, on the way back, I spoke to Lew, Rick's friend. Afterwards I learned that he had called Rick and asked, "What is wrong with Diana? I just got done talking to her and she didn't understand a word I was saying. She asked me to slow down, but that didn't seem to help much."

Midday, my boss scheduled a short group meeting to reunite me with his team. En route to the reunion I encountered an old acquaintance and became too involved in the conversation to realize I was making myself late. I arrived fifteen minutes tardy to my first group meeting since the accident, creating a bad impression. Drawing on my green note card of deficits, I admitted to my colleagues that I was returning to work with disabilities and, in shame, listed some. After the ten-minute meeting, I continued the conversation with my boss. I recited more inadequacies and restrictions until I couldn't contain my sorrow over my brokenness. Tears streamed down my face faster than I could wipe them away. *Crying at work? Really! At work? Uh-huh. On my first day back? Yep. In front of management? But I NEVER cried at work. Who had taken over my controls and spun the ship off course?*

Chris, witnessing my struggle, agreed to allow me to telecommute part-time. From his office we called a third party to discuss arrangements. Because I could not absorb the instructions, my supervisor took notes for me. I truly appreciated his help. On the other hand, he took an additional note of my reduced, way-reduced capacity from leading groups to needing spoon feeding. I cemented the impression fifteen minutes later when I returned to his office to retrieve my forgotten briefcase. My supervisor, on the phone, gave me an exasperated look when he realized what I had done.

For the remainder of the day I deleted e-mail, unable to make sense of the acronyms strewn within the messages. My loss of vocabulary spelled T-R-O-U-B-L-E A-T W-O-R-K, or TAW, since there was not a sentence on the job that did not contain an acronym. Astoundingly, I had forgotten every one, including the capital-lettered word creatures I had used every day for years. Translation: The brain sloshing was affecting part of my long-term memory, and the indication of a deeper injury, retrograde amnesia, terrified me.

After six hours at work, my boss visited me at my cubicle. From the doorway he must have seen me—eyes straining, posture droopy, voice moaning. Too mesmerized in e-mail deletion, I didn't notice him there until he spoke. "Diana, go home. You look wiped." Following his direction, I packed my briefcase and left. The next day, mainly I slept.

I returned to work again on Wednesday. In the morning, a maintenance man came to my office in response to my light turn-off request. He left the area and then returned. "I'm back to complete the job." I was flabbergasted to learn from him that we had met ten minutes before—the re-encounter with the woman on the sidewalk at my one-month mark of brain injury long forgotten—as I had absolutely no recollection of our acquaintance. As a teacher I'd impressed my students on the first day of class by memorizing all of their names. Every first week of classes I'd matched over a hundred names to faces and rarely did I forget one. Now, recognizing one relatively-new face was beyond my brain. How would I make new contacts, a weekly occurrence in my job?

The maintenance worker removed the fluorescent light sticks over my office, but the lights on the periphery bothered me. Weeks later, a work friend would solve my problem. He would create a partial roof over my cubicle from white poster board, and then I could genuinely say, "I work in a box." Standing in the center of the cube, with a lean or a stretch, I could touch any of the cube's six surfaces.

Inside the box, my main chore that Wednesday consisted of trying to dull my Vivitron. An unnecessarily complicated task, I discovered that the monitor had a brightness button which changed the lightness of the screen. I would learn many such tricks across the months. I could modify the set-up scripts, in a hybrid shell language which ran during a computer boot, to change color for certain windows—the clock or the UNIX windows. Other applications, such as the word processing program or the internet manager program, had their own methods to switch colors and were trickier to learn. Most distressing of all, some computer applications required for my job had no way to globally change the window's hues.

This self-imposed color assignment kept me busy until day's end, when the fire alarm suddenly blared. The ear-rupturing honking rattled my nerves and sent me into overload. Like a chicken with her head cut off, I ran around my office in small circles, agitated. Getting a grip, I ransacked my desk for essentials. Snatching keys, purse and briefcase, I scrambled to the closest stairway which quickly filled to capacity. Panicked and overwhelmed in the tight crowd, I pleaded to God for instant rescue. Getting suction-vacuumed out of the building seemed a good alternative. For a long ten minutes, I exited in an orderly fashion while resisting my instinct to push and scream. Once ejected out of the emergency exit and beneath the open sky, the rushing winds on my back propelled me to my car. Home beckoning me, I climbed inside and drove away. For my first week back, I'd logged a total work time of twelve depleting hours.

Over the weekend, on my birthday, I spent most of the hours upset and crying for one reason or another. Having a birthday reminded me that time was passing, at least for a day, and a familiar tension returned that had begun in my late twenties and had continued up until the day of the accident. With each tick of my biological clock flashed my desire: a satisfying marriage and then kids. At thirty-seven, my eggs were running out of my hourglass. Spinning myself into a tizzy, I worried, *Instead of working on family planning, I am relearning old moves and rebuilding my broken body and brain. My dream is slipping away.*

As a birthday present to myself, to get out of the house, I drove to the community pool for a favorite activity: swimming. I loved feeling weightless and strong with confident, even, streamlined strokes. Sometimes I'd pretended to be a sea turtle sinking to the bottom in a ball. Or I'd frolicked like a dolphin, pushing off the bottom and breaching on the surface. Gliding in water felt as natural to me as breathing. Water signaled daydream and play.

But on this day, floating in the water disturbed me. The buoyancy clarified the pain in my shoulder, arm and hand, and highlighted the twisted knots along my spine. My little finger became numb instantly, then my right arm, then my right leg. I didn't move fluidly as before; I lurched. My favorite stroke, freestyle, felt lopsided because my right arm raised only as high as my shoulder. After a short splash session, I emerged from the pool dripping in fear. My body was wrecked.

The rest of the day I searched for something that would make my birthday special, but didn't know what special was anymore.

The following day I dragged, trying to get over the sadness of my birthday. Although my compass still pointed toward family, the time-related tension vanished again (and even at forty-four has not returned). By evening, I lifted out of my mood. I would need all the energy I could muster for my second week back to corporate life.

At work, I attended an intimate presentation to our group. Even though I'd been an expert on the topic, I couldn't grasp most of the talk. To slow things down, I posed many questions, but had to leave the room when I became unable to concentrate on the answers.

The next day that I drove into work, I discovered my computer in the middle of a log off, compromising, for the first time, the security of my account. After shaking off this stunning news, I set to work on a solitary first assignment. In my journal that night I summarized my experience: "Working by myself is the easiest type of work to do." Not that I perceived work as easy. My second week's productivity totaled another draining twelve hours of work.

On Saturday, even though I was experiencing serious pain, Rick and I attended the wedding of mutual friends. Upon arrival at the reception, I couldn't find my jacket. When Rick retraced our steps, he determined that I had left my blazer at the church. He drove me back to the church to retrieve it and then back to the reception. The interrogation-bright lights and the moving-lipped people overstimulated my brain and again, conversations garbled in my head. When the DJ started up, the music squawked many decibels too loud and conversation became downright impossible. By the end of the night, I ached in excruciating, throbbing, screeching distress.

The next morning Rick tended to my agony—massaging me, stretching me out, icing my head, recommending a hot shower for my taut body, and calling my chiropractor for an emergency appointment. Finally, the body manipulator's adjustment released me from the I-can't-withstand-the-pain mode and resumed me to chronic, slightly bearable pain.

(Although the chiropractic treatments released me from agony, they did not seem to help in any other scenario. When my mother became concerned with the violent force chiropractors apply, and when she worried that a wrong move might damage me further, I followed her oft-given advice. Eight months after the accident, I stopped going for chiropractic manipulation. A year and a half later, when my masseuse recommended chiropractic care, I went back to the chiropractor having forgotten my mother's counsel. After a few sessions, my mother's concerns re-surfaced in my mind and once more, I stopped taking treatment.)

After a few spine pops and back at home, I positioned myself in bed in the only way that allowed sleeping: a heating pad on my back and my usual five pillow set-up supporting the right places. I can still picture myself lying on my good side, partially fetal, with my rigid right side resting on a fictitious soft-bodied person—bones removed.

This intense pain scenario repeated itself every other week. Two weeks later, in mid-August I would write in my journal, "my moods swing from 'I don't care' to depression to intense anger to oblivious happiness." By the last day of August I would physically hit rock bottom: "I want to be dead so that the pain will go away." Even though I remember long periods of stultifying pain, I don't remember anything about this intolerable day or its build-up. I don't even remember wanting to die. Yet this self-revelation stares at me starkly from the journal page. Unswayable, my memory is of continuous mental and physical endurance to a type of pain I'd never felt before.

Was I experiencing neuropathic pain, common among the brain injured, which latches on in the brain, possibly the thalamus, and doesn't let go? I suspect so. After the accident, I stopped wearing jewelry and whenever I could, I stopped wearing clothes—especially underwear and other tight fitting articles—because they induced more hurt.

The third work week, the last week of July, began in achy misery. Thus, I performed light work: reading e-mail and straightening the papers on my desk. I had lunch in the cafeteria with a close friend and got tripped up again in following easy conversation. Unable to decipher her voice pattern, especially in the too lively, loud and distracting cafeteria, I asked her to repeat and repeat and repeat. At least with voice mail I could replay a message three or more times without any more energy required from a messenger.

After six hours of virtual work, I felt exceptionally dizzy and spacy. I must have overdone my efforts. While in this out-of-body state, my boss called to give me feedback on some work I'd done, on the only real work I'd done since returning.

"Diana, I'm looking at the report you modified. It is missing the tape column."

"Tape column? Is this a new requirement?"

"No. Last week I told you to add in a tape column."

"But you didn't give me any requirements for this report."

"Yes, I did. Last Wednesday. I saw you copy down my request."

While I have my boss on the phone, I search my desk for a synopsis that seems to belong to somebody else. Remarkably, buried under a pile of papers, I turn up sketchy notes in my own handwriting on a requirements conversation with my boss. A tape column is one of the requirements. Holding the startling evidence in my hand, I have no dispute and no defense. I weakly acknowledge, "You're right. I'll fix up the report." I didn't know that I was that far gone.

The big questions were: What would I forget? What would I remember, and for how long? No one *with* a short-term memory can accurately answer these questions about themselves. Yet, the solid bet rode on my forgetfulness, quite immediate—if only I could remember how forgetful I'd become.

By week's end I decided to pull out of the yearly, company golf game. The intent of the friendly competition was to loosen up, make new contacts, and bond. With my constant pain and my inability to converse with multiple people, socializing with upper management would drop me down the rungs of the career ladder, not lift me up. In my boss's office, I delivered my retraction. I felt like a lone house teetering on the edge of a cliff, unable to hold onto normal life among the inland houses that made up the town. "I can't contribute fully to the company," I blubbered. Some of my tears soaked into his work papers and dimpled his reports.

The next morning a dream jolted me awake. People were talking to me, but I couldn't comprehend what they were saying. The dream's interpretation came through clearly—I had a recurring problem haunting my attic. Spooked, I later turned down a wedding and rehearsal dinner invitation from my sister's childhood friend. My R.S.V.P.: I am not well enough to attend.

When my sister flew into town for the wedding, we met for the first time since my accident. The giggle sisters, as coined by a former boyfriend, chatted face-to-face again; however, we didn't giggle at all. I'd lost the rhythm of our sisterly speak. By the end of the evening with her, I was crossed wires.

I'm handicapped?

At work I used to behave like a personable walking computer. I had memorized about a hundred customer six-digit problem numbers, which was obscene considering that numbers dropped off and on the list each day.

Regularly, engineers visited me. One might have said, "Diana, we have a permanent patch for that problem with the faulty customer-interface screen."

To verify we were talking about the same problem, I'd have asked from the top of my head, "Do you mean problem 943215?"

He'd have looked down at the number written on his paper. "Yeah. How do you do that?"

I took to numbers. As a kid I could recite phone numbers after hearing them once. Sometimes I surprised myself because I could recall phone numbers given out in somebody else's conversations. My brain naturally gravitated to digits even when I wasn't aware I was recording them.

I'd also mentally stored personal information, including complete conversations. The sight of someone had flipped my bits to the section on unresolved work/personal questions/issues, the latest personal data, a history of how we had treated one another, and an extrapolation on how I could expect this person to respond. I'd automatically known how to pick up where we left off on both a personal and a business level. To my version of events, most people had acquiesced.

Brain injury changed all my relationships. Instead, I started conversations by giving the other person, as well as myself, a clean slate. I couldn't recall recent events nor unresolved transgressions in the pre-BI past. Although I could remember the pre-BI past later, my brain did not bring off-topic long-term memories to my attention while in conversation. Engagement sequestered me within the moment.

Starting clean was loving and peaceful and mellow. A deadly silent brain doesn't worry. To other people, however, the loose ends remained loose—they didn't get back the document they had lent me—and more issues were created in the process. They became frustrated and angry with me.

While trying to resolve our past, they would get caught in the net of explaining events from square one. "Don't you remember saying that you were interested in the latest test plans and then I loaned you my document?" If I could understand them I'd still look quizzical, trying to figure out if this really did happen. "I have no interest in test plans. Why would I say that? Why would I have your test plan document?" Spending time in recall took the punch out of their anger.

If past events were not explained, I'd wonder why people acted angry. But then, after five minutes, my mind drifted back in the moment and soon I forgot the conversation took place.

People expected me to apologize for previous acts. I couldn't even remember missing their deadlines, let alone know to apologize for it. People expected me to ask them about their families. I couldn't recall if they had a family and would avoid the topic. I sounded selfish talking about myself. I would have sounded more foolish talking about them, asking things I should have known but could not recall.

At the urging of my therapist, I contacted Carla, a fellow car-induced closed-head-injury victim with a four-year perspective. We shared many of the same symptoms, although, some of hers were more severe than my own. Carla taught me that BI can cause sleep disturbance. I had not related the two even though my own sleep pattern had become remarkably different since the accident. The transformed me, a night person, stayed up late—three or four hours later than my pre-accident 10 P.M. bedtime. Contrary to the asleep-before-my-head-hit-the-pillow sleeper whom I was, I usually didn't fall asleep quickly. Slumber lasted at most four hours and then getting back to sleep took at least another half hour. During the daytime, I catnapped to adjust for the inadequate night sleep.

Carla fatigued easily as did I. She'd overdo on the good days, far and few between, and then pay later in exhaustion. I had the same oversight. Taken over by the excitement of rare energy, I seized at the illusionary chance of catching up to my responsibilities and fell short each time as they galloped forward. We were on the circular track of the Runaway Train at a Six Flags amusement park: inching up, screaming down, never level. Four years post-injury, Carla still had sleep and fatigue problems, and was in the middle of a job change. Her skills no longer matched her occupation: trial lawyer.

A month and a half after returning to work, a call from a coworker opened my eyes to how others resented me. She clearly stated that my job was up for grabs. Restless all night and unable to sleep, the instability of my work future trickled in. My faint memory, strong enough to chip away at my self-esteem, reminded me that I was useless at work.

In front of my therapist I became unhinged over my job's precariousness, and the potential loss of wages and career.

"Who do you know at work with a handicap?" she asked.

"Uh, let me think about that." Of the hundreds of people at my job site, I could not think of one person with a missing body part, with a missing function that caused blindness or deafness, or that required a wheelchair. Until she brought it up, I didn't even realize that I fit into the handicapped category. "Uh, no one." *Uh, me, I guess.*

She continued. "I thought that might be the case. I believe that your coworkers are most likely ill-equipped to deal with you because they have not been faced with the handicapped in a work situation.

"Have you ever worked with the handicapped?"

"Yes, when I was a teaching assistant, I shared an office with a blind man."

"How did you treat him?"

"Like one of the gang. My office mates and I did a few extras to help him. We occasionally read school-related books to tape. Or we walked with him arm-in-arm calling out obstructions or changes in terrain so he could walk without his cane."

"Is anybody helping you?" my therapist asked.

"No." *I need help from coworkers?*

"Okay. You need to continue to do good work and to guard your reputation. Since you forget a lot, you need to get in the habit of rehearsing important information. Can you do this?"

"Yes."

"Now, is there someone in your group who can fulfill the role of spokesperson for you with the others?"

"Maybe."

"I suggest that you find someone soon."

I'd wanted a job coach, a go-between person specialized in working with the brain injured who would bridge the gap between me and my boss. If I had shown up to work drunk every day, which was similar to showing up to work with an MTBI, my good, costly health insurance would have paid for the expensive rehabilitative services. However, my insurance did not cover people with an MTBI for evaluations (such as neuropsychological testing), job-appropriate training, and work interfacing—even after I submitted the appeal below. I sent a letter which took me hours to write, a letter eight years later I consider emotional and unconvincing, but my best attempt at the time:

> Thank you for your consideration of my claim. However, I am disappointed in your decision—not because it went against me, but because the question, "Does this policy make sense for the situation?" was not asked. I feel that the bureaucratic response was given; I'm just a number. I long for the days when I feel a sense of community, where people know one another—our pains, our joys—and from that vantage point make a decision.
>
> Please treat my claim as medical rather than psychiatric even though the insurance billing codes are psychiatric codes.

That benefits administrators considered the physical injury to my brain a psychiatric matter, with less coverage than medical matters (they were paying for my physical rehabilitation), irked me. Furthermore, if I had applied to the Social Security Administration (SSA) for long-term disability benefits, a daunting process for someone with a brain injury to figure out, SSA also would have categorized my disorder as mental rather than neurological. On my work insurance claim, I'd imagined I had one of the worst illness classifications—the hopeless case of mental derangement which was not worth spending money on for medical care. (In fact, William Winslade in *Confronting Traumatic Brain Injury* cites that 95 percent of persons with brain injury don't receive needed rehabilitation services.)

Because my doctor had returned me to work, I had no other choice than to try to integrate with the able-brained using the few resources I could marshal. In my mind I saw a sign over the company's entrance that read, "Only come back if you are whole," whereas this hologram, tilted at the management angle read, "Only come back if you are competent."

Work was more than generous in allowing me to falter without retribution, but they were as lost as I was on how I could contribute. They graciously agreed to let me telecommute and bought a computer for my home, but I couldn't figure out how to set up my system to talk to the work computers. The computer support team had specific instructions not to help anyone with a home computer, even if he or she was approved for telecommuting. Six unproductive months would accumulate before I had found enough people who would break this rule and help me figure out the company-specific protocol. When we finally hashed out the set-up procedure, we had twenty pages! By 2000, technical support streamlined this protocol and made it available to all employees. Back in 1996, I felt lame, on my own, trying to solve problems above my head, problems I would have had difficulty solving even without a head injury. I had an unreasonable assignment that did not affect anyone but myself. Amazingly, I still got paid for ineffectiveness.

As work progressed, my incompetence was becoming clear to me. I was unable to answer questions in areas that had been my forte. Instead, I found information and passed it along rather than formulating my own answers. I sent out dyslexic e-mail. While carrying out procedures that I had written, I riddled my work with mistakes. New information dropped out of my mind, including how to use new computer programs, and I spent hours in relearning. On several days I'd forgotten my computer passwords and each time, took an hour or more getting authorization to access my own accounts. I was fatigued, stressed and contemplating a career change. How long should I wait to heal, I wondered, before I could decide if a new career was necessary?

Over the Labor Day holiday I cried for the lost summer of cancelled plans, emotional traumas, physical pain, and flat-out confusion. Too unhealthy, the warm months had slipped away without a vacation. Why should the last weekend of summer play out any different? Once again, faced with battling pain, I scrubbed all my arrangements. Instead, I took another down weekend of stretching, icing and relaxing.

After the holiday, I returned to work with ignoble status and felt the scourge of the group. Coworkers were mad at me for not fulfilling my duties. I was mad at them for expecting too much, such as attendance at several meetings a week, and turning a deaf ear to my disability. Each day at work typically ended with me weeping in my office, highlighting my loss of equanimity.

I could no longer command respect from others since it appeared that I did not respect myself. As I found out, respect requires a memory. I couldn't remember deadlines because I would forget to write them down or when I did write them down, I would forget to put them in my date book or if they were in my date book, I would forget to look at my date book or if I looked at my date book, the deadline would fall on a later date and it would slip through the black void in my head. Did people meet my deadlines? No. Did I remember that they weren't met? No. I did not appear true to my word because I could not remember my words. Would people follow my directions? No. Some went out of their way to digress. I still respected myself, but I couldn't get any.

I led a Mr. Magoo existence, creating havoc everywhere I went. People saw me walking on a tight rope yet my myopic viewpoint was that I stepped on solid ground. Talk sprouted behind my back and my responsibilities dwindled to those that could do no harm. With no power left, what was society going to do with me, a single, brain-injured woman living alone? What was to become of me, a formerly whip-smart lead engineer?

PART II
Just Deal

10

Trying on New Glasses

FIRST YEAR
CONCENTRATING

My life became a TV show run by the TelePrompTer.
I was the writer, the card flipper and the actress.

"The logic is kindergarten," I'd started my therapy session. From the cues of the week's events written on a red 3x5 card, I reconstructed the milk debacle. "Each day I discover something out of place, like a gallon of milk on the kitchen counter. When I touch the container, it feels warm and I know then that it has sat out for an hour or more. But thinking back over the day, I have no recollection of drinking milk. I want to accuse my roommate of being the culprit because *I* certainly didn't sour the milk. Yet, I live alone. Logically, the only person I can accuse is *me*."

"But Diana," the psychologist said, smiling with the beam of a light bulb moment, "you can fault that other person living inside of you, the one that the brain injury brings out. Let's call her Marcia."

With the smack of a hammer splitting a rock, Shazam! Marcia was born.

I considered her my evil twin. Marcia left the doors to my car and house unlocked and sometimes open. Other times she locked me out of the house for hours in the cold, underdressed, until my boyfriend or a neighbor with a spare key or a policeman with a crowbar arrived. Marcia left the indoor cats outside all night. Marcia hid my things, including my car, in the most unusual of places. She heated the oven all night long, burnt most of my meals, and started kitchen fires that turned my pans to charcoal. Marcia left tasks half-completed as if she had been kidnapped in the middle of a job. I'd walk into these scenes—half of the laundry folded or a dryer door open with wet clothes inside—incredulous at her lack of concentration or her distractibility. Marcia was hard to live with. I could get angry at Marcia. I could laugh at Marcia.

As I got to know Marcia and her antics, I saw a need to take back some control from her. No pills and no treatments exist to combat evil twins (although many people on the outside insisted I hadn't done enough to heal or that I was smarter than I was behaving). Instead, about all a doctor could do in 1996 to help a patient cope with an injury that directs the show was teach compensatory strategies—the tools of adaptation.

Each compensatory strategy needs to be matched to the level of the injury as education is matched to age. If the brain is not ready or needs rest, it will not learn. Give the brain injured too many tactics when we cannot parallel process and we overload, rendering the ideas useless. Tell the brain injured to rest for an hour at two each day when we have lost the concept of time, and we miss some of the rest we need. A compensatory strategy is only as good as its probable execution.

With my therapist, we developed a game plan. (Others with better medical insurance might undergo rehabilitation.) She was the brain of the operation.

"Diana, my biggest concern for you at home are those regular kitchen fires. We need to put measures in place so that they don't happen again."

"Uh-huh."

"Now, one kitchen fire scenario goes like this. You start rice on the stove, leave the kitchen, and then forget that you are cooking."

"Yeah, I do that a lot."

"What you need is a reminder that you are cooking."

"Okay."

"Do you own a microwave?"

"Yes, I do."

"Before you leave the kitchen, I want you to set the timer on the microwave to alert you when the rice is done cooking."

"Uh, I don't cook rice in the microwave. I cook it on the stove."

"No, no. I don't want you to cook the rice in the microwave, I only want you to use the timer on the microwave."

"Uh, don't I have to cook something in the microwave to use the timer?"

"No, you don't. It has a timer function. Okay, let's scratch that plan. Do you have a kitchen timer?"

"Huh? What? What is a kitchen timer?"

By the end of the session I had written down: *Set timer to indicate when food is done.*

At home, I examined my microwave because, like a mathematical challenge, having been told I couldn't solve a problem motivated me to try. Still technologically savvy, within minutes, I figured out how to use the timer. Remembering to set the timer, however, was my impediment. I had to burn meals to remind myself of my frustration with cooking, which might or might not have led to recalling my timer solution. I might have needed to see the note from my therapy session, and then, immediately, to create a large sign: *USE TIMER FOR COOKING*, and then to place my sign in an obvious location next to the stove. When cooking, I might not have seen that sign and then forgotten to set the timer again. After a month or two, I might have turned using a timer into a habit. Yet, after I had established the habit and taken down the sign, I still might have forgotten to use the timer and consequently burned my food.

Say I remembered to set the timer. As soon as I left the kitchen, I forgot about the timer and my cooking. Sometime later, perhaps while I sat in my living room, I'd hear the timer ring and ask myself, *What was that noise in the kitchen?* Curious, I stumbled to the kitchen and magically, like I was rich and had a professional cook on my staff, I found a hot meal on the stove with pan unscathed. Learning new habits was hit or miss, a smidgen of luck, and an operable brain day.

When Rick saw the timer sign in my kitchen, he jumped into the act and helped me to develop more cues. Tackling his biggest worries for me, my unlocked/open doors and my erratic driving (sometimes I drove okay and other times not), he suggested signs: *Are the doors locked?* and *Am I conscious enough to drive?* I copied his words on Post-it notes and stuck one at eye-level along the stairway to my bedroom and the other on the steering wheel of my car. I could never tell if I was conscious enough to drive. As it was, I always answered Yes to that question. In retrospect, a better set of questions would have been: Did you get a good night's sleep? Have you spent most of the day in a quiet, dark environment? If not, have you done any brain-intensive activities today? If so, has your brain had enough rest?

After awhile, the note on my steering wheel prompted me to think about my driving. Soon, I devised some of my own Rules of the Road. Before putting my car in gear, I required myself to adjust my mirrors, buckle my seat belt, and turn on the fan; I could not do these things and drive at the same time. Since music distracted me, I did not allow myself to listen to the car's radio or cassette player. (At my one-and-a-half-year mark, I could drive and listen to classical music, and then at my four-and-a-quarter-year mark, driving and listening to any radio station was safe.)

Some techniques were concocted, but others I came by naturally. If a pen and paper were not available, I repeated one short sentence over and over, unbroken, until I could write it down. If my doctor, Rick, or my boss assigned me a task, I completed it immediately; inept at managing multiple tasks, waiting increased the chance that I would not get it done. At work, I found myself doing what other less skilled people did to offset their bad reputations. I dressed in fine clothes. I agreed with management regardless of my own views. I became unavailable—not by design—which gave me the side benefit of slowing down the pace of work.

Across the next months, my therapist worked with me to customize more tactics. In speech, I got stuck trying to remember simple and complex words. One time I paused, spoke a filler word, "U-h-h," then called my young adult self "am-bi-dex-tri-ous" when I meant to say "versatile." So, to help with word recall, my aphasia problem, the psychologist recommended working crosswords. I would have benefited more if the crossword answers were everyday conversational words instead of words like "eta" or "toga." But I still think the puzzles stimulated a floundering portion of my brain. I cheated when I was stumped, which was quite frequent and quite helpful.

My therapist, pleased that I was keeping a journal, suggested that I change its purpose. Instead of recording events because they seemed unusual, she proposed, "Have the journal compensate for your memory. Write down what you want to remember. Then you can reference it to fill in the blanks you will have later on." In the same session, she added, "The act of writing increases the chance that you will remember what you wrote about. So, you may not even need to reference an event in your journal because, instead, you have remembered it." After this discussion, we referred to my journal as my memory book.

Months later, I determined one more motive to write in my journal: the unpredictability of my life's course was fascinating. My former life had been foreseeable. Study hard. Get a degree. Find a good job. Buy a house. Nowhere in the plan did I read: Get in a car accident. Become whimsical. Unravel.

At my home and office, visitors noticed how slovenly I'd become. Stacks of papers littered tables and desks. Numerous Post-it notes, *Don't forget your keys* or *Buy milk at the grocery store*, were affixed to vertical surfaces. On the floor sat several items in the middle of a path, forcing one to step over them to pass. At entrances lay a line-up of goods—borrowed possessions, dirty clothes for dry cleaning, my leather briefcase—which made it impossible to open or close a door without moving the obstacles first. My surroundings, an eyesore, contrasted my old image—the neatnik. Uninformed observers concluded that I'd slipped down a muddy hill and into the pits of squalor.

They didn't recognize that I'd expended great effort to arrange my environment this way; the disorder possessed an order. The top layer of papers corresponded to tasks needing immediate completion. The Post-its, scraps of my brain, reminded me to do things I otherwise would have forgotten. The laundry basket in the middle of my living room floor dislodged the memory that I was washing clothes. And the location of my briefcase forced me to pick up the case before I could leave the house or the office. The messes represented a positive sign that I was learning compensatory strategies.

Six months into the BI, I devised a somewhat nutty method for remembering to hang up the phone. First, I embellished the problem definition. After BI, while conversing on the phone, invariably I would need some information in another room. I'd leave the phone to get the data and then pick up an extension. At the end of the phone call, I only hung up the receiver I was holding. My remedy for the "dead phone problem" was to turn on the light in the room before I answered the phone. After hang-up, eventually, I'd notice the light. *Why did I leave that light on?* I questioned, and while turning off the light, I would notice the off-the-hook phone.

Eight months into the injury, my therapist helped me to address my high frustration and stress level from trying to fit into a high-functioning brain life-style.

"At the end of a day at work, after a long phone call, or when you feel anxious, try listening to classical music. You'll find it calming."

"Classical is the only type of music that doesn't make me jumpy," I stated, which she already knew. "But out of my large CD and tape collection, I only own about two classical recordings."

"Who is your favorite classical composer?"

"Hmmm. I guess I don't have one."

"Well, I just happen to have a catalogue of classical selections." After she found the brochure, the psychologist pointed out a ten-tape compilation containing a variety of composers: Mozart, Beethoven, Bach. "Here, you can have this. To order, dial the 800 number on this ear-marked page."

From home, I charged the "Meditation: Classical Relaxation" series on my credit card. When the ten tapes arrived, I played the first tape again and again. As a teen, my sister had blasted the same David Cassidy or John Denver song repeatedly until I'd cracked, "Turn that song off!" I hadn't listened to music that way. I hadn't reread a book or re-watched a movie. Blessed with a strong memory, I had no interest and saw no purpose in repetition. I'd sought variety. With BI, the replaying of music and movies, and the rereading of books was variety; they were fresh to me each time I experienced them. A month or so later, I switched to the persistent playing of Tape Two.

Besides music, the other key to reducing my stress was a detailed well-balanced schedule. With my therapist's help, I reorganized. I moved from a week-at-a-glance datebook to a month-at-a-glance calendar to widen my vista. In the monthly view I combined my work activities with my social activities with my to-do list with my phone book, previously kept separately, and retained my memory bank within arm's reach as best I could.

Each Sunday Rick worked with me to schedule the next week's activities, coordinating his schedule with mine. Around my seventh-month mark a dab of planning capability returned, which gave Rick something to work with during our lengthy scheduling sessions.

To create my schedule, I rated activities on a scale of one to ten based on their brain intensiveness. On the low end of the scale sat physical therapy and massage sessions. More stressful activities, fives, included walking to a small grocery store to shop or to the bank to get cash. Social activities with several people talking at once rated a ten, as did working at the corporate office, as did driving.

From the experience of using this system, I later refined the driving grades—strong ten, average ten, weak ten—dependent upon the busyness of the roads, the mileage of the trip, and the weather conditions. Rain ranked a strong ten because others' headlights refracted through the rain, and the rain on the windshield decreased my visibility. Fog, on the other hand, rated a weak ten; the fog blocked the other cars from my view which allowed me to focus more on the actual driving. Snow, the other weak ten, was the only condition under which I could drive at night. Against a light snow backdrop, taillights and headlights did not blind. However, a blanket of snow changed the appearance of places and I made more wrong turns, even on the rote route to work. Every other weather state started the grade at an average ten. On the days I'd scheduled a drive, I prayed for fog and snow, my least favored motoring conditions pre-injury.

Driving, nonetheless, strained my brain. To recoup, my scheduling rules required non-driving days to follow driving days and rest periods to sandwich a drive and other heightened events. As Rick and I played with the schedule, other strict rules developed: We prohibited talking on the phone past eight because active thinking spun me up and made falling asleep improbable. On my calendar, we added "note writing," an hour long event, after each work meeting. Sundays became my cooking days with Rick when we prepared an army portion of chicken stir fry, spaghetti or vegetable soup, and froze it for consumption later in the month. (See Appendix B for a more complete list of my compensatory strategies and scheduling rules.)

Even with all this scheduling, my life whirled out of control. I was impulsive, lost track of time, would forget to look at the schedule, and frequently got sick. Unforeseen things happened, such as having to spend an extra hour to retrieve a purse I'd left in an ice cream parlor. Some days I woke up too exhausted to follow the schedule. All of these circumstances impacted my adherence to the schedule and forced revision. Off-kilter, I scratched off social events first, then driving into work and meetings in person, and then work itself. Resting, physical therapy exercises, and doctor's visits became my top priorities. The on-the-run person, me, turned into a recluse.

Spontaneity died. I couldn't say impromptu, "Let's shop for groceries tonight," because the sky might have been dark and the ground not covered in snow, or I had driven my allotment for that day, or the next day's schedule was a killer. Even if I ignored or forgot my rules and drove to the store with a list, I might not have functioned well enough to shop for the groceries, pay and drive home. I risked finding out in the middle of the activity, like driving, that my brain couldn't handle the event. When I sank fast, I thwarted the activity, at times abruptly, and quickly got myself to a safe place. I didn't want to harm myself or others. Sometimes I ran from embarrassment over what my sorry dysfunctional brain had done, over knocking over a cereal display in Jewel.

For the longest time, I thought that I could tell the state of my mind by how I felt. But crazy people can't tell from the inside how crazy they are. After a year, I understood that the internal measure on my steering wheel—*Am I conscious enough to drive?*—was ineffective. The only way I could gauge my brain's ineptness was to watch what happened when I tried to do something. Like a pilot checks out the plane's equipment, I learned to test myself for failure. *Walk okay? Check. Read okay? Check. Play card game Solitaire okay? Check.* Dissimilar to a captain's assessment, a check meant no more failure than usual.

Many times I didn't test out okay. After an excessively stimulating activity, like a wedding, my schedule's full day or two of rest was not enough of a down period—even if I instituted the no TV/music rule and spent my time sitting in silence or walking. With no other viable strategy, I waited and hoped that sometime soon my brain would refresh like a computer screen degausses.

With my therapist, I added more methods to aid my fidelity to the schedule. Because I'd forget to execute my physical therapy exercises at home, she suggested I follow the rule: Dinner is contingent upon the completion of the PT routine.

This edict worked marginally. My hunger became my cue that I should exercise. However, exertion while famished felt too unpleasant and soon, I stopped enforcing the rule altogether.

At work, I wouldn't remember to go to meetings, so my therapist advised that I enlist another person to remind me. I did as told, but he too, forgot, or thought that an adult should be responsible for following her own schedule, or possibly wanted to see me fail in public as backlash for picking up the bulk of my work, or surmised that I would be better off sitting in my cubicle since I no longer contributed in a meaningful way. Consequently, I continued to miss meetings.

Then, all the managers at work got Palm Pilots. I saw what the electronic scheduler could do and requested one. Because of my mis-execution of my work schedule, the department head granted my request for a Palm Pilot as long as I did not flaunt that I, a non-manager, owned one. Immediately I transferred my schedule to the Pilot. Like a mother reminding her daughter, it beeped me fifteen minutes before a meeting and flashed the message, *PREPARE FOR GROUP MEETING* on its screen. Five minutes before the meeting's scheduled start, another beep sounded, prompting me to leave my cubicle. For physical therapy and psychotherapy, the Palm prodded me, and also when my wash was ready to be taken out of the dryer. With my personal prompter, I could follow a schedule as long as I did not misplace the Life Pilot or let the batteries run low.

About a year and a half after the accident, my whiplash pain, which lessened at a glacial pace, started to break up. With a little more energy, I decided to add yoga to my schedule, an excellent strategy.

The first year of class was like unsticking a body after a vat of rubber glue had been poured over it. The rubber kept pulling at my arms, legs and back in opposition to the way I was supposed to bend. Not only couldn't I perform the moves, but also I had trouble aligning my body in the correct position at the right time and coordinating my breathing to the sequence. During the Triangle, Fencer and Thread the Needle movements, commonly a classmate guided my hand or pointed to an out-of-place foot, hip or elbow. After a while, I started taking a tape recorder to class so that I could learn the exercises at home.

In class, I always felt glad when we got to the last ten minutes: relaxation. As we rested on our mats, the teacher spoke softly, "Quieting the mind is hard to do. We all live busy lives and fill our minds all day long. Now is the time to relax. So, clear your mind. Don't think of anything. But if you have difficulty, like we all do, then do what I do. Think of white."

I had been one of those people. Silence was a gap requiring fill and I had trained my mind marvelously. When I was growing up, my parents didn't get along and would go long periods of time in angry silence toward one another. Anxious in their joint presence, I'd either talked to one parent at a time or else brought my mind to other topics—to homework problems or a girlfriend's upcoming birthday party, anything but to a fight that would never resolve. Staying with my parents' uneasy silence had seemed a deadly option.

Constant head chatter carried into adulthood, during work, driving, even relaxing. I'd had problems to solve, events to plan, memories to replay. During each pre-brain-injury week, I'd meditated to break from the mental parade. But soon into the trance, my mind would stop chanting or blanking out, and instead, would maneuver back to a stream of side thoughts. Playing sports, another tactic, had slowed down the flow, but had not squelched the shooting ideas. Inner silence, my lofty goal, only had entered my awake-life for seconds at a time, with a single exception. Once while in college, I'd paid to float in a dark, enclosed tank—naked. After I'd entered the small pool and laid supinely in the water, my mind had sped from idea to idea, until, drifting in the blackness for several minutes, my thoughts quelled. Because the temperature of the salty water matched my own, soon I couldn't sense my body. In my disorientation, I also couldn't tell where the outside world ended and where I began. Terrifyingly, I'd lost my "self" while at the same time, inconceivable in a logical sense, "I" became one with a powerful silence of greater breadth than a galaxy. More mute inside my head than not, I'd hung in cosmos-limbo, about forty-five minutes, until the attendant startled me back to reality by banging on the tank. For the next two months, from one brush of an angel, I'd carried peace deep inside of me, the same peace I'd sensed once before, emanating from a Hawaiian surfing instructor I'd met while on vacation.

Like hovering in a flotation temple, brain injury connected me to an absence of words which mysteriously washed a sereneness over me. So when the yoga teacher calmly whispered to still our minds, I thought, *I have no trouble thinking of nothing. My trouble is thinking of* something. Easily, I blanked my mind each session; nun-like, Zen-like tranquility described my now natural state. As if making up for years of head noise, my new genius (everyone is a genius at something) became silence of thought and in-the-moment living.

Great at relaxation, but awkward in movement, sooner or later, my self-consciousness in the exercise portion of the class was outweighed by the friendly classmates, the knowledgeable teacher, Janet, who gave me the individual attention I needed, and yoga's benefits: pain alleviation, health restoration, freer movement and a peaceful inner center. Ultimately, I caught on, started helping the newcomers, and reaped more advantages.

After your memory improves to the point where you can remember that you have a bad memory and you understand what behaviors occur because of this, the dynamic changes. Take the discovery of milk on the counter. I no longer asked, "How did this happen?" I knew that I had left the milk out even though I had no recollection of doing so. Without hesitation, I dumped the milk down the sink and in the process realized that the milk was cold. I did not leave it out for hours, only minutes, and could have kept it. Recognition of my problem was progress, a progress that cultivated my yearning for recovery. Whatever recovery looked like, I was growing doubtful that it would molt me back to the pre-BI me.

11

The Conference

The effects of mild traumatic brain injury can be loss of or reduction in
short-term memory, logic, emotional control, physical coordination and
balance, information processing speed, initiative, sensory input, time
concepts or ability to discriminate/plan/multi-task.
—some of my most prominent symptoms attributed to mild traumatic
brain injury

Each year the Brain Injury Association of Illinois (BIAI) hosts a brain injury conference. The brain injured and the network of people needed to support the brain
injured—family, friends, medical professionals, lawyers and activists—meet to
exchange knowledge and to give encouragement. Six months after my injury, I
signed up for the one-and-a-half-day BIAI conference held at the Radisson Hotel
in Lisle, a western suburb of Chicago. I needed to know more about the illness
that was orchestrating my life.

I don't know why Rick didn't accompany me to the conference. But in my
journal I counted seven half days that he took off of work to bring me to a hospital or a doctor's appointment. I can understand why he didn't or couldn't take off
another day, a Friday. Yet on Saturday, he wouldn't have worked. Possibly he was
taking care of his kids that weekend.

Thus, I entered the hotel alone. In the open areas I saw people at different levels of brain injury—some clutched a cane or sat in a wheelchair, some flapped
their appendages or spoke too loudly, one stared at nothing in particular with an
arm curled against his body, and others, like myself, appeared "functional." Typ-

ically, a mother or wife accompanied the brain-injured person. More rare was the father or husband chaperone.

Standing among the less fortunate, a surge of gratefulness welled up in me. Factors that could have been different on the day of my accident—a less-vertical position of my seat, a shorter distance between my car and the car ahead, a harder hit—could have caused me greater injury than I sustained. As I looked at the people around me, I noticed into whom I *could have been* transformed.

Brain injury was not selective. It nabbed a hard-edged man with tattoos, a retiree, an artist with a hand-painted scarf, a doctor in a suit coat and tie, a black woman factory worker from the South Side of Chicago, a white teenage girl, a janitor wearing a brown shirt with his name on it, a housewife, and me, a college-educated businesswoman wearing my professional clothes from my professional life.

A man in a suit coat and tie—I don't recall his name or his place of employment—walks up to me and introduces himself. "Hi, I'm Dr. So-and-So, a neurologist at Such-and-Such. What hospital are you affiliated with?"

Taken off-guard, I stumble. "Uh, I'm not a doctor." I recover somewhat and tell him, "Uhm, my name is Diana, and, uh, good to meet you." Quickly, I leave, elated that a physician with brain-injured patients did not notice, at least from my physical mannerisms, that I belonged on the other side of his stethoscope.

By the end of the conference, though, I would feel a penetrating connectedness negating any doubt that I might not be brain-injured, that my diagnosis was all a mistake. Undeniably, I had the same affliction as those sitting in wheelchairs and those using canes. This class of people was my best social fit, and I was crushed and angered at my circumstance. I once considered myself in the "movers and shakers" grouping; in a flash, I reluctantly landed in the handicapped one.

Yet, as happens to those with bad memories, lessons become unlearned. Personalities split. By the end of the conference, in another moment, I was still conflicted over my identity. I also felt a deep awe and reverence for the brain injured—them over there, not me. *They* possessed courage to continue through the pains. *Their* communication beat pure, direct and simple.

Years later, my identity crisis resolved, I would have my most memorable experience with a pure, direct and simple communicator. While I was walking up to a railroad crossing next to a train station, a man with a grin approached me. Moments before I'd seen him speaking, face animated, to another stranger who was inching away. The smiley man was effusing about trains. He told me that the train which had recently passed through was brand new. He pointed at its picture in several spots of his railroad magazine. The photographs did look like the actual locomotive.

He rattled off several facts. The train was owned by Union Pacific which was headquartered in Omaha, Nebraska. He went on about some other train-related information, more technical in nature, that I can't recall.

Even though I dislike noisy, massive, air-polluting trains, his joy was infectious. In that moment I loved his trains. He wasn't using trains to persuade me to sleep with him, to vote for him, or to buy him some coffee. He was enthralled about trains and was expressing his rapture to anyone who would listen. His communication beat pure, direct and simple.

After his spiel I was happy, very happy, and the fluttering butterfly inside stayed with me all day long.

While at the same train station a half year after meeting the train man, I met another brain-injured man. We were both waiting for the train to arrive when a message blurted out over the loudspeaker, "Please move to the Main Street railroad crossing. Passengers will be able to board the train only from that location." As the crowd moved to the new pick-up point, I watched the wheelchair-bound man struggling over icy cobblestones in his motorized people carter. He was making slow progress.

When he pulled up next to me, I noticed that his nose was running from the brutally cold wind. Extending common courtesy, I offered him a tissue. While he reached out his atrophied hand to accept it, he grunted, as if to say thank you. Then he raised his crooked finger up to tell me to wait a second. Patiently, I watched him fumble through his basket. He picked up a black notebook, flipped laminated pages, found the right page, and pointed to words, "Thank you." His eyes told me that my kindness melted his heart.

He continued flipping and pointing. "Train late all week. What you think is happen?"

We continued small talking. He had a good sense of humor and I enjoyed our conversation. I also noticed that the other huddled people gave us a wide berth. I sensed from others' avoidance of eye contact that they wanted nothing to do with this crippled and odd-sounding man. Earlier I had watched people flee in the other direction just from the sight of him.

I had to ask myself, would my before-BI self have talked to him? I might have. I was a nice person who treated others respectfully. As part of my academic requirements, for a psychology practicum, I had spent two years at McKercher Rehabilitation Center teaching brain-injured people basic work skills. What I would have missed had I not experienced brain injury, too, what I had missed at McKercher, was a brain-injured person's value and beauty.

In the fairyland of the conference, non-brain-injured people listened to the brain injured. While two men walked past me, I overheard exactly two sentences. The non-brain-injured one asked, "How old are you?" The brain-injured one replied, "What year is this?"

Most people reply instantly with their age, or some younger age. They remember how old they are. Many brain-injured people can't keep track of an entity that marches across time and instead, rely on calculation. Ironically, the age calculation depends on knowing the current date, or at least the year of the current date, another marching time concept.

So when I heard, "What year is this?" I immediately identified with the inability to track time. Ever since a car rear-ended mine and for four-or-so years thereafter, I'd had the same problem.

At the conference, I thought of myself as a static 36 years old, my age on the day of the accident. I was one step ahead of the what-year-is-this man; I could still track the slow moving year and knew it was 1996. But I did have to calculate my age each time I was asked. The formula I used to figure out my chronological age was (I still reasoned in formulas like the consummate mathematician I used to be):

$$A = Y - 1996 + 36 + B \quad \text{where}$$

A   = my age
Y   = today's year
1996 = the year time stopped for me
36   = the age that I stopped aging
B   = 0 if it was before my birthday and 1 if it was after

Non-brain-injured people always want to know your earth age, whereas brain-injured people want to know your brain age. In brain years we started our clocks at 0 the day that our brains became damaged. I was reborn on April 9, 1996.

Living outside the concept of passing time, unsynchronized to the rest of humanity, has had dramatic effects. Most of the day, I used to think of nothing—my brain turned off, blank as a 3 A.M. TV screen. I floated in emptiness, an

"anti-time." Void of retrospective thought, I did not miss people nor feel senti-
mental, and "I miss you" became a figure of speech. Neither did my thoughts
drift to the future. I hardly ever knew when my menstrual periods were coming
or when an appointment was approaching, even if these events were marked on
my calendar. Yet, if someone asked me about the past or future, I could have
answered because the question happened in the present and I still understood the
concepts of yesterday and tomorrow. For example, I could have described my sister's wedding day if asked, but I wouldn't have actively thought about it unless
prompted. Until I could readapt to time, I existed before the brain-age of worry,
remembrance, and forecast.

For the first time in my adult life, I lived solely in the here and now, a pre-BI
goal; my mind was always where my body was or else it was nowhere at all. Frequently, as I became aware of a new environment—possibly only a room
change—I would have a flash that I had no recollection of how I'd gotten there.
Chunks of time were absent as if someone had beamed me there or transported
me while I was sleeping. Without the grappling hook of time, I lost my consis-
tency of thought. Instead of a continuum, my mind represented time as discrete,
unrelated events. To a lesser extent, several years later, it still does.

Generally, these problems don't entirely go away. After a while, you get used
to it, you work around it, it doesn't seem as bad. Sometimes, if lucky, your brain
rebuilds itself and the problem is indeed lesser.

A row ahead of me, in the Symposium Theatre, the only room with stadium seating, a severely brain-injured person was amused with another brain-injured person's beer belly. He playfully poked the belly, repeatedly, like a Pillsbury dough
boy is poked. I, too, had often become preoccupied with a small detail that had
caught my attention to the exclusion of all others. Throw in too many new details
and the exercise had become too intense, frustration set in, and failure was high.
That was me in the morning trying to find the hotel—too many buildings and
signs in the way of the building and sign that I needed to see.

In survival mode, I reserved my brain power. If a speaker didn't resonate with
me, I turned away from the bright lights and amplified voice, and strode out to
my car for a peaceful rest until the next talk. In the morning, I walked into the
windowless keynote speaker's ballroom and sat down at one of many long tables
covered with a white tablecloth. Thirsty, I grabbed the heavy pitcher of ice water
on my right and filled my crystal drinking glass, spilling some on the pristine
cloth. Fifteen minutes into "Power of Humor in Communication," I walked out.

I had a headache from the busy environment and I did not find the dumbed-down jokes funny.

I rested in my car for an hour and then returned to a small conference room several lobbies away from the ballroom for "Improving Interpersonal Skills and Conflict Resolution for TBI Survivors." Ever since I became a survivor of traumatic brain injury, I had been fighting with others. To my neighborhood's yard-waste pick-up service, I had complained loudly that the garbage men had not hauled my packaged leaves, that they had ripped off the yard-waste stickers attached to the cans. Actually, I had been the one at fault. I had forgotten to put the required stickers on the leaf containers. At work I had raised my voice to the departmental secretary for being slow to fill my supply order. Again, I had been culpable for not having the proper signatures on my order form. Worst of all, Rick and I seemed to argue with each other most of the time. Some people, who had continual negative contact with me, fueled my outbursts and took pleasure in getting a rise out of me.

The main tenet of the conflict resolution talk was to replace the "you message" with the "I message." Instead of saying, "You make me angry," say, "I am angry because—" This was sound psychological advice, but it did not address my issues. Through more embarrassing experiences and more lectures, and with improvements in my brain's functioning, I eventually pinpointed my problems. I lacked emotional control. I was unable to read a situation correctly, but did not know it. I was more like a two-year-old, only able to view a situation from my own point of view. Granted, being self-centered was better than my earlier stage of not being self-aware; still, I was not advanced enough for adult interaction.

In retrospect, I have come to understand why, after the brain injury, I became self-centered. In the first stage of injury, I was disconnected from my body, my senses and my actions. As I started to heal, I became aware of my body and my actions, but I was only able to focus on one item at a time. If someone else was in the equation, I was not able to focus on both the other person and myself. Since I could feel my body, it was easier to focus on me than the other person. Add in my short-term memory problem, and events happened on their own, rather in context. The easiest context I could put an event into would be a context I had experienced prior to the injury.

Take the day I drove to Rick's house. On the phone my boyfriend warned me that he was packing for a trip. He would not have time to do anything fun, he said, but if I wanted to come over, I could. By the time I arrived, I'd forgotten our previous conversation. So the context I created was that I was at Rick's house to have fun. Oh, was I disappointed to find out that I was there to watch him pack. My contexts never seemed to match reality and appeared self-serving.

On the second day of the conference, I awoke with no idea of how I would get through the day. My brain was exhausted from two and a half hours of listening the day before and sleep had done little to refresh it. How could my blob of a brain listen to more lectures? drive safely to and from the conference?

Although my brain did not have stamina, my body energy had started to rebound the week before. I'd been ravenous—eating three full meals, snacks in between, a snack before bed and waking up in the middle of the night to eat. I'd not known this hunger before and welcomed the healing it implied.

The key speaker was Dr. George Prigatano, a renowned neuropsychologist, who would open and close the second day. Even though the Symposium Theatre audience consisted of many brain-injured people, the doctor delivered a fast-paced, premed-level presentation. To compensate for my inability to comprehend, I furiously copied as much as I could. Within the first quarter-hour, I could recognize that the talk was packed with useful information.

In "Disturbances in Self-Awareness After TBI: Importance for Diagnosis and Rehabilitation," Dr. Prigatano described some of the problems associated with brain injury. A car accident that causes frontal and temporal lobe damage may produce a lack of emotional control and an inability to perceive the intentions of others. Problems with memory and vision might ensue. An ophthalmologist's tests might show that vision is 20/20, as in my case, and yet the temporal lobe might be damaged, causing vision problems, also my situation. Socially, when trying to follow a conversation, the brain injured may get fatigued and then withdraw. *Would you say that again? My brain is slowing down.* In monkey studies, the brain injured lost their perception of social rules and relationships; eventually their peers ostracized them. Other monkeys could not predict what the brain-injured monkeys would do.

Other doctors mislabel the brain injured "in denial" when in reality we lack insight. Here was a neuropsychologist who corroborated my thoughts, which I would later try to explain ineptly to my own neuropsychologist.

The most troubling data Prigatano reported were the employment statistics for those with an MTBI. A third were unemployed three months post injury and the percentage jumped as time increased. By four years post injury, 27% were still non-productive. Persons with an MTBI function too well for employers to consider us as having a "long-term disability" that would land us in the work junkyard of the disabled. Yet, we are not well enough to perform our pre-BI jobs and are subsequently more likely than our able-brained counterparts to be laid off or fired. If it had not been for the Americans with Disabilities Act, as well as my connections at work pre-accident and my stellar work record, I probably would have been jobless within the first year since injury.

Another perturbing tidbit from Prigatano was that the brain might shrink one year after injury, slowing thinking speed. My thinking crawled. I could not fathom the prospect of an even slower rate.

I was in a mentally depleted state. But I knew it was crucial that I stay for Dr. Prigatano's second session. He was describing someone I did not know well enough—me! I skipped the small concurrent sessions. Instead, I called Jeff, a friend who lived close to the conference site and who was fascinated with the brain. I persuaded him to attend Dr. Prigatano's second session with me. He could listen to those sentences with the big words that my brain could no longer decipher. Jeff could figure out the meaning—he could be my brain.

I met Jeff in the hotel lobby and we rushed to the lecture hall to attend "Mechanisms of Recovery Following TBI: A Neuropsychologist's Perspective." Dr. Prigatano confirmed my therapist's approach: compensatory strategies are the best coping tools a doctor can teach a brain-injured patient. He said that previously doctors recommended rehab between one and two years after injury, but that in 1996 brain-injured patients were in rehab much sooner. Later in the talk he warned about starting rehab too early, as doing so sets up situations and expectations that the brain injured will be unable to meet. These statements are akin to Jean Piaget's child development theories. Piaget identified four stages of cognitive development: sensorimotor (0–2 years old), preoperational (2–7 years old), concrete operational (7–11 years old) and formal operational (11 years old and up). Learning has an order and teaching a concept before a person is cognitively ready will end in failure.

As with the first session, the second session left me with disturbing news. Some problems may get worse across time, such as sensitivity to stress, lack of interests, and temper. *Wait a minute. I assumed that each of my problems would either get better or stay the same. I can get worse! I didn't know that I could get worse.* To recover, the brain uses up its reserve left for aging, which sets up persons with a BI for brain aging problems, like memory loss or reduced processing speed, years sooner than our contemporaries. I wondered, *Will the accident make me feel 75 when I turn 50?* And then the implication seeped in: *I have a lifelong illness to manage.*

After the lecture, Jeff quickly left for a planned lunch with someone else. As soon as he was gone, he slipped out of my mind. Utterly spent, I chuckled to myself about the oxymoron of us brain injured attending premedical presentations and flashed back to another incongruent conference. As an undergraduate, I'd attended a psychology convention in Milwaukee as part of an elective activity for my psychology major. Other psychology majors and I stayed at a hotel that was hosting two conventions: ours and one for blind bowlers. In the lobby, the elevators, the hallways—everywhere—we saw the blind with one hand holding a cane, a seeing-eye dog leash or another's arm, and the other hand toting a bowling ball bag. They crossed in front of us. They crossed behind us. They criss-crossed each other, traveling to and from the bowling alleys. It seemed sci-fi. Up to that point, I had no idea that the blind could bowl. I certainly did not know then that many brain injured were once smart people who still had the smart inside.

PART III

A Change of Season

12

The Winds of Autumn

MONTHS SIX THROUGH NINE
FURIOUS

Take shelter now. A tornado is in the area.
—warning over the intercom at my job when the 1990 Plainfield
tornado wiped the town off the Illinois map.

The fall weather brought changes to my body. My teeth loosened like someone had hit me in the mouth with a basketball. My soft tissue contracted from the cold, amplifying my pain, and my sinus cavities filled in reaction to the pollen-releasing ragweed. Darkness enveloped the day sooner, and since I had to be home by dark due to my night blindness, it felt like I was folded and tucked into my box well before playtime should have been over. Pending doom was coiling its tendrils around me and my brain frazzled mad while it tried to adapt.

With the leaving sun, I worked to close down my garden: clipping dead perennial leaves, picking the last vegetables, shutting off the hose from the inside, and storing fencing and garden tools—the Claw, small rakes and shovels. In my half-conscious way, my feet tangled in the fencing. I tumbled swiftly and solidly on the lawn, jamming my knees and wrists. Grass-stained skids covered my outfit and skin. Every day I bore the telltale marks of a life of hard knocks—a soiled wardrobe—and even the cover-up of new clothes provided immunity for only hours.

During the same period, finances depressed me. I could see from the daily mail that I owed lots of money. Unable to keep track of what was due and when it was due, medical companies, credit card companies and utility companies sent second and third red warning notices and tacked on late payment charges. My neurologist's medical practice put a lien on my house, the consequence of my

117

inability to work effectively with the correct insurance company to pay my neurological bills from four appointments. (I now wonder how many neurological patients with loose screws have neurologists whose office staff severely penalize their patients for not being able to figure out how to pay their bills.) Should I have relied on my medical insurance, my auto insurance or the insurer of the person who hit me? I took on treatment first and then tried to manage payment later.

The more I could feel the consequences of being street-post dumb and the more I could see what my life was like, the angrier I became at the negligent driver. He drove his honking-big vehicle into my medium-sized car, a sitting target, and reduced my brain to rubble: tiny unconnected pieces of gray matter that sparked uncontrollably.

The reason for the accident was still unclear. The rear ending driver had told me that he was adjusting a mirror. Yet his insurance agent told me that the driver was reaching for a tissue in his glove compartment because his nose was running. I had two contradictory stories and without further contact with the driver, came to the conclusion that neither were true. Wouldn't the motorist have adjusted the mirror during the ample time our cars were stopped? Why would he lean across the passenger seat for a tissue while his car was moving? I wondered, too, about his glassy eyes, but his insurance agent said that the driver had drunk an over-the-counter medicine to relieve a cold. I kept going back to the negligent driver's reluctance immediately after the accident to tell us he had a cell phone, until I finally deduced: He was on a cell phone when he hit me! (I have no evidence that this distraction was the cause of the accident, but it is what I believe today.) Every time I screwed up—I fell down the stairs, I couldn't converse cogently, I couldn't satisfactorily complete a work assignment—was because this man had diverted his attention, most likely, to his cell phone conversation while he was driving a one-and-a-half-ton crushing machine.

This man lived in my town. In my imagination, we had similar upbringings with similar values. He was probably a friendly neighbor, a loving husband, and a wonderful dad. He also had a slip in judgment, perhaps daily, when he decided to talk on a cell phone while driving. The crash was unintentional, for sure. The results, my results, were years long and totally life changing.

I can picture the day when I took my first neuropsych tests. I see myself driving through chaos, searching for a legal parking space, racing around while looking for the test area in the hospital, interacting with the test administrator, taking the tests, sweating, getting wrong answers, and talking to the doctor, answering on fumes alone. The day jolted my sense of self, a long full day's trauma to remember. Then my memory turns blank.

The second time I took the neuropsych tests, at a different medical facility from my first round of tests, I have one memory of being in the parking lot and another of sitting in the lobby. But I can't be sure if this memory is from that test day or another, follow-up day at the neuropsychologist's building. I have to rely completely on my journal to know what happened the second time around:

> At my six-and-a-half-month mark I was reevaluated—neuropsych testing—by a different neuropsychologist and hospital. I felt that these tests did a much better job of trying to expose my difficulties. Many of the tests were the same (exactly), but it seemed each portion of the same test had a much more difficult section. Or more tests from a test suite were given. For example, the math test had a couple polynomial questions, where as the first test did not. So that brought the test up to 7th grade math (which certainly did not stress my math skills). At both places I was given the "put the pegs in the hole" test. But the second place also gave me the finger tapping and grip strength test. I wish I could have had those tests at the first place so we could have a comparison point (I know my grip strength was much less—it is only through physical therapy that my strength has increased). In general, I felt I did much better on these exams.
>
> For the first time, the week before, I had a breakthrough in the area of planning. I asked, How would I feel if I were to go to a tennis match? My boyfriend remarked that this was the first time since the accident that I was thinking ahead. My general feeling has been that I've been thrown into situations and back pedal out of them. By doing this advanced thinking, I know better the situations I'm walking into. I also did advance planning on the "put the pegs in the hole" test, looking to see ahead of time how to match the notch of the peg to that of the hole. I didn't do this in the first test.
>
> Another positive result—that I had more stamina during the second testing. The first testing I was exhausted throughout and thinking was a huge effort. The second test I was tired and overstimulated, but at no point did I feel on the verge of collapse. I also had energy to drive home. I have been excited this last week because my physical energy is returning.

If someone would have asked me immediately afterward what questions were on the first neuropsych exams, I would have been unable to say. But amazingly, months later, when given the test again, I was able to recognize it as the same test. I couldn't remember many things I had recently written and was surprised daily by notes in my own handwriting. I could not recognize reruns on TV; they appeared to me as brand new shows. I could not remember people I'd recently met and was amassing people I didn't know who knew me. Yet I could recognize tests I had been given a few months before. My brain was inconsistent. Under the right circumstances, it could recognize. It recognized a novel trauma.

Also, I knew that I didn't have the finger tapping and grip strength test because I had written notes on a neuropsychologist's talk at a brain injury conference. My notes said that these tests were standard to any neuropsych examination. At home, when reviewing the notes, I looked up my own neuropsych report from my first examination; these two important tests had not been administered.

While I was waiting for the results of my second neuropsych examination, I dug out the test results from the first neuropsychologist again. I reread that I was a hypochondriac of average intelligence with mild traumatic brain injury whose comprehension and attention were not compromised, but whose "conceptual and problem-solving skills were limited."

This time, the findings seeped in under my skin. In a delayed reaction that lasted months, I oscillated between deep sorrow and livid indignation. My sorrow was that of a fallen star who had lost her most prized gift: intellectual ability.

In college I'd studied seventy hours a week to master algebraic topology (AT), one of the most conceptual and analytic branches of mathematics, whose practicality has yet to be discovered and whose abstractions can't be pictured. The only woman in AT classes, I'd studied various mathematical spaces, such as infinite-dimensional ones. You live in one type of three-dimensional space. With great imagination you can picture a four-dimensional object—the Klein bottle, a figure-eight-ish container twisted into itself where the inside is the same as the outside. But you can't envision any five-dimensional space, and infinite-dimensional spaces are one degree worse because the dimensions don't end. Most everything else that I'd analyzed while a graduate student was as abstract as mathematical space multiplied by itself to an infinite degree.

The algebraic topology classes didn't even have books because no text completely covered an entire course's ideas. Occasionally the professor handed out other mathematicians' papers, either in German or English, which proved a recent theorem or corollary. In this innovative atmosphere where papers came hot from a conference, before translation, where the rest of the material came by word of mouth, where we'd thought that maybe twenty, fifty or one hundred years later someone would find a use for this field of study, I'd felt close to a small pocket of people on the mathematical frontier. Understanding most of the concepts, I'd frequently volunteered to go up to the board and prove a theorem. In a flurry of chalk clicks, like an overzealous puppy, I'd illustrated key concepts in mathematical symbols and the Greek alphabet as succinctly as possible.

In my minor, mathematical logic, the other purely abstract branch of mathematics, I reveled in infinitely many infinities and their different properties. I immersed myself in the meaning of questions like Russell's Paradox: Define the set A to contain member X if 1) X is a set and 2) X is not a member of itself. Is A a member of A? (Both yes and no answers lead to a contradiction.) I ruminated about Gödel's Incompleteness Theorem which basically states: Within any logical, consistent system, some assertions can't be proved or disproved. The crux of the argument hinges on trying to prove: "This statement is unprovable." Because self-referential statements posed trouble, I'd wondered, *Did Gödel's theories extend and imply that I could never wholly understand myself (assuming I could create a logical, consistent system to explain my behavior)? Could science, so closely tied to mathematics, never explain everything? Would man always be searching for truth in an ever-expanding universe?* A star can never reach a brightest point and thus, will always feel like her potential lie untapped.

For an exam interpreter to state that my conceptual, problem-solving mind was limited based off an exam which couldn't even measure my usual ability, was absolutely, positively, mind-blowing. I'd fallen from mathematical heaven and crash landed on my head.

I now had a head with a brain that could hold only one thought at a time and that thought free-floated in space, unconnected. It may have been pushed into my head from another thought or an environmental cue or somebody's comment, but quickly it untethered itself and became unrelated. Cause unhinged from effect. Reason and worry tumbled into their graves. Ulterior motives, doused in gasoline, vanished in a whoosh of fire and smoke.

At times I appeared as if I could reason, but these appearances came from my long-term memory, from having devoted my existence to reasoning. I knew what cause and effect were. I could look at the dark sky and say it was about to rain, but I couldn't piece together new cause and effect relationships. I couldn't deduce that I shouldn't drive, that I shouldn't turn the burner on and leave the kitchen, that I should go to the doctor. People had to tell me these conclusions, which didn't make sense to me, and they had to tell me with conviction and they had to spend an hour explaining it to me and they had to tell me multiple times. Their conclusions conflicted with my long-term memory driven self-knowledge: I *was* a good driver, I *could* cook, I *knew* when I needed a doctor.

Moreover, my view of myself had never been solidly average. Now, everybody has a talent. Some are phenomenal singers. Others can persuade people to do things they normally wouldn't do. I was great in academics, particularly mathematics. I'd always strived to be the best and in pursuit, spent a decade in college toning my intellect. My talent opened doors for me wherever I went.

I don't say this to boast. In fact, it pains me to remember my aptitude, to remember what was seized. Like Julie Andrews who lost her spectacular singing voice after surgery—a voice that took her to great heights, a voice on which she hung her career, her life-style, her identity—a calamity wiped out my significance and my gift. When it was all gone, I was left standing in a field on top of a hill, spinning with open bent arms, looking out into the world, eyes barely able to open, head droopy, crying, "What do I do now?"

Remembering how brightly I'd shone, how protective I'd been toward my brain—rarely drank liquor, kept a regular schedule, rarely took medication, got enough sleep, exercised every day, ate a balanced diet—makes me weep. My gut constricts, sadness drips down my internal organs, the loss permeates. A profound enveloping of grief; my first brain vaporized before its potential was met, its power doused like a flood extinguishing a five-alarm fire. To think about my top-notch qualities in detail, to write about them, chops me off at the knees. Sniveling, I'm reduced back to my bed, unable to cope. For the next few days I'm in the most dour of moods.

Four years after the brain trauma, I threw out many of my handwritten notes from graduate school to reduce the clutter left from a life that feels dead to me now. So when I reminisce about my history to pick out three stories that best capture my talent, you know I've ruined my next block of hours. I only return to mathematics graduate school in my mind for good reason: to illustrate my decline.

One semester I took a math class taught by a giant among mathematicians, known as such because he had fathered a branch of mathematics. I felt honored and blessed to learn from the best, the creator, in a class which had a reputation of extreme difficulty. Unknown to the professor, to survive, the students banded together into teams to tackle the assignments (this was the only graduate-level class where I was aware that cheating took place). One such group invited me to join them, but I declined because I didn't cheat, I would learn more if I did the work myself, and I was confident in my abilities (so confident that I didn't even bother to take the prerequisite course). The only student not on a team, I toiled more than the others, putting in an average of forty hours each week for this four-credit elective class. My diligence paid off. Periodically, the professor announced that only one student had solved a problem and that student was me.

Another semester I took a theoretical computer science class and discovered that I could solve some of the problems with mathematical solutions. The math proofs were more elegant and much shorter than the taught, brute-force, computer science methods. Soon, I began staying after class to teach the professor these prettier and more general methods and began turning in assignments with these types of solutions. Yet, for some of my homework answers, the teacher could not understand the mathematics I'd used and thus, gave me half credit. Upset over losing any points but especially because my work had contained no error, I complained. To resolve the issue, she collaborated with a mathematics professor to produce a fair grade. In that class, I'd stood out, abnormal, a pain in her side.

My last semester in graduate school, for extra credit, I'd solved a chunk of someone else's computer science PhD thesis—about twenty pages of proof. The only such student to do so, I'd picked the hardest way to receive extra credit because I'd wanted a challenge.

I feel grateful to have had any talent at all and to have had the opportunity to share it, through teaching, with over a thousand college students. But having reached a crest, having placed all of my effort in that direction, in retrospect I wonder why news of mediocre scores on elementary-level neuropsych tests and the implied prognosis of intellectual normalcy (which, in actuality, was not quite that), hadn't fazed me sooner.

Though I'd acted emotionally flat since the time of the accident, reminders of the hypochondriac label eventually fired up my anger. I wasn't making up the illness to get attention, medical or otherwise. Why else did I rely on others—the policeman, my psychologist—to push me to see a doctor? Why else would I leave out symptoms when I talked to my doctors? Wouldn't a hypochondriac show a false concern about her illness rather than tell the doctor, as I did, that she was "worry-free"?

I was incensed. Supposedly, I had an inclination to develop physical complaints when none were warranted. But, I hadn't complained. Someone told me to go to the doctor. I did. The doctor asked me what was wrong. I told him. The test administrator told me to answer true or false to a bunch of questions. I did. *They* led me, not the other way around. I could not manage my life and my mind wasn't capable of a hidden agenda. I was not that "together."

When I think about my false identification, HYPOCHONDRIAC stamped permanently in my medical records, I boil for days with excess energy brimming over my rim. I cry. I punch the air. I scream. I am bereft over a doctor's claim backed up with a so-called objective test. His word carries more weight than mine—I'm a patient, not to be believed. He robbed me of my credibility about my illness and for a long while, the illness robbed me of my credibility in every other area. In doctors' offices, at work, in society, I am invalid, someone to be treated with suspicion and disgust, someone with whom all conversations about illness need to be cut short, thwarted, diverted.

Doctors' own fears about their brain-injured patients may lead them to a hypochondriac misdiagnosis. According to Diane Stoler, a psychologist with an MTBI, and Barbara Hill, in *Coping with Mild Traumatic Brain Injury*, in a section about the stress of putting a patient through too much testing, "Some practitioners may even hesitate to pursue testing that will spell out the precise causes of MTBI-related symptoms because of concerns that graphic descriptions of brain injury may lead to psychosomatic complaints that will hinder a patient's recovery."[1]

How can someone have psychosomatic complaints when test results show a real problem? Would a doctor withhold testing for or knowledge about a condition such as AIDS, cancer, a leaky heart valve for fear that acknowledgment would deteriorate the patient's condition? Why in the medical profession is withholding important information from brain injury patients acceptable? How prevalent is the problem of faking a brain injury that doctors are on guard and provide a lesser quality of care? Is that one of the reasons why the neuropsych test administrator kept reminding me to give each exam my full effort? From a doctor's perspective, why are brain-injured patients more prone to hypochondria than non-brain-injured patients? Is it because we are given the Personality Inventory where our typical brain-injury aftereffects—headaches, dizziness and lack of deep sleep—are woven into the hypochondriasis questioning and so we test out positively as complainers?

The brain-injured people I know generally have bad memories, react rather than plan, and have lost the ability to immediately comprehend the full picture of their own malady let alone keep their symptoms in the forefront of their minds. How exactly would hypochondria manifest itself in this population of people?

Besides, who owns information about a person's health? Holding back such knowledge is unconscionable because, like wearing Kick Me signs on our backs, it prevents us from compensating for problems we don't know we have. As a result, a doctor's decision to minimally investigate a patient's problems or to remain mum about certain results is more of a culprit, hindering a patient's recovery, rather than a cushion for a patient's initial reaction to learning about problems.

Not only that, in my own case, concentrating on hypochondria diverted my money, time and energy. Doctors railroaded the discussion to focus on reducing complaints versus compiling all physically-originated problems affecting my mind and their corresponding solutions. Branding me a hypochondriac allowed doctors to do nothing about my actual issues. Effectively, I was discredited, shut up, abandoned. As did insurance companies and as would have the Social Security Administration's offices, neuropsychologists labeled my problems as psychological rather than neurological, implying that I was faking my struggle. Instead of helping me to heal, the mind doctors threw in an albatross and then deserted me.

Yet, I cannot overlook my own contribution to my unpalatable label. In Dr. O.'s office, when he had rattled off the findings, rapid-fire to my ears, I'd not fought for my good patient reputation. My silence to the hypochondria tag, instead of interpreted as a typical brain injury response—of acting slow to understand, unskilled at reasoning, incapable of responding to multiple points put forth—must have been interpreted as agreement. The very injury that was the reason why I became a patient of this doctor in the first place, abetted his misdiagnosis.

Contrary to my neurologist's opinion, I know now that I needed help. I needed to try to understand my injury even though my capacity to understand was reduced. I needed information so I could speed up my progress, not slow it down. Ultimately I found the hypochondria label destructive to my health, to my employability, and to my self-worth. I cried for many nights.

My sorrow and anger carried over toward other test results, to my "strong attentional functioning and appropriate comprehension." If that were true, why, then, could I only last fifteen minutes in conversation before I had to take a break? Why could I not follow the characters or plot in a TV program or a movie? I thought it was because I was overwhelmed with words and images. Why could I not understand my work? Why couldn't I tell who was next to go at a four-way stop sign? These experiences were consistent each day. My answer was that the tests were not designed appropriately or their results not interpreted correctly or their reliability was too low.

If a person's long-term memory is intact, what is really being tested? Why not get a person's background and then devise an exam series rather than judge the person from a basic elementary school perspective? Isn't brain injury a comparison of what a person could do versus what he or she can no longer do? Shouldn't the tests indicate how a person with these abilities will succeed or fail in society, in his or her life, and more specifically, in his or her current job? Dr. O. and the first neuropsychologist gave me the impression that my social and vocational areas were basically unaffected. My life did not require all of the brain power that I had previously brought to it. I later concluded that BI, especially MTBI, cannot be adequately measured without knowing the brain's functionality prior to injury—an MTBI person's success in life cannot be predicted without knowing the life.

Testing the mind is tricky. When one neuron pathway shuts down, another pathway is tried. People with an MTBI may still get to the right answer, just not in the same way as before. For example, I could subtract numbers, but my new way to subtract was slower and left me mentally exhausted. A correct response doesn't mean that our minds are undamaged. Are testers sure of what they are testing?

To check my memory, I listened to a recited story, a recited grocery list, and recited numbers. Then, immediately after each recitation, I told them what I'd remembered. In real life we need to remember longer than that. Why not include a test where there is an interval between what is told and when information is asked back, such as immediate, one minute, half hour, one hour, two hour, three hour, eight hour, next day, and one week interims? Include some non-emotional and emotional material. See how good the patient is at learning names, learning a computer protocol, remembering to call the doctor back the next day without aid of a note. Throw in some surprises. In the waiting room, drop some confetti on the patient. While talking, put on a clown's nose. Get creative. In some persons with brain injury, emotional memories stick better than factual ones.

Besides bad test designs or misinterpretations, a test's reliability may be a factor. When doctors give results, they say, "You have a tumor," or "You don't have a tumor," or "You don't have an attention problem." They don't tell you that the tests are only 70% accurate or have a 30% failure rate at false positives or have a 30% failure rate at false negatives. They tell you like it is gospel. As patients, we or our on-site advocates need to start inquiring about test reliability and insist that the release of reliability information become part of an American medical-practice standard.

In another delayed blowup and later collapse, I raged over the doctor's term "mild" to describe my injury. If my brain injury was mild, why was my life turned on its head? Why did cooking a meal end in smoke? Why did I open myself to theft by leaving my purse in public places, by forgetting to lock my doors, by believing scam artists' sales pitches? Why did I sail through the air every day for one reason or another—I tripped on a crack in the sidewalk, I misjudged the stairs, I didn't see the tree branch, walked right into it, and flipped back?

My best friend, a counselor, softened the blow. She explained that there were three classifications of brain injury—mild, moderate and severe. Even though I had the mildest type, brain injury doesn't affect anyone mildly.

In fact, I didn't even understand brain injury. No neurologist of mine, and I saw three different ones, and no neuropsychologist of mine, and I saw two different ones, took the time to explain it to me. They merely said I would get better—it may take a couple of weeks, or a year or two. They labeled my injury mild traumatic brain injury, but I didn't understand how they arrived at this diagnosis nor what the diagnosis meant. Two neurologists offered a prescription for rehab, but indicated that it wouldn't be useful to me. They all sent me out of their offices on my own to wait for good fortune to visit me again.

Perhaps the lack of treatment for brain injury conveniently divests a doctor from these cases. Perhaps mild cases are not a neurologist's cash cow. Perhaps the more complicated severe and moderate cases are more interesting to a brain doctor. Or, maybe my doctors were simply ignorant of or lacked experience with MTBI cases.

What I am about to say next, I don't want to say. I wish I didn't feel this strongly about what it feels like to have a brain injury. I know only one mild case from the inside, mine, which I believe is on the harsh side of the spectrum of mild brain injury cases. Many of my problems are not going away. Through a mildly brain-damaged mind, I have observed mild, moderate and severe cases. My view may be tainted.

I fear saying that, yes, my mild traumatic brain injury has had major impacts, but if you have a moderate or severe case, then your case is probably worse. I don't want anyone to have been worse off than me. My experience was hard enough. My experience limited my life enough.

The readers whom I fear for most, initially, are not patients themselves, because it may take years for a brain-injured person to fully understand and it may take months for a brain-injured person to connect with the emotion of it due to the injury itself. I am afraid for the invested loved ones, who can comprehend much more rapidly what I mean.

I preface my standpoint some more. Brain injuries are individual. Within each category of mild, moderate and severe, a wide range of cases fit. (How useful can these categories be when there are wild fluctuations within each one?) This doesn't sound astounding, but consider this. I once asked a nurse who had once worked in a hospital and then had switched over to specialize in brain injury, "What in your mind sticks out about the brain injury population?"

She responded, "I never know what to expect because one patient is very different from the next. This is so unlike other patients with other conditions; they and their illnesses were much more predictable."

The mild, moderate and severe terms seem incongruous with how brain injury feels. These terms seem as far off as calling a tornado, which has turned houses into splinters, a breeze. Or telling someone that they have a mild case of AIDS or a mild gunshot wound to the heart.

When I floundered, but appeared able to do better, my mild TBI felt devastating. I imagine that others who might be labeled with a moderate TBI, who show obvious outward signs of trouble but can still inch, feel destroyed. And then the worst off, those with severe TBI who need constant care, if they can feel, might feel decapitated. Brain injury is tornadic; I wish I could shield the afflicted and their loved ones from the undoing of BI and doctors' diagnoses, but I can't. Out of compassion to handing out a blow, I can understand why medically neutral terms—mild, moderate and severe—evolved. But I know from experience that mild, moderate and severe do not even hint at the initial reality. Ploughing into the storm is ultimately in the patient's best interests. A patient and the family need to know what they are looking at to be able to respond appropriately.

Even though a brain-injured person's symptoms may be overwhelming today, continue to hope. Across several years, my brain continues to heal and my quality of life continues to improve. Brain scientists are advancing the field rapidly, via gene and stem cell research, and may discover ways to better our lives. If ever there is a period in history to hope, it is today.

So, how did my doctor categorize my brain injury? He listened to my description of my alertness after the accident, he noted my alertness at the time of questioning, and he applied the Glasgow Coma Scale. On the scale, a doctor awards points based on a patient's eye opening response (or coma duration), verbal response (or post-traumatic amnesia) and motor response. A scale so simple used to describe something so complex; brain injury reduced to a number. Because my eyes blinked, because I could answer and understand most short and easy questions, and because I could move my body appropriately to verbal direction and painful stimuli, I must have scored a 14 or a 15 on the GCS. Scores from 13 to 15 fall into the Mild Brain Injury category.

The term "mild" unraveled me. I cried accumulatively for hours over my perceived misdiagnosis, over the minimization of my symptoms, over the lack of validation for my symptoms, over being told to carry on with my life when all I had left were splinters. I had lost my ability to perform my job and I could no longer do well what I had enjoyed doing: sports, reading and socializing. At my nine-month mark, worry started to kick in, and I asked, What type of life did I have left?

At the time, I was as distraught as one can be with a weak memory and consciousness. Mainly, my pendulum swung with the moment: high highs when I saw a baby bird in a nest and low lows when I felt misunderstood. In the beginning of my emotional suffering phase, I had short crying outbursts. I couldn't hold onto feelings for long, I couldn't remember how bad things were, and I wasn't fully aware of the present. As my memory improved and my awareness of the moment increased, my crying spells stretched from five minutes up to an hour or two. (One exceptional day, I did cry most of the day.) When the pain came, it was deep and wounding. My awakened consciousness brought a view of life as a series of emotionally draining events. What accumulated, overpowered. I couldn't get up from the couch or out of my bed. Then my tears dried as an event drifted out to sea. I'd eat a bowl of strawberries, then be smiling and ready for the next misadventure. Depression with a BI twist, a horror peep show, was forgiving.

In *Looking for Spinoza*, Antonio Damasio describes some key elements of anguish and joy.[2]

> When we face each new moment of life as conscious beings, we bring to bear on that moment the circumstances surrounding our past joys and sorrows, along with the imaginary circumstances of our anticipated future, those circumstances that are presumed to bring on more joys or more sorrows.
>
> Were it not for this high level of human consciousness there would be no remarkable anguish to speak of, now or at the dawn of humanity. What we do not know cannot hurt us. If we had the gift of consciousness but were largely deprived of memory, there would be no remarkable anguish either. What we do not know in the present, but are unable to place in the context of our personal history, could only hurt us in the present. It is the two gifts combined, consciousness and memory, along with their abundance that result in the human drama and confer upon that drama a tragic status, then and now. For-

tunately, the same two gifts also are at the source of unbounded enjoyment, sheer human glory.

The standpoint of an improved condition allows me to realize that my extent of brain trauma is correctly labeled mild. My long list of symptoms—short-term memory loss, illogical reasoning, social immaturity, lack of motivation, loss of balance, changes in all senses, self-centeredness, to name a few—are typical after-effects. What I didn't understand for a long time was that mild categorized the trauma, those few seconds my brain was jostled. Mild did *not necessarily* label my outcome. In fact, up to 15 percent of patients with mild traumatic brain injury have life-long problems. Additionally, Dr. Peter Letarte mentioned in lecture "Improving the Lives of Persons with Brain Injury and Scanning the Spectrum of Care: A Neurosurgeon's Perspective," that one study reported good outcomes for 4.1% of people with a GCS score of 3, 6.3% of people with a GCS score of 4, and 12.2% of people with a GCS score of 5. In other words, people with severe traumatic brain injury and of whom it is initially hard to imagine major improvement, can indeed dramatically regain function. In severe traumatic brain injury cases, if a doctor makes a predictive error, it is usually an overly pessimistic prognosis. Oppositely, in mild traumatic brain injury cases, a doctor's predictive error is usually one of false optimism.

Isn't it time to stop dropping the "mild" grenade in patients' laps, potentially misleading them and triggering further pain than is already caused by becoming brain-injured? Confused minds become more confused without an accompanying explanation repeated many times over. I'd much rather have spent my crying over the injury than the deceptive label.

Religion is a volatile subject that divides my family and my extended family. When I was little, my parents had shouting matches over my dad taking me to a Lutheran church. Conflicted over her own Lutheran upbringing, which was tied to physical and emotional cruelty, my mom could not raise her own children as Lutherans. After a while, my dad and I stopped going. Besides the smattering of church services I attended—Lutheran with my dad, Catholic with a girlfriend and her family several times in junior high and high school, Presbyterian with another girlfriend and her family a few times in junior high, Unitarian with my mom a few times in high school, and Christian Science with my mom a few times in high school—organized religion was mainly absent from my childhood.

However, religion was one of my mom's favorite topics, and I picked up the subject by listening to her views. She taught me that God lived in everything, including myself, and that we were all hooked into the grand consciousness. She interpreted the Bible metaphysically, not literally, and taught me open-mindedness toward all religions, even Lutheran. She bought me books by Joseph Campbell and Thomas Troward. She never questioned God's existence, but allowed me the space to decide for myself.

I tried to lead an ethical life as religions teach. I believed, Do unto others as you would have others do unto you, Try to understand others by walking in their figurative shoes, and Mankind should live in accord with nature. I did not believe that the Christians had a lock on the true God. I didn't like the follow-the-leader feel of organized religion: the chants, the imposed guilt, the formality, the idolatry. I thought religion was more personal than group worship, yet understood the societal need to pass on ethics and morals so that each citizen could become self-governing. Despite the deliverance of the message, I viewed the church community as among the most loving, compassionate, and safe communities on this earth.

Occasionally, my mom, my sister and I received letters from fanatically religious relatives trying to save our souls. If we would convert to their religion, then God could heal our wounds and forgive us for our sins: my mom's depression, my sister's divorce, my bachelorhood. One of my proselytizing relatives refused a doctor when she had gangrene. Instead, she waited for the Lord to work to save her. Miraculously, she survived without amputation.

At heart, I was a scientist who'd shelved God. Mainly, I felt ambiguous about God, yet comfortable among the unexplained or unexplainable. I could see that there were natural laws, like those of physics at work, which kept a spiritual order. The natural laws centered around giving, intention and purpose. Instead of praying to a particular God, I meditated.

That autumn of 1996, profoundly lost, I turned to something outside of my reality. Not prone to do so in a crisis, I turned to religion.

I came to the paradoxical conclusion that believing in an all-knowing almighty God brought more value to one's life, yet at the same time, an omnipotent God didn't exist. I simultaneously believed in each pole more strongly than at any time in my life; brain-injured minds are not bothered by such contradictions.

My nonbelief in God was not because of the reasoning, How could God, any god, do this to me? Rather, BI showed me how connected my brain was to all aspects of myself: personality, emotion, skills, and perceptions—including belief in God. I'd turned from a morning person into a night person, from an emotionally stable person into an unstable one, from a budgeter to a free spender, from a person with conscientiousness to one without.

Even though I was taught oppositely in college, I concluded that Descartes's Dualism theory of 1641 was wrong: my body was *not* separate from my mind. In fact, my body reacted first, and my mind's awareness of a feeling occurred second. Damasio has shown many times over that indeed this is the case. Many of our body's signals occur without our conscious awareness; we don't recognize that we have released an excess of dopamine, our circulation has slowed, or we have begun to perspire. Unaware of our body's workings, we think that our thoughts have more control than they actually do. Astonishingly, body signals can alter short-term memory, attention and reasoning. Furthermore, much of our thinking is patterned—rapidity of thought, type of thought—based on our precedent body reaction and prior body-emotion/mind-feeling experience.

Brain-injured, I felt that I didn't have a soul; I had a body that reacted, to the best of its ability, to stimuli. My thoughts were part of the reaction package and my impaired brain narrowed my choices which constricted my free will. Because a change to my brain altered my view of the essence of who I was, I felt inextricably tied to my body. God didn't alter the course of our lives. Our bodies did. Our environments did. God didn't work miracles. Miracles were just another name for something we didn't understand yet. The application of religion became useless to the brain injured who lacked self-control, those who couldn't feel social emotions of embarrassment, guilt and shame.

Accordingly, to me, the laws of nature described God far better than immortalization and omnipotence did. Suddenly, I understood why the priests of the 1600s, when religion was more important than business in society, felt threatened to their core beliefs if body was not separate from mind and why Descartes, the reluctant originator of the mind/body-separateness idea, saved his mortal soul from papal ostracism with his Dualism theory.

Contrarily, I found that I needed an omnipotent God for spiritual peace. I experienced that no single mortal, not even I, a talented analytic, could see the way through my brain injury problems. To keep my own sanity, to survive, I decided to pretend-believe and created my own God. I put my faith in God to show me the route back into my life. I didn't get fanatical, I became quiet and personal. I started internally talking to God.

When I was in great need, abruptly uncertain about myself and the world, God was solacing and secure. God couldn't be taken away or defined differently or disappoint me because God couldn't be disproved. I invented my God because God made me feel better. I found comfort in knowing that God looked after me.

I sought the feeling that I was still loved. Reality was distressing, but God was magical, hopeful, safe. Whether God was real or not became immaterial. What God could mean to me was more important. I was survivalist in God's pursuit, and soon, I'd forgotten that I was pretending to believe.

The omnipotent God became part of my reaction to severe body and emotional distress. My belief didn't mean that God was real.

Assuming we can adequately define God, the existence of God may not be provable as true or false using man's logic. If not, existence arguments are futile. Instead, I have to return to faith, a faith that even catastrophic events happen for reasons higher than my own knowledge potential, a faith that I belong on this earth "as is" and still must commit to strive toward my fullest possibility.

13

Thanksgiving Meltdown

*Generally the suicide rate increases between Thanksgiving and
New Year's Day, which are times of stress for most people.*
—Tina Oman, EdM, LPC, psychotherapist

A month before Thanksgiving, Rick invited me to the company's annual Patent
Awards banquet. Because he and a team of engineers had created a new and sub-
stantially important software algorithm for which the government granted a
patent, Rick's name appeared on the list of honorees. As his partner, I wanted to
show my support for his phenomenal achievement. As a disabled woman, I didn't
want to reflect badly on him. I hemmed and hawed on my two options until I
decided that I would attend.

When Rick asked me what I would wear, I realized that my wardrobe lacked a
formal, business-like dress. We headed to the mall. Doing more than he custom-
arily did, Rick picked stores to browse in, looked through the clothes on the rack,
and gave me his opinion on the formal wear I lethargically modeled. Never before
had a man taken this much interest in my apparel purchase, which impressed
upon me the importance of the evening for Rick as well as how much I'd slipped
in keeping up my own appearance. Aware of my limited energy, he shopped efficiently. A couple stores into the hunt, Marshall Fields, I think, his face lit up
when I paraded back and forth in a long-sleeved, black velvet dress with a short
collar and a zipper down the back.

The mid-thigh length of the dress seemed rather short to me, but Rick
gleamed, "I think this is it."

I looked at the price tag hanging off my sleeve. "But it's $100."

"Don't worry about it. Every woman needs a black dress that makes her look good."

He purchased the dress and I felt valued again.

By the time of the banquet, though, I'd gained weight from hours of resting and instant foods, and the black dress now felt snug. I didn't think I looked as nice as when I'd gotten it. Nonetheless, I looked better than I had in months, and Rick appreciated my effort. Of course, he looked great in one of his finest suits and his hair fine-tuned.

Rick drove us to the fancy hotel. At the entrance of the banquet room, a table contained hundreds of elegant cards with names and table numbers. We picked up our card and then entered the grand room of twenty-foot high ceilings and bright, bothersome lights. The noise level from people talking disturbed me. The cold air in the room chilled me. Searching the expanse—squeezing between chairs and chatty people—we found our seating location. Rick's boss, his boss's wife and the others at the table stood up, and introductions followed. Compared to the boss's wife's evening gown, my hemline was too short.

Throughout the perplexing conversation, I nodded or gave short replies and said little else. Soon, people stopped talking to me and turned instead to converse with Rick. To freshen my mind, I took frequent and longish bathroom breaks during cocktail hour, the dinner hour, and the dessert portion of the evening.

After the waiters cleared our plates, the lights dimmed, the audience quieted down, and the Smothers Brothers took the stage. With one Smothers Brother talking at a time, I could concentrate, understand a majority of the show, and laugh. Momentarily, it felt good to get away from the living room couch and enjoy myself.

After the Brothers loosened the stiff engineers, the award presentation began. A master of ceremonies introduced the ideas behind each patent, and even though I worked at the company and at one time had understood some of these ideas, I no longer grasped the general descriptions. I tried quite hard to comprehend when the MC introduced Rick's patent idea, but again the topic and the acronyms, in a metered speech, went over my head. When Rick strode up to receive his reward, which included a hefty bonus check, I wildly applauded. Shortly after the end of the ceremony, experiencing a whopping headache, I convinced Rick to leave early.

In retrospect, my inability to mingle must have disappointed Rick. That night, I didn't act like the wife whom Rick desired having, like that person whom I used to be: interesting to talk to, interested in others, involved. Even with our lopsided coupledom, our frequent spats, and our sparse sex life, Rick continued to date me. He didn't have to try to make the relationship work; we weren't married. Maybe he felt loyal because I'd stayed with him through the sour moods of his custody battle. Then again, like the me before injury, he was the true-blue type.

From my perspective, our relationship's expectations and needs rose like mountains springing up before my eyes—steep, high, insurmountable. Not only did I, a veritable wallflower, flounder socially at the banquet, but I routinely found myself stretched far beyond my means and unable to deliver in other situations. For example, one time Rick arrived at my house to find nobody home even though he'd phoned me before he drove out. I'd forgotten about his call and felt surprised to see Rick, livid, when I pulled into my driveway. We only got ten minutes together before he had to leave. In another instance, Rick expected me to celebrate his son's birthday. But when the day came, I cancelled due to exhaustion. Another time, Rick wanted to spend the weekend with me in Phoenix, one of his business trips' locations. But, I'd not felt well enough to travel. Steep paths. High ridges. Insurmountable obstacles.

Leading up to Thanksgiving, serious doubts about my career crept into my thoughts as well. By this time I could work two days in a row, but by the third day I blew up frequently and made more problems than I solved. Business was all stress. I arrived late for meetings and daily found evidence of things I'd forgotten to do. I still hadn't figured out how to dial into the company via computer. Instead of moving forward with the team, I lagged behind trying to pick up new information.

I strained neurons while reviewing others' documents. Like reading Shakespeare, I couldn't keep names and strange words straight nor follow the story lines easily. Critiquing took me hours in a quiet environment with notes to myself. Then, I needed to repeat the information multiple times to cohere it to my brain for a while, until time washed it away again. I slogged an inordinate amount of hours for something that I used to do in a half hour and with only one reading. My job had become foreign to me.

My new personality now behaved similarly to my friend John with ADD (Attention Deficit Disorder). In a recently-found commonality, we both ground gears at the changeover (called cognitive inflexibility), lacked a sense of time and required extra repetition to learn. We both struggled at our professions. However, John had a loyal set of work friends. To the contrary, colleagues stopped returning my calls. I think they expected me to be me, and instead, Marcia, the creator of pigs' styes, botched job after job.

With regularity, my boss reprimanded me for sloppiness. Despite my tenuous employment situation, I felt angry at him. Often he changed his mind about what he wanted from me. Such requests would not have frustrated me if I could have completed my duties facilely. As it was, I had to summon all of my capabilities to understand an assignment and produce output. The act of throwing out the product and starting over because of somebody else's lack of foresight disheartened me.

Reality began to sink in. *My career is over* shone across my internal screen. Apparently, my chosen occupation was not at all suited to someone with a BI; my brain needed to function at a much higher level to perform my job capably. In a mental state of loss, I began the Thanksgiving holiday.

For Thanksgiving weekend, Rick drove me and his kids to his mom's home in Michigan. The six-hour car ride collected its toll from me, requiring extra stops and long stops to calm down my nausea.

That night, the next morning, and at Thanksgiving dinner, talk centered around pregnancy, new jobs, vacations—good news, happy-time events. Mary, Rick's sister, was pregnant for the first time and brimming over in anticipation of starting a family. Her husband, excited as well, effused about his new promotion. He looked like a proud papa-to-be, chest inflated, stomach paunchy, and face glowing, pleased to contribute financial support to his growing family. Rick's brother and sister-in-law, recently back from a vacation to the Caribbean, regaled us with island tales. And Rick's sons, a preteen and a teen, talked about their accomplishments at school and in sports.

At the end of a thread about business, I snuck in, "I am back to work now." But no one asked me any questions. Instead, the topic was changed to a concert someone had seen.

I tried again during a long break in conversation. "I went to the Brain Injury Conference." Rick's brother trampled my introductory comment. "So, what do you think of the Detroit Lions this year?" a question posed to my counterpart.

Later, weakly, when talking about achievements, I gave it a third try. "I've been improving in physical therapy." Ignored again, I shrunk at the table. Mention of struggle was not allowed, not over a holiday weekend.

Before brain injury, I had never cried during slumber. But afterward, on the day of the electronystagmography (ENG), on the day after Thanksgiving, and on other despairing and fearful days, in the strange territory of emotional instability, my tears formed and fell while I slept. Silently they trickled across my cheek, crept around my nose, and dropped onto my pillow without an accompanying dream.. At daybreak, I came into consciousness with a thousand pounds of pressure bearing down on me. Hazily, I perceived my wet face, a salty taste in my mouth, and a mood so suffocating that I awoke more crisply than usual gasping for air. In bed, I cried not knowing what I was crying about.

On that Michigan morning, bereft and desperately inconsolable, I couldn't stop weeping. Not only that, I couldn't find the will to get up. Even the fact that I was company at my potential mother-in-law's home, that I was trying to make a good impression on my potential stepchildren could not motivate me out of bed. With no way to contain my confusing sadness, I laid there balled in the dank basement room—hopeless, faithless, and overcome by grief. I oozed out all over the place.

Rick checked in on me every now and again. Each time he entered the dark sanctuary, he witnessed me fetal and tearing, a hill of used tissues piled nearby.

"What's wrong? Why are you so sad?"

The questions triggered me to cry harder. After catching my breath, I squeaked, "I . . . don't . . . know."

By mid-afternoon, red, puffy and tender, and low on energy, I found a crumb of volition. I guess I must have eaten a little before I forced myself to get ready for a walk. Rick slipped on my winter boots, tied them, held my coat open so that I could slip each arm in the respective sleeve, handed me my hat and gloves, and walked me, an arm around my waist, to the door. Through the window of the storm door I took my first glimpse outside. Low-hanging grey clouds filled the sky and a foot of grey, melting, sloppy snow covered the ground. Rick gave me encouragement: "A walk should cheer you up." While I roved, he and the others planned to have fun at a touristy attraction.

I can only imagine that I looked slovenly. Instead of my previous fashion sense, my stylishly coiffed hair, jewelry galore, and coordinated clothes, I now routinely left my shirt tails untucked, did not wear jewelry (because it bothered my pained body), and wore mismatching colors. Most of the time my hair looked dirty as did my skin, even though I'd rinsed them. Too much trouble to do otherwise, I wore an outfit two or three days in a row and I regularly spilled food on my ensembles. I don't remember ever appearing this way, but the evidence adds up. I must have looked like someone to stare at in a bad way.

Stepping out of the house and into nature has always had a calming effect on me. Yet, that day, the tears continued to flow down my face and into the snow. Expending the least amount of effort to move forward, I wandered alone, looking in lighted homes at people who smiled and laughed. As I shuffled through piles of slush on the dreary, cold day, nobody's path crossed mine.

A couple miles into the walk, slouched, toes dragging, I came to an empty park on the outskirts of town adjacent to a cemetery. There, too, I wept, sitting on a swing, twisting right, twisting left, plotting to hitchhike to the train station, drawn like Dorothy and Toto to home.

I peered at a family in the ranch house across from the park. Every room beamed as if the house itself was the sun on an ashy horizon. In the kitchen, two parents washed and dried dishes. After the father put a plate in the cupboard, he hugged his wife from behind and they rocked back and forth. As in a silent movie, I couldn't hear the china clinking or the couple cooing. In the living room, a boy and girl played a board game. They were the other half of the Norman Rockwell portrait: The Quintessential American Family on the Day after Thanksgiving. Occasionally, one of the kids jumped with joy, the window muting the squeal. They looked as happy as I was sad. Mental images of plastered smiles danced diabolically, the lips curled up, bold red lipstick outlining their shape, mocking me like Batman's Joker. I cried harder. Brain injury had stolen not only my abilities, but also my dreams. Unable to multi-task, handle commotion or meet my own needs, let alone anyone else's, I could never become a wife or a mother now. My destiny did not include any grown-up role in an American family.

Chunks of life fell away. Not only did the possibility of a daughter or son with my previous intellectual abilities slip out of reach, but so did gainful employment and travel. The swing's metal links creaking from small movements to and fro, I thought of myself as more likely to get fired than promoted and projected that I would never become well enough to take a fun vacation. One by one these asteroids plummeted with a thunderous splash into the sea of woe. My rocketing-down soul hit bottom and I felt myself shatter.

For a half hour I sat on the swing, destitute, until the coldness of my body could no longer remain ignored. Prying my gloved, frozen fingers from the chains, raising my head ever so slightly, and unkinking my knees, I rose out of the hard plastic seat. I didn't want to head back to the house until I stopped crying. But, maybe Rick could hold me. Tired and trembling, and on the edge of twilight, I trudged back, squishing the slop beneath my boots, toward more lives I would never have the potential to lead.

The only memory I have of laughing that trip is when I was climbing the stairs. I had trouble negotiating the stairs' ninety degree turn, bumped into the wall and fell down the stairs. Every day I bumped into walls. Every week I fell down stairs. Never had I thought that I would do both at the same time. As if God was saying, "This is your life now," that exact moment I made peace and discovered humor. The others in the room at the bottom of the stairs—Rick, his mom—looked at me with sadness as I laughed irrepressibly at my crazy life.

Thanksgiving changed how I felt about Rick, not that I mindfully recognized the shift. With little ability to reflect, analyze or reason, I hadn't connected my feeling that I shouldn't have kids with the obvious fact that Rick already had two sons. Also, I didn't specifically recognize, and thus couldn't address, Rick's shortcomings that weekend. He failed to rally his family behind me, or at least to talk to them about their avoidance of me, which felt like I was Rick's pathetic secret hidden in the basement. Something I've only done once in my life and care not to repeat, I cried uncontrollably for twelve hours straight. At somebody else's house. While the hostess entertained family. The soulful scarring brewed under my consciousness afterward. Whether I overtly knew it or not, I needed a break from Rick. And I think the reverse held true for him. Thanksgiving tripped the beginning of the end.

14

Subtraction of Self

I admit I am powerless over brain injury and my life has become unmanageable.
—Step one of the Alcoholics' Anonymous twelve-step program
where "alcohol" is replaced with "brain injury."

In my daydreams V. S. Ramachandran, one of the most inspirational brain researchers currently living, would have asked me a series of well-thought-out questions about my condition. He wouldn't have assumed that he was all-knowing because the god stance is a dangerous position to take when so little is known about the workings of the brain.

I first saw Ramachandran on TV in the NOVA special *Secrets of the Mind.* An Indian, he spoke confidently and logically as he took viewers through hand-picked cases of brain-altered people: a brain-injured man who thought his parents were imposters, an epileptic who talked with God, an amputee who experienced pain in his missing hand. These patients fascinated Ramachandran. As wild as their claims were, his rigorous investigation into anomalous cases would cause him to believe that they indeed perceived themselves and others as described. The general public might have called them "lunatics," but Ramachandran could see that they held the key to solving twentieth-century mysteries about the brain.

Secrets of the Mind led me to Ramachandran and Blakeslee's book *Phantoms in the Brain.* In *Phantoms,* the authors elaborate on several cases of phantom limbs, a well-documented phenomenon. Typically after amputation, patients still sense their missing parts. Some amputees report that the phantom appendage moves, such as hand gesticulation while speaking. Yet, others describe the opposite—the phantom limb remains frozen in place, possibly in an awkward position. In either case, many experience a debilitating, constant ache in the absent hand or foot.

For more than a century doctors have speculated about how one can feel pain in a body part that is missing. Some psychiatrists believed that the amputees' distress was "all in their heads." While some physicians theorized that neuromas, scar tissue at the amputees' nerve endings, caused the suffering, and advised more surgery. But the relief from pain was short-lived. Usually, in time, the phantom pangs returned and became worse than before the neuroma removal.

These tough medical mysteries, with potential for a solution involving the brain, engaged Ramachandran's intellect. Skeptical in nature and open to alternate possibilities, Ramachandran relentlessly picked apart amputees' stories and then conducted simple experiments to verify claims. During his questioning of Tom, whose hand had been amputated, Ramachandran found out that whenever Tom smiled or touched his upper arm, he simultaneously felt sensations in his phantom hand.

The basic human body is wired this way. If someone strokes your chin while you have your eyes closed, the signal travels to the section in your brain reserved to interpret the chin pat and then you feel the sensation. Different body parts connect to different neuronal segments, and the mapping of head, toes, limbs, etc. superimposed on their corresponding brain sections looks like an upside-down baby sucking his thumb. Except, some parts on the map are not adjacent to one another as in the picture of a human—the genitals are below the feet and the hands are next to the face, for example—and some parts, such as the hands and lips, are exaggerated in relative size. (In the 1940s and 1950s, a Canadian neurosurgeon, Wilder Penfield, created this body map from experimental data obtained during brain surgery. Specifically, Penfield electrically stimulated locations on patients' brains and then asked his conscious subjects what they felt.) Researchers knew that our brains form our body maps at birth. They said that the Penfield map remained static throughout our lifetimes. However, in 1991 Dr. Tom Pons of the National Institutes of Health discovered a case where a monkey with a paralyzed hand exhibited an altered body map. Similarly, the Penfield map did not correspond with Tom's plot.

Ramachandran began to think that this schema was alterable in humans, and he set out to discover Tom's map. While tapping the areas of Tom's face and upper arm with a cotton swab, Tom, blindfolded, reported the spot on the phantom limb where he experienced sensation. From the information, Ramachandran drew a couple of segmented handprints on a picture of Tom's face and upper arm. Somewhat replicating Penfield's work, but with the aid of advanced technology, Ramachandran then ran the same experiment while he took neuroimages of Tom's brain. When he tapped Tom's face this time, the Penfield face and hand area on the brain lit up. When he tapped Tom's upper arm, the Penfield upper arm and hand site on the brain lit up. Apparently, on Tom's brain, the face and upper arm body image area had leaked over to the adjacent brain cells originally reserved for Tom's hand (called brain plasticity). In essence, Tom's body map had changed, disproving the Penfield map's immutability and providing a key puzzle piece for the phantom sensations (see *Phantoms in the Brain* for more key results).

Dr. O., my second neurologist, had read the results from the first neuropsychological report to me. But now that I'd switched neurologists again, the procedure was different. This time my neuropsychologist, Dr. G., who was also the test interpreter and report writer, would perform the second report's readout. Possibly because I barely understood the first doctor's readout, but primarily because Rick wanted to understand my condition better, Rick took off a morning of work to listen to the neuropsychologist's conclusions with me.

But when we arrived at Dr. G.'s office, his assistant informed us, "I don't have you down for an appointment today."

"Why not? This is the day I've written in my calendar."

The assistant plausibly explained, "Well, you must have copied down the wrong day."

"I didn't copy down the wrong day." Although I usually couldn't recall much of anything as boring as setting a date, for some reason I foggily remembered an appointment conversation with the doctor. My plausible explanation was that *the doctor forgot* to tell his assistant of our arrangement. So I added, "I think the doctor messed up here."

"I doubt the doctor made the error. He is away at a conference and wouldn't have booked any appointments for today."

Obviously the neuropsychologist's believability factor rated higher than one of his memory-loss patients. Still, I rejected her version of events. "But he booked *my* appointment for today."

Rick, on the other hand, focused on the goal. "So you mean that we can't squeeze in to see him at all?"

"I'm afraid not. The doctor isn't here."

"Oh, no." A look of exasperation flashed on Rick's face. "Diana, I took off from work to get your results with you. I rearranged my day."

"I'm sorry. But this one wasn't my fault."

"Uh-huh." This scenario has repeated too many times for Rick.

"Really, it's not," I protested. "Nobody believes me." In my calendar I'd not only scheduled the neuropsychologist's appointment for the morning, but thoughtfully, I'd scheduled an appointment with my psychologist to discuss the readout with her. (Of all the schedule mix-ups from that year, I believe today that this is the only one not caused by me.)

"Well, I can't stick around. I've got to get back to work."

"Sure. Go. There's no reason for you to stay here."

On the day of my real appointment, Rick couldn't afford another morning off from work. So, on the first Monday following an emotion-rattling Thanksgiving, I set out alone. After finding the right path through the maze from my house to Dr. G.'s office, I finally got in to see him. I sat with open ears ready to discuss the implications from the latest battery of exams.

My IQ had jumped seven points from the initial testing which confirmed what I'd thought all along: I was doing better. Furthermore, seeing improvement brought hope of better days ahead. The sparkling news aside, the doctor boiled the results down to these four interpretations/recommendations (consolidated from my journal entry):

1. I had the brain power to reconstruct new strategies, working within my new limitations, to deal with everyday problems. My employed processes would feel different on the inside from the ones I used before. He [the neuropsychologist] concluded that I could get there.

2. I needed to stop trying to be whom I was and put my total energy into reconstructing this new person—new likes/dislikes, new ways of doing things, new personality. My old strategies no longer worked for me. Comparing myself to my before-the-accident self was detrimental and frustrating. Instead, I should contrast myself with my one-month-after-the-accident self and feel good about my progress. This tactic would pave the way for a new me to arise. He thought I could remake myself to be effective in the real world again within a year or a year and a half.

3. The reconstruction would only materialize through hard work.

4. I needed to stick with some of the good strategies I was already using—relaxing to classical music when stressed/frustrated, working on one project at a time, taking periods of rest in between major activities, leading a balanced life (work, social, exercise, rest), writing things down that need remembering, removing myself from situations when over-whelmed, etc.

Although I accepted most of the specialist's conclusions, I became quite emotional about the readout of his second point. My thoughts tumbled out in a garbled, irate, tearful mess.

"Huh? I'm in denial of myself? No. I'm not."

"I need you to listen to me. I want you to snap out of this denial stage and stop pretending you are someone you are not."

"Pretending?" I cried. "I'm not pretending."

"You are chasing the self before the accident and that is not working for you. You are not that person anymore. For your own good, you need to accept your new limitations," he scolded.

"What? I'm not chasing anyone," I said, unable to explain myself any better.

He showed no sign of understanding what I was trying to say and moreover, he didn't treat me as if I had valid input. Instead of exploring my issue, he re-emphasized. "Diana, you're not going to get very far if you continue to deny who you are."

My frustration escalated. Wiping my wet cheeks with my hands, I shouted, "No, you're wrong! You don't know me at all!"

My response was probably what he'd expected since the results from my second MMPI-2 test indicated that I "lacked self-insight and was intolerant of suggestions that I might have problems beyond my ability to solve or control." But Dr. G. didn't tell me this during our session nor did he divulge the second confirmation of my hypochondriac label (again, the honest reporting of my headaches, dizziness, ringing in the ears via the MMPI-2 gave another neuropsychologist the goods to betray me). On paper he called me "essentially free of any significant disturbances in higher-level cognitive processing ability," recommended "strongly to continue her psychological treatment," and projected a "reduction in her complaints . . . with increased self-confidence and greater cognitive efficiency and effectiveness." Face to face, the doctor chose to run the other direction with a denial theme.

Five years later reflecting back on this incident, I think the neuropsychologist viewed me as a textbook case. To him, I was a mildly brain-injured patient experiencing loss, so he applied Elisabeth Kübler-Ross's five stages of grief: denial/isolation, anger, bargaining, depression and acceptance. In his opinion I was at the denial stage and he was helping me acquire acceptance.

I felt the doctor was saying that I was in denial of my reality, when, in fact, I did not fully grasp yet what my reality was. I was trying to insist that you cannot deny what you don't understand and don't remember. Furthermore, continuing to compare myself to my pre-BI self seemed important since it helped me to understand who I was now, to determine my loss and to mourn it, and to envision what smart was and to recreate intelligence (which was the dangerous reason bundled in my hope chest; this reason for keeping my old self around bordered on unrealistic dreaming and its abuse threatened to hold my development stationary). In the thick of an identity crisis, stronger than the one of my teen years, starting from nothing was not possible nor was it going to pop me out the other side. Whoever I was, would have been easier to answer if I'd been a healthy child with a tabula rasa rather than an adult with BI who already had a fully developed, enmeshed personality and had difficulty learning.

My brain remembered my original self and only months later would I have the capability of remembering bits of my new self. Today, several years later, my brain mainly remembers my first self first and then overlays the image with my new self. The first who of who I am, developed when I was a youngster, is etched permanently and deeply in my psychic structure. An unerasable haunting from the grave, my self-image is always of a bright person. Like the sensation of a phantom hand profoundly embedded in my neurons, my brain-iac self doesn't go away.

In some brain injury cases Antonio Damasio indirectly makes a case for promoting the retention of the developed pre-BI self-image.[1]

> The findings and interpretations regarding the adult frontal lobe patients become especially compelling in light of the recent description of young adults, barely in their twenties, who sustained comparable frontal lobe damage early in life rather in adulthood. . . . Just as in the adult cases, they do not exhibit sympathy, embarrassment, or guilt, and seem to have lacked those emotions and the corresponding feelings for their entire existence. But there are remarkable differences as well. The patients whose brain damage occurred during the first years of their lives have an even more severe defect in social behavior; more importantly, they seem never to have learned the conventions and rules that they violate.

My original version, a model of a working, actualized, internal self fortified across thirty-six years of living, is an invaluable asset to me that brain-injured children don't have. I credit my comparison to it for shaping my new self to my old self. I attribute the contrast for helping me to act within social norms.

Yet, some psychologists are quick to have you throw yourself away like tossing a clean paper towel in the trash can. At a brain injury conference, I debated with a psychologist who'd worked with brain-injured patients and offered mainly sound advice, except for her counsel to stop before-trauma/after-trauma self-comparisons. She viewed voicing ways that we can no longer function as a form of self-punishment. Although chastising comparisons happen—a husband once introduced his brain-injured wife to me: "She didn't used to act this way. She is not the person I married."—I argued that comparisons need not scathe. If we'd not been rushed to leave the room for the next presentation, I would have talked about how my comparisons evolved. My self-judgments seemed to follow a pattern. At first, for a particular difference, say my inability to feel embarrassed, I hadn't noticed that I had changed. Later, after an embarrassing situation occurred, either someone would mention the change in me or in a moment of higher consciousness, I'd have figured out the difference and felt surprised. For the next months, each time I'd done it again, I reacted with surprise. As the number of humiliating situations mounted, my surprise became subtle, like an after-the-fact nudge, which eventually turned into shock that my difference was significant. Shock led to sadness and the mourning of loss alternated with a short anger phase (directed at the driver who'd caused my injuries). Months afterward, the behavior became somewhat old hat, accepted, yet with potential for change. Comparison of selves wasn't detrimental, but instrumental to my growth. Accordingly, I believe that the best advice is to learn how to use comparison to your advantage.

Why do psychologists always explore our childhoods? Why do late-stage Alzheimer patients revert back to the era when they were children? Why is it important to our brains to maintain our original self-images?

From a brain science point of view, two opposing constructs play out within our heads when an anomaly to self-image occurs. For instance, I was walking into tree branches even though I knew I was coordinated; I wasn't remembering phone numbers even though I considered myself a whiz with numbers. The simplified theory states: The right side of the brain lobbies to change the self-image to account for the anomaly; whereas the left side, the gatekeeper of the operation, attempts to keep the self-image the same by explaining the irregularity away. Only when the right side presents enough evidence, does the left side comply with an image change. This setup allows us to build up a body of knowledge and to retain stability in our lives. In support of the theory, anosognosia patients, unaware of their own illnesses and clinging to their old, well images, have right hemisphere brain damage in common.

In the beginning of my injury the anomalies seemed odd, but that was as far as my thinking proceeded. I didn't need to rationalize them or modify my self-image because, after a few minutes, the peculiarity disappeared from my conscience. No integration required. What forced my identity crisis was an improving memory, a reviving consciousness, and the constant chipping away of ignorance that my internal image did not match reality. For longer periods of time, I began to awaken to the many facets of a changing self. With other diseases, you can separate self from the disease and say, I am not the disease. With brain injury, however, every aspect of my personality had shifted. I became the malady and paradoxically, my self-image remained unaltered.

I believe that the psychological component of BI is distinct from other illnesses. Not wanting to look at and deal with an amputated hand was not what I was doing. I looked and what I felt each time was my hand. When my appendage hadn't worked right, I might not have noticed, or I'd wondered why, or I'd remembered for a moment that my hand was gone and then the next time I'd looked, I'd perceived my hand again. My first problem was in seeing my illness, not in playing denial mind games. This blindness was my new brain's modus operandi. Psychologists shouldn't apply the Kübler-Ross model precisely to damaged frontal and temporal lobes which frequently forget new information, which cannot link events to embarrassment or sadness. (In retrospect, I feel as if I'd skipped over Kübler-Ross's denial and bargaining stages.)

What if denial is partly a memory issue? Until you have enough experience with the change and the change overrides the old experiences in your memory, then and only then do you have a choice to deny it, get angry at it, bargain for its return, grieve it or accept it.

With short-term memory loss, you cannot assimilate new readily. If you possessed a remembering brain, how long would it take you to stop almost every ingrained habit and replace them with new ones? Don't turn on that oven, you haven't set the timer first. Don't answer that phone, it is after 8 P.M., the quiet-time zone reserved for calming your hyper-electric brain. Don't buy those size seven pants. After months of inactivity, those jeans won't fit. Instead of mimicking the old me, the new me was on automatic pilot, my plane in a tailspin, whirling toward the ground. To be me felt natural. I just was.

Reflecting again seven years later, I see that I argued with the neuropsychologist from my understanding of the definition of denial: a refusal to accept a usually obvious, disturbing truth. However, the medical community's standard definition with respect to brain injury included not only a refusal of, but an *unawareness* of the truth. Some doctors attribute the unawareness to memory loss while others finger it as a Freudian defense mechanism: repression of a traumatic fact.

So I have to ask: Did I avoid facing brain injury by repressing my symptoms? When I scrutinize those initial months, I remember that, at first, no single brain injury symptom felt traumatic to me—my forgetfulness, my incomprehension, my clumsiness. Instead, I reacted with indifference, humor or surprise. Only when I began to grasp the gravity of my problems, did they become unpleasant and "memorable." The unpleasantness forced memory, not unawareness.

I still find it hard to believe that unknowingness is accepted as part of the medical definition of denial. Instead, I call it ignorance. So yes, I agree, I was ignorant of my injury. On the other hand, professional arrogance probably influenced my neuropsychologist; he was "in denial" of my ignorance. (I admit to a devilish satisfaction in projecting back the specialist's words.) Otherwise he wouldn't have admonished me for my slowness to comprehend my new self, a limitation that the brain injury imposed and in all truth, a limitation with a side benefit. Not seeing the totality of my injury allowed me to plod forward, blissfully much of the time. Old-me vision let me carry on with, not cower from, my new life, a continual attempt to dig out of an avalanche of mistakes.

After I'd cooled down in a location away from the galling neuropsychologist, I decided to include a new strategy in my routine: comparing myself to my one-month-after-BI self, at least as much as I could remember about that self. Noticing advancement would elevate my spirit. Yet, back in the psychologist's office, the leadenness of arduous months ahead weighted my body. I sunk out of the session feeling reduced and misunderstood.

15

Breeding Brain Injury

MONTHS EIGHT THROUGH TWENTY-FOUR INVESTIGATIVE

I have company.
—realization of the staggering number of
Americans with a story like mine.

Re-examination of the Accident

When I'd first sought treatment, I'd done so for the whiplash, not for my head. Although they could tell that I wasn't acting like myself, my brain malfunction slipped right on past my boyfriend Rick, my good friend Steve, my boss Chris. Only another close friend, Jeff, and my therapist, knowledgeable about brain injury and in particular, BI related to car accidents, could tell that something was wrong with my brain. Jeff thought he had convinced me to seek additional medical care. But soon after our short conversation I'd forgotten what he'd said. Only the trained psychologist possessed the skills necessary to convince an irrational me to seek diagnosis from a brain doctor and to help a forgetful me follow through with the advice. Once at a neurologist's office, Dr. A. almost pronounced me healthy. But the description of my damaged car and Rick's recounting of my character aberrations—critical evidence—changed the diagnostician's rash opinion and led him to ascertain that I'd sustained a concussion. I felt lucky to have stumbled into an accurate diagnosis within a week of the car crash.

For those who hit their heads with no witness and no visible signs an accident even occurred, proper syndrome identification may never happen. They are the walking wounded with sudden personality changes, distancing friends and family, declining at school, losing jobs and committing crimes, maybe diagnosed with the sudden onset of a psychiatric illness.

Once a neurologist labeled my injury a BI, I still didn't know that I'd knocked my head. Months later another neurologist's such suggestion induced me to contemplate the question. Banging my skull was easily deniable because I hadn't sensed my head striking any object. Afterward, I did not "see stars." Furthermore, I'd remembered the traumas of the first day. Yet, wouldn't whomping my cranium have qualified as memorable? Re-examining the accident details—struck at a moderately high speed while at standstill, not knowing I'd smacked another car, and not witnessing that my car even traveled—kept me wondering if the doctor was right.

To answer the question, I obsessively studied slow-motion car crashes shown on news shows. In Insurance Institute for Highway Safety simulated car crashes, dummies thrashed in the cab section as the space around them compressed. They always thrashed, so I must have too. I glued my eyes to the screen when an offset test with a 1995 Nissan appeared. The car I had bought mindfully to protect me during an accident, the one involved in the crash, had a 1993 Nissan body. The test car drove at 40 m.p.h., the estimated speed at which my car was rear-ended and then propelled into the stopped car ahead. (From my lawyer I learned that the driver who had crashed into my car had confirmed my belief: He had not braked before his car hit mine. I then judged his speed, without braking, to approximate 40 m.p.h.—the average speed that the cars drove during the last "go" period prior to the accident.) On TV, I saw what must have happened to me. Pulled down a track by a steel cable, the test car sped forward and crashed into a cement wall. Frame by frame, the dummy's head sailed forward, then snapped back and smacked the seat. After the test expert studied the dummy, he announced that the mock driver had received a head injury. At last, a month shy of my two-year anniversary of the accident, I'd uncovered answers. I *had* struck my head on the back of my seat. I *had* sustained a brain injury. The car accident *had* caused my brain trauma. Any gaping or niggling doubt around these issues vanished. I could stop channel surfing for mannequin reenactments.

Dummies only batter their surfaces. They fail to replicate how real humans' innards move during sudden acceleration/deceleration. These pseudo crack-ups with pseudo drivers and passengers cannot uncover internal bleeding nor coup/contrecoup brain injury. The abrupt stop of a fast, forward-moving head harms the frontal lobe, the most injured brain area in a car accident, and/or the temporal lobe. A similar backward motion deceleration hurts the occipital lobe. A person need not receive a head hit to undergo brain damage.

In further comparison, this simulated accident represented only the tail half of my sandwich accident. For my final analysis, I'll replay my window of the collision. A monster SUV with driver unaware, perhaps talking on a cell phone, is barreling down on me. My car is stopped. I'm listening to the radio, maybe leaning forward in my seat to flip channels. One second before impact, the SUV driver sees what is about to happen, possibly drops his phone, and tries to swerve left of my car, but does not brake. BOOOOOM! Our cars smack, buckle, splay glass. I'm thrown into my seat, the back of my head whipping into the head rest, my foot parted from the brake. My car abruptly accelerates forward. BOOOM! My car slaps the car ahead and car parts crack, crease and crinkle. I fly toward the windshield. My seat belt clicks, catches my left shoulder, which quickly decelerates me and flings me back into my seat, causing my head to strike the headrest a second time. My seat belt held back one shoulder. When the impact shot me forward, my body and head rotated. Not only did I experience coup/contrecoup injury, but also the rotational diffuse axonal injury. Potentially, every lobe of my brain had acquired damage.

The vehicle that clobbered mine was an SUV, much larger than my automobile. My ears perked up when news stories started surfacing about sedan/SUV accidents. One newscaster stated that the number of SUVs on the road was increasing, and accidents involving an SUV with a smaller car caused a third more deaths than accidents involving only sedans. In conclusion, he reported that injuries to a person in such a car are more deadly/serious when hit by an SUV. This deduction made sense. Energy transfer is based on differential mass, differential speed and alignment. My car's smaller mass hadn't a prayer in the collision; I'd born the brunt of the impact.

During impact, my brain sloshed around in my skull, soft tissue twisting, tearing, bumping into bone, outer layers of brain more damaged than inner layers. After impact, my brain must have done what the soft tissue in my neck did—swell. My neck had room to grow. My brain, though, must have squeezed my capillaries, reducing my neurons' oxygen, and pressed against my skull, crushing neurons. Brain cell death triggered the release of an avalanche of chemicals and set in motion a chain of events that would culminate in the suicide of healthy brain cells. During the first forty-eight hours or more, my brain killed parts of itself. With this amassing destruction, who I was shattered as well.

ER doctors typically do not offer any treatment to reduce brain swelling in people diagnosed with mild traumatic brain injury—existing treatments are probably inappropriate and ineffective for these cases, and possibly damage from swelling may turn out to be minimal. But the adult diagnosed early with a severe brain injury, if in a good trauma center, is routinely monitored for intracranial pressure. If above the threshold, for lack of a better method, a neurosurgeon treats the patient with strong coma-inducing medication, removes small amounts of fluid from the brain, cools the brain, or performs brain surgery.

In 1996, the year of my accident, trauma specialists couldn't adequately stop brain cell suicide. But in 2004, drug developers are gaining ground. An injection exists in test at Northwestern University (currently with undesirable molecular composition) which targets the enzyme DAPK, released in the early stages of the death march, and foils the suicidal attempts. A New Jersey company, Pharmos, expects to receive FDA approval in 2006 for dexanabinol, shown to prevent brain swelling and to block neurotransmitter glutamate (released in surplus following injury). However, the patient must receive the medicine within six hours, and preferably within three hours of the traumatic brain injury or stroke to stem secondary brain damage.

Before I had done any research, and after I had figured out that I'd banged my head, I spent months more asking myself what my physicians wanted to know: Was I knocked unconscious? I replayed the events immediately after the accident trying to get an answer. When did the teacher (the driver of the fourth car) and the third car's driver exchange information? What was I doing at the time? Crying uncontrollably? Nothing—sprawled and unconscious? How much time had passed between the cars crashing, each of us moving his car out of the way, and my conversation with the teacher? I'd assumed time had flowed like always—one event streaming into the next. In the beginning, the hidden assumption of sequential time flow didn't jump out immediately. Only across many post-accident experiences—meeting people who claimed they'd met me minutes before, not knowing how I'd gotten to places, thinking somebody else must have put my clothes in the washer—did I discover that time was gapped. Did I lose any time on the day of the accident? Some days I was sure I'd become unconscious and others not (a loss of consciousness is not necessary to incur permanent brain damage). In the end, I have accepted that I may never know.

Mallory Ref

A friend of mine, an office manager, answers mail and phone calls for a non-profit organization. One day he tells me that a correspondent is driving him insane.

"Mallory Ref—she sends me a letter and leaves a phone message every week! I respond only to receive another letter and another phone message ignoring or misinterpreting my reply. How do I get this to stop?"

Immediately I think that the manager is dealing with someone who has brain problems. I feel drawn into the dilemma. "Let me talk to Mallory," I offer. "To you she is a burden, but to me, she is an angel." I want to figure out Mallory's brain-related issues.

"Well, now, she is a pain. She keeps telling me to send her a free patch and I keep responding that only members get free patches. She is not a member. Then, last week, she sent in a money order for a patch. Now, I know from talking to her that she wants to become a member, yet the money order does not cover the membership fee."

"You might want to try explaining things simply. Be patient. She is doing the best that she can. Besides, you don't see this yet, but I expect she will eventually warm your heart."

Weeks later, the manager gives me an update. Across way too many correspondences, Mallory successfully paid for a membership and other club merchandise. Of the more than a thousand members of the organization, Mallory was also the only one to send a Christmas card. Inside she wrote a personal message professing her love for the club. The holiday card changed my friend's feelings toward Mallory. From a softer frame of mind, he is sympathetic to her limitations. He has figured out that Mallory remembers parts of sentences and transposes words. "Get a free patch with membership" becomes "Get a free patch" or "Get a free membership with a patch." With an adjusted attitude, he helps her.

My next objective: I'm working on persuading the manager to involve Mallory in the club more, to give her a job at which she can only succeed. He doesn't think such a job exists. "Create one," I retort. "You volunteer for a benevolent organization."

Brain-Injured People Everywhere

Throughout my life I'd met many people with MTBI, yet I did not know they were brain-injured until I'd suffered one myself and then could spot the behavior. Suddenly I saw my best friend from college as brain-injured; she lacks a good memory, sense of direction, and sense of time. When I asked her if she had ever slammed her head, she recalled an incident when she was ten years old. While away at camp, she fell backwards off a top bunk and bashed her skull on the concrete floor. Dazed, her eyes couldn't focus in the spinning room, noises became too loud, and her head pounded. A doctor diagnosed her with a concussion and told her that she would feel better in two days. She believed the authority and continued on in spite of her headaches, bad vision, and sudden inability to do well in school. Decades later, when she saw the effects of BI on me and compared them to her own behaviors, her life-long problems made sense through the BI light.

When I queried a coworker if he'd once hit his head, he secretly confessed to me about a motorcycle accident and head injury. In the same vein, I told a good friend that I suspected her brother, a drifter, had a BI. She agreed with me and recounted several childhood incidents where he received blows to his head. Then she added, "He vehemently denies that he has a brain injury."

There were others I knew who had bumped their noggins, but I wasn't close enough to them to discuss the subject. Like the recovering alcoholic, when more clear-headed, I recognized the behavior of people who were just like my blundering self.

Brain-injured people surround me. A poll of people who reside on my block and one block down, fifteen households, turns up four people with BI, all enigmatically living in corner houses. Among my fifty aunts, uncles, cousins and grandparents, four live with disabilities resulting from TBI: two from car accidents—the leading cause of TBI, and two from falls—the second leading cause of TBI and the leading cause of TBI among the elderly. My uncle died from TBI: a gunshot wound—the leading cause of TBI-related death.

According to the Centers for Disease Control and Prevention, an estimated 5.3 million Americans, about 2% of the U.S. population, live with TBI-related disabilities. Although this statistic is based off of 1994 data from a sampling of hospital discharge records, as recently as 2004 the CDC still recites this estimate as fact. The immutability of this number seems odd in light of another 1994 estimated statistic: annually, 1.5 million Americans get a TBI, and another fact from 2003: trauma medicine has improved significantly such that more people survive a severe brain injury than ever before.

For other reasons, 5.3 million is considered a low 2004 estimate. First off, survivors of war contribute big surges to the brain injury population, and recently, the U.S. military has been fighting in Afghanistan and Iraq. Secondly, MTBI cases in particular, which constitute up to 75 percent of all brain injuries, are infamous for misdiagnosis and underdiagnosis (recent advances in technology will provide physical evidence which in turn will assist doctors toward more accurate diagnoses). Obviously, statisticians couldn't count undiagnosed cases. Lastly, not all brain-injured people are admitted to a hospital—I wasn't. Despite the difficulties in classifying brain injury, particularly MTBI, and the decision not to collect data from private practices or hospital emergency rooms, the CDC and other organizations did a phenomenal job at great expense to tally the brain injuries that they did and extrapolate statistics. But to regurgitate 5.3 million brain-injured Americans as the lower limit, ten years after compiling the data, only hints at the magnitude of the problem. Clearly, there are many more neurologically-impaired people among us than touted.

Regardless, in 2003, the 5.3 million brain-injured community outnumbers those with AIDS/HIV, MS, spinal cord injury and breast cancer combined. This high saturation and that car accidents, gun shot wounds and falling are common to American life leads me to conclude that most Americans are bound to know someone brain-injured. Look around. Who do you know?

PART IV
Just Deal

16

Guidelines to Return to Work

THE FIRST YEAR
REGRETFUL

. . . I view my crippled life . . . as a project, in which others must participate if it is to prosper.[1]
—Nancy Mairs, *Waist-High in the World*

If I had been the pope with Parkinson's disease, my assistants would have supported me in my role and filled in for the jobs I could no longer do. Perhaps they'd have attended some meetings on my behalf, provided meeting and report summaries, nudged me about upcoming sessions that I had trouble remembering, defended me against character attack. Providing an extended support would have sustained my position; the outside world would have continued to look upon me as a worthwhile person whose image I'd worked hard to earn. I would have maintained an honorable reputation albeit with diminished capacity.

But how does American society handle the run-of-the-mill handicapped person? I intently watched the story unfold of a not so run-of-the-mill handicapped person, professional golfer Casey Martin, whose situation still applies to lots of other people with disabilities. Martin has a circulatory condition which restricts blood flow in his right leg. Because walking an eighteen-hole golf course is painful and unduly fatiguing for him, Martin had requested a special allowance from the Professional Golf Association (PGA): the use of a golf cart. In response, the PGA stood as steadfastly as Augusta National Golf Club did in 2002 on not allowing women members; unequivocally, the no-golf-cart rule applies to *all* PGA Tour golfers. Walking is part of the physical competition, PGA officials argued, and thus, letting one golfer leisurely ride in a cart would give an unfair advantage. Besides, if the PGA rescinded the regulation for Martin, then the admission gates would fly open and other golfers would request carts for aching backs, sore knees and other reasons.

As Martin saw the situation, using a cart allowed him, an elite golfer, to integrate and compete with his able-bodied counterparts and without the cart, he couldn't participate in the game. Treating everyone equally with a one-rule-fits-all philosophy was not only unfair, but insensitive to people's essential differences. A testament to the resolve of both sides as well as the gulf that existed between them, Martin and the PGA swung their clubs of arguments all the way to the Supreme Court. In the final decision, Martin won the right to ride in a golf cart while competing in PGA tournaments. The court deemed the cart a "reasonable accommodation" for his disability and upheld that cart use by a walking-handicapped player did not "fundamentally alter the nature" of the game.[2] Score an eagle of justice for the physically challenged

I should have gone back to work with a fleet of golf carts, armed to the teeth with experience in using each one. Fervently, I had tried to procure rehabilitative services and cart-like job coaches while on disability leave. But medical insurance, owned and run by the corporation for which I worked, wrapped a golf club around its own neck and denied my requests and appeals. Left with only a psychotherapist for an assistive cart, I leaned on her to walk me through the course of my job. Immediately she recognized what I couldn't: without more compensatory types of carts, management would bar me from the business world's fairways and greens. The responsibility was mine to figure out my deficits, address them, and ask for what I needed. Considering the small amount of time that she saw me, the psychologist prepared me for corporate life as best she could teach a learning-disabled adult. A year would pass before I understood 90 percent of my deficits, and another year before I had an arsenal of effective tactics, and another year after that before I consistently employed most of the strategies. Only in retrospect do I characterize the work-arounds, coupled with the act of working, as my cognitive rehabilitation program.

A few months after the accident, my neurologist made the decision to send me back to work based on my normal EEG, ENG and MRI results, my near-normal neuropsychological interpretations, and on the improvements I'd reported. My hearing had returned. My eyes' focus had improved. Even my memory was better (although miserably deficient and compromised). Moreover, I didn't object to returning to work. I'd been gone three months, which had sounded like an eternity for idleness. If only time could have been the deciding factor . . .

Pitched back into the competitive atmosphere of American business, sud-denly, I was no longer able to compete. Since strapping ten-pound weights around my competitors' legs was not ethical, quickly I'd needed to assemble and learn how to use some golf cart-like job-related behavior and to substantiate a golf-cart-allowance case. On the first day back, I'd won the therapist-recom-mended telecommuting golf cart, but computer support held onto the keys to turn it on. Effectively, my only substantial cart was a dead cart.

On physical golf carts, my supervisor willingly approved dimmer lights, a back-supporting chair, a Palm Pilot. But when I requested slight behavioral changes, many coworkers met me with resistance. I'd asked them to spell out acronyms, to talk one person at a time, to speak slowly. Clearly, to belong, *I* had needed to fit into corporate culture and not the other way around. Because I wasn't pulling my own golf bag's weight, I'd sensed that they felt justified in withholding my needs.

Besides receiving opposition, making the behavioral requests in the first place felt taboo. The work culture included the hidden expectation that employees compartmentalize their lives; illness, love and family issues should not enter office conversations. Years after knowing a coworker, I learned through company gossip that he was a diabetic. I'd also witnessed a coworker thrash about in his office chair (he was having a seizure and I called for help). Within a few months, the competent worker had left the company. Although most of the labor was done at a desk, over the phone or in a meeting, no one I saw at work sat in a wheelchair. Like an oversized golf umbrella is to rain, the corporation seemed to repel visible "disability."

Today I wonder what my manager and coworkers thought of me when I hadn't remembered to go to their meetings, I'd forgotten their deadlines, I'd pro-duced work of poor quality—characteristics antipodal to the pre-accident me. Maybe their thinking pattern had mimicked a friend of mine's. He said about an employee of his who'd been in a car accident, acquired memory problems, and started showing up to work uncharacteristically late, "I'd like to slap her and say, 'Stop it.' But I know she can't help it. She had been such a good employee." Now, this employer had attained the benefit of intimately knowing my memory woes. Perhaps some of my colleagues, having never heard of such problems, didn't realize that I couldn't help it.

Knowing now that my performance was subpar when I returned to work and that the company wasn't legally required to carry me on their books, I feel a deep gratitude to my employer for giving me many chances and not firing me. Par-tially, though, I credit the old me for my fortune. I'd been a dedicated engineer up for promotion into management. According to a previous boss, I'd done the work of two or three people. Shaking his head back and forth, he'd explained how he initially had felt reluctant about hiring me. In the interview I'd told him, "Don't expect me to consistently work overtime," and consequently he'd surmised, incorrectly, that my productivity would amount to an average output. Instead, I had stuffed a bundle into the workday. In order to maintain a racing speed, I was letting my prospective employer know that my brain and body required a sufficient balance of work, fun and rest.

On another occasion, a supervisor from a different department took me aside to talk about a self-assigned project I'd just completed. As one of my side jobs, I'd taken the company's manual system of operation, and within a couple of months, had automated and updated the antiquated method. I had leaned on my mathematical ability and training to produce solutions quickly. In mathematics, I'd studied specific examples, looked for patterns and generalizations, and played with conditions to determine what was necessary and sufficient to obtain a particular result. Adept at digging into the details and simultaneously viewing the big picture, the systems I'd created worked efficiently for all cases and were easily adaptable for foreseen future cases. About the novel and labor-saving implementation the supervisor had gleamed, "I wish I was that clever and had thought of those ideas myself." Because of my glowing reputation, management wanted to do right by me even though they grappled with what exactly right was.

One more reason may have accounted for my continued employment. Rick was a manager at the company and we worked in the same department. The first time my name came up between Rick and the department head, Rick divulged that we were dating. He didn't want involvement in any improprieties and recused himself from having an opinion. After knowing of our relationship, the department head would sporadically ask Rick how I was doing and Rick would give him a short update. Possibly this exchange in and of itself gave me a type of favoritism. I stayed employed despite my fallen review rating from the top of my classification to the bottom. Possibly the department head thought, *Don't fire the manager's girlfriend.* I will never know.

Yet, while feeling thankful for a job, for many years a residual anger tainted the mix. Abandoned in the sand trap, I kept swinging the Big Bertha, missing the Top-Flite ball and spraying sand on myself and the grounds. Instead of waiting, teaching me, rescuing me or offering emotional support, most of my buddies had played through the hole and were three tees ahead. Today I have forgiven them, for they didn't know how to respond to me, and from a political standpoint, acting too cozy with me might have jeopardized their own careers. For my misdeeds, I hope that they have forgiven me.

No doubt about it, I returned to my job too soon, too broken, and with very little preparation. Consequently my brain injury put a heavy burden on others. As Casey Martin had done, I'd mainly sought "reasonable accommodations." In contrast to Martin and without realizing it, I had also "fundamentally altered the nature" of my work. In the process, I ruined my reputation at work and never recouped it, even after I became competent again in an easier job (I still had restrictions).

Generally, character doesn't spoil when you break your arm. In such cases, a doctor might tell a patient: no lifting, rest the arm. But when a brain is hurt, what does a physician say? No living? Everything requires the use of a brain. Weak-armed patients can go to rehabilitation to strengthen muscles and to take tests which determine the arm's capabilities. Based on the results, a doctor can speak specifically to a patient's problems and write an explicit note for the employer like: the employee can lift no box greater than five pounds. If the patient is a mover for a living and the disablement is permanent, he might as well find another occupation. But if he is a paper pusher, then his career remains practically unaffected.

To determine the ramifications of my brain's damage, I had taken the neuropsychological tests (not covered by my medical insurance). However, the results inaccurately described my cognitive functioning and the brain doctor misjudged my competence. Unaware of my therapist's pursuit of compensatory strategies tailored to my deficits, the neurologist sent me back to work without operating instructions. His note simply read:

This patient is under my care and may return to work part-time [starting] July 8.

17

Grabbing at Tree Boughs

LEADING UP TO FIRST CHRISTMAS WITH A BRAIN INJURY LOST

It is one matter to forget things when you have a million
thoughts flooding your mind and quite another to forget
when your head is as empty as a looted store.

Christmas Season

"I recommend that you attend my Monday night support group," my neuropsychologist advised during an appointment midway through autumn.

"I can't drive at night. Is there a service I can use to get a ride to the meeting?"

"No, we don't have a service. You should ask a friend or family member to drive you."

"Most of my friends and family don't live close and the meeting place is a half-hour drive from my house. No, no one would take me. The drive is too big of an inconvenience."

"Ah, you'll figure it out." And he left it at that.

I really wanted to go, but the only time I "figured it out" was for the brain-injury support group's December meeting and Christmas party. While Rick worked in Phoenix, my normal-brained friend Steve drove and accompanied me as his Christmas gift to me. Instead of flirting, dancing and drinking, his normal party behavior, he graciously listened to story after story of accidents—hit by car, onset of a stroke, fall on the head—and the aftermaths, many recitals told while we waited in the slow moving line for the buffet. In the party room of a medical clinic, we ate food and drank soda pop amid anecdotes of brain operations, doctors' visits, and physical malfunctions. In between stories, people raved about my tasty cranberry salad, showcased in my favorite crystal bowl.

At the end of the evening, while Steve and I walked out the door to leave, he remembered to go back for my expensive bowl. Slowly he was learning to compensate for my Swiss-cheese memory. The week before, at a zoo's gift shop, I'd left a previous purchase on the counter after buying a calendar. Steve picked up my zoo cup and waited for me to realize I had forgotten it. Not until we got outside did I have a feeling of something missing from my hand. I had lugged *something* all over the zoo. Steve brought the cup from behind his back with the comment, "I count 1, 2, 3, boom, she forgot."

But even he forgets. Back at home, while unpacking my crystal bowl, I recalled that I'd brought a spoon too. Some other person with a brain injury must have ended up with my spoon, and that seemed just. I felt happy to give to someone who was always losing things, even if the recipient never realized the new acquisition. Backhandedly, I imagined myself as someone's top-secret Santa.

Before my brain injury, friends and family most frequently answered, "Organized" to the question, "Besides smart, what word best describes Diana?" Typically, by the end of a Thanksgiving weekend, I'd completed Christmas gift making, Christmas gift shopping and Christmas card writing. Between Thanksgiving and Christmas, I decorated trees, attended numerous parties and Christmas programs, and hand-delivered gifts with time to spare. Compared with others, I had operated ahead of schedule.

My first Christmas season with a brain injury, December 1996, the pattern reversed. At the three-week mark before Christmas, I still had numerous gifts to buy and mail, and curiously, I hadn't even felt the seasonal pressure. That winter I learned that Christmas tension necessitates a brain which remembers time and time of year, and a brain which remembers, period. Memory is essential to circulate those background, self-created pressure loops, "Twenty days left till Christmas and ten people left to buy for."

One day during that period: I woke up and put on a short-sleeved shirt and shorts. Stepping downstairs, a cold chill galloped up my spine, too cold for a summer day. I looked outside, saw snow, and then knew that the season was winter. On another winter day, I walked around the house barefoot. When I turned on the TV, a commercial for Barbara Walters's *Ten Most Fascinating People of 1996*, a Christmas standard, played across the screen. Suddenly, I shivered. *Oh, it's winter.* Again I'd thought the season was summer.

Christmas didn't feel imminent. I relied on the constant stream of holiday reminders: Christmas ads, the chime of Salvation Army bells, and Christmas decorations. These were my absolutely necessary, wouldn't-happen-without-them memory joggers to go Christmas shopping. After enough glances at my neighbors' lighted shrubs and trees, I found my way to a mall.

In the lot I circled rows of parked cars until an owner arrived and cleared a spot for me. Hoofing past car after car in the cold, ten minutes later I arrived at the mall's entrance. Inside the people-packed plaza, my eyes opened wide to the scene. A thirty foot tree, surrounded by Santa's village, stood in the center and stores lined the outskirts of the village. In the display windows, velvet outfits, gigantic gift-wrapped boxes and fake snow enticed me inside the stores. The shoppers, toting several bags apiece, moved with purpose. The busyness of the locale and tightness of the crowd made me somewhat woozy.

Caught up in the consumer frenzy, seduced by merchandise displayed so prettily for holiday shoppers, I made my first purchase—a pair of black suede shoes with buckles and striped heels. At another store, disregarding price again, I purchased a second pair of black suede shoes, which were lace-ups. Since the car accident, shoes were exciting me. I bought shoes I didn't need, shoes I would rarely wear, shoes I would forget that I owned. I bought high-heeled shoes that I had to squeeze my feet into and shoes that I would discover months later were the reason my feet hurt daily. These newly-purchased shoes, which didn't fit my feet, I would later decide to give to charity. Having gotten two new pairs of shoes, I came to my senses and remembered the aim of my trip. *I'm supposed to buy presents for others,* I told myself. Then I added teasingly, *Duh-uh, silly.*

I must have bought gifts for friends and family because I did give presents that Christmas. I do remember mailing many of them. When I was done taping brown paper around each package and addressing the outside, I noticed the rolls of shiny green and red paper sitting next to me. *Damn it.* I'd forgotten to wrap the gifts. Angry at myself, I removed the brown paper layer, gift wrapped each present, rebundled the gifts, readdressed the packages, and mailed them. When I got back from the post office, I found two gift-wrapped presents in the packaging area of my house. *Ugh!*

Did I send out Christmas cards in 1996? I have no evidence that I did. I suspect that I managed to get a few cards out to some family and some friends.

Did I buy a Christmas tree? My journal tells me that I purchased a tree on December 16, which was late based on my previous standard. I probably wanted to keep my tradition of getting a tree even though I was ill (it would involve hard work: I was in pain and lacked energy) and because I was ill (it would lift my spirits). But the tree I brought home that day prompted me to write in my journal, "since the BI, I do most things 'half-ass'-like."

The tree wouldn't stand straight because of its crooked trunk. The branches, which had been tied together, sprang open cock-eyed with sparse areas. The needles were long, unlike the short-needled trees that I'd grown up with and loved. This couldn't have been the tree I'd purchased. But there it stood, in my living room, my Charlie Brown tree.

After the lights were strung, the tree glowed bright—too bright for my light sensitive eyes. I hadn't thought about how bothersome colored bulbs would be; I'd only thought about how I long-term remembered lighted trees. If I could have thought shorter term, I would have remembered walking through a nearby zoo seven nights before for an annual festival and viewing rows of lighted, blinding trees. Unconnected to my recent past, I spent a couple hours stringing Christmas lights only to turn them off and keep them dark for the season.

Internalized

Early on I looked at brain injury as an eventual advantage. I was only temporarily "out of service" until I could rewire. The rewiring part didn't scare me because I was familiar with the process from childhood. With each skill and fact I'd learned, I linked neurons to form operational pathways. Never satisfied with my speed of recall or breadth of knowledge/skill, I honed my paths to the most efficient and piled more information into my gray matter. "Sure, you've learned to write cursively with your right hand, but can you train your left hand to write as well?" I had challenged myself in third grade. My constant vigilance on self-improvement and learning produced a fine brain, if I may say so myself. All I needed to do was to apply this knowledge to the second brain build. Happy as a skylark, I repeatedly sang the Don Henley lyric "Building the Perfect Beast," to myself. I felt certain that I would become smarter after the rebuild. For this reason I considered myself lucky, yes, lucky, to have a brain injury. Not everyone gets a second chance at brain construction. Not everyone gets to turn out better.

Looking back, I can clearly say that only a damaged brain produces delusional thinking of this magnitude.

Having brain cells with busted parts and fewer brain cells overall, a remade brain creates slower, less efficient thinking than the original. In older people, replacement pathways may never redevelop (called a reduction in brain plasticity), especially when large areas of the same functionality are damaged. My recovery would conclude with a still broken brain, patched with millions of myelinated band-aids. As I sobered up to daily pratfalls, constant confusion, dwindling friendships, and career blunders, I descended the spiral staircase of distraught, despair and dearth, sometimes tripping down two, three, stairs at a time, a definitive sinking down, spinning down, going down. I sobbed daily for half of a year (suffering is prolonged when each mistake is experienced as new). I would end up dumber. I was dumber.

In the thick of it, in between Thanksgiving and Christmas, I dreamt about how my brain worked before BI and how it worked after BI. The before brain had the precision of the Dewey Decimal System. The picture of this brain showed white tabs sticking out of it, each tab with a clearly-marked label, each label in a pre-defined order. I used a shorthand method to store all incoming information in the right place(s). To get information out, I immediately knew in what category I had stored the information and where that category existed on my brain. Recall was immediate.

Oppositely, the after brain had many disconnections. Sometimes I did not comprehend the incoming information because it raced at me too fast, was brand new or was communicated in a confusing style, or because I was spaced-out and not listening. Under those conditions, I stored nothing or else I stored jumbled pieces that I couldn't recall. Storage, when it happened, was based on the time of entry rather than by content. To recall information, I had to travel across all sections of my brain until I found it. A recall would have turned out more successful if someone had told me what to look for. Then, I could have pattern matched. Many times, the system broke down. This brain was a file cabinet with unlabeled files thrown in.

I woke up with the notion that the key to my recovery was to label and reorganize my internal files. I had one question, "How do I sort out my brain?"

I am Looking for a Christmas Tree

I'd like to tell you about shopping for my 1996 Christmas tree. However, I have no notes in my journal on this topic and my mind is void of any detail. I don't remember what lot I was in or even if I was standing in a Christmas tree lot. I don't remember choosing a tree or the look of the tree when I selected it. I don't remember who sold me the tree or how much it cost. Maybe I have this information somewhere up there buried deep in my head.

One night, sometime after 1996, I am in a writing class. We're doing a group meditation to dig for details. I focus on my brain's temporal lobes—nothing—on my parietal lobes—zilch—and then on an inner section—my amygdala I'm thinking. At first I feel a weak signal, an emotion. Sadness. I stay with it and it grows to miserableness and then to an elephant-sized, all-encompassing depression. As I'm feeling this, I have no words. My despondency is not attached to language or to an event. Instead, it connects to that time of year, that year, that first Christmas season after the car accident which left me brain-injured. Immediately after meditation, I write about shopping for a Christmas tree while in the throes of a raving mental disturbance. Here is what spills out.

> I wake up with searing pain in my shoulder, neck and lower back. The knives are still inserted, as they have inflicted suffering for the last nine months. I feel tired because the constant pain has worn me down, because I can only sleep for four hours at a time, and because I struggle in every aspect of my life. I spend the morning and early afternoon trying to rouse my brain.
>
> Around three o'clock I decide that I will get out today. As I am leaving, I read the post-it note on my back door. It tells me to buy a Christmas tree, so this will become my big activity for the day. I probably wrote the note when I looked across the street and saw my neighbors' Christmas displays. I grab the note and my purse, and remember my keys. I remember my keys now because of my rule of three which states that I must take three items with me when I go out the door.
>
> After I get into my hatchback, I read the note on my steering wheel—Am I conscious enough to drive? I must be. I read the note okay. I always read the note okay. I check that my mirrors are in the right position, buckle my seat belt, and then turn on the car. The radio will remain off because I am unable to drive safely while it is on. I turn on the defroster, put on my sunglasses and wait for the lens fog and window fog to clear. If I waited for my brain fog to clear, I would continue sitting in my car for years. Finally, I give myself the go-ahead to put my car into gear.
>
> Lacking energy, I plan to head out to the closest busy road to look for a tree lot. I know to do this because I repeat the phrase, "I am looking for a Christmas tree lot," over and over without break. At a four-way stop, I don't know who is the first to go. I wave the first layer through before I feel safe enough to pull forward.
>
> At a stop light, I am the first car on red. When I hear people honking their horns behind me, I look up to see a green light and then turn onto the busy road. Within the first block I spot a Christmas tree lot, but can't think far enough ahead to turn into the lot. I drive right past it, turn around, and pull into the lot on the swing back.
>
> I am two miles from my home in a Jewel parking lot, which is usually bustling with shoppers. Today, however, the lot is nearly empty. I still tell myself I am looking for a Christmas tree lot. If I stopped my mantra now, I would forget why I was there, see the Jewel sign and go grocery shopping instead. I

park my car close to the trees. This is my first time shopping for trees in this lot. I feel disoriented and confused; I slip into my black hole.

A passerby might think that I was waiting in my car for someone to finish shopping.

Sometime later I snap out of my mental blackout. My car is turned off. The key is in the ignition and I am sitting in the driver's seat. My last moment of recall is sitting in my home. Now I am in a parking lot in front of Christmas trees. I must have arrived here to buy a tree. I glance at my purse on the passenger's seat. It has a note attached which confirms that I am here to buy a tree.

The key won't come out of the ignition. I try for some time and it won't budge. Didn't this happen recently? Yes, my boyfriend figured out that I had forgotten to put my car in park. I look down. My car is in drive. I put my car in park and the key comes out.

The perimeter of the lot is fenced off and is strung with bare round light bulbs above. The hum of the generator is the only sound in the air. It annoys me. Above, the sky is filled with investigative-bright sunshine, and below, the ground is covered with shiny white snow. [For non-brain-injured non-light-sensitive people, replace this line with, "Above, the sky is filled with low-hanging gray clouds, moving swiftly, and below, the ground is covered with gray and black snow." These are the types of days that depress you.]

At the entrance is the owner's warming trailer. He is inside drinking coffee as I enter the lot. I am his only customer, and he fails to ask me if I need help. On the ground is a thick electrical cable, which I don't see, and I trip over it. I feel myself falling, quickly make body corrections and pull my neck and back muscles, but land upright. I am stunned. I have forgotten that I am now a clumsy person. As my muscles tighten, I notice how cold I feel. My right side is much colder than my left and is in fact numb. I will spend the entire winter this way, split in two, cold right, warm left. Brain freeze. I won't stay here long.

I walk down two rows of trees and don't see anything the right height. At the end of the second row, right in front of my face, though, is a nice looking tree lying against the fence. The pine is about six feet tall with branches tied. I am closed into myself like this tree. Yes, I will buy this tree, my tree. I do not touch it. I do not smell it.

As I walk to the trailer, I trip on the cable again and curse under my breath. I know if I worked here, I would trip on that cable all day long. I knock on the door to tell the man in the flannel shirt that I have selected a tree. The cost is a pricy sixty-five dollars. I have not brought sixty-five dollars and convince the man to take my check. He grabs my tree, cuts off a small portion of the trunk and loads it into my car. The treetop sticks out of the trunk, so he ties down the trunk with cheap rope. He advises me to put the tree in water within the hour. I repeat this information to myself until I write it down on my note.

Back at home I work on getting this big tree out of my trunk. My car is parked on the downward slope of my driveway, which gives me a disadvantage. I am lower to the tree than I'd like to be. My right arm does not raise above my shoulder, so I place it on the bumper of my car and my left hand around the tree. As I pull on it, the tree branches hold onto the sides of my car and the lip of my trunk. The pine is resisting its new home. With all my might, I pull and the tree gives me a foot. I rest. I pull. I twinge from exertion. This tree will not defeat me. Foot by foot, it comes out of my trunk. I drag it to the side of my house. Its branches are mostly broken and hanging by the bark. I follow my note, and place the tree in a bucket and add water.

Exhausted, I go inside, lay down on my bed and fall asleep. When I awaken, I forget that a tree is leaning against my house. I will discover it the next time I go outside, three days from now. It will have a ball of ice around its trunk.

My physical limitations in the Christmas tree story were daily occurrences and according to my journal, the branches were tied up at purchase. But besides that one fact, I have no idea if any part of this story is true. The fable's truth lies in the depressive feelings it evokes, and in the plausibility of it happening: it feels like a typical outing for me (which makes me conclude that without my eraser of a memory, I would have locked myself in my house and refused to go out again). That Christmas, I was trying to latch onto something positive and good. I desperately needed the tree of my dreams. Yet bringing me down, in a corner of my living room, stood the tree of my realities. The tree's pathetic demeanor reflected my ailing state. I was dumber.

PART V
Death and Life

18

A Pill Short of the Netherworld

**FIRST CHRISTMAS AND NEW YEAR
STRESSED**

Brain injury can kill.
—almost a firsthand experience

Dealing with brain injury would have been enough. Around the corner slithered more.

Two weekends before Christmas, while getting out of my automobile, I slammed my head on the underside of the car roof. Immediately, my daily headache got bigger. The hammering continued to worsen throughout the day until it climaxed by evening—just before the head-explosion stage. I didn't think to call a doctor. Instead, I rested. The next day, still alternating between sleep and wakefulness, the incessant throbbing in my head worried me. *Did I have a second brain injury?* I asked myself.

Some weeks before, I'd attended a brain injury conference and grabbed the Traumatic Brain Injury (TBI) Fact Sheet. Among other succinct facts, I became aware that: A person who has acquired his or her first head injury is three times more likely to sustain a second one than people who have sustained none. Since I had already acquired one brain injury, I had concluded that my heftiest challenge in the first year would be the prevention of a second head injury, specifically because of my continued disorientation around objects. Squirming in bed, I wondered, Had I failed to keep myself safe? Had my biggest fear materialized? If so, then I was in big trouble. *The effects are cumulative*, another fact obtained from the conference and heard from the brain injured and a rehabilitator, echoed in my head.

On the next day of pulsating, I developed a fever and sore throat. In and of themselves, I hadn't found these symptoms unusual. After the accident, my immune system had become fragile. Now susceptible to picking up the latest flu bug going around the closed-air-system office, fevers/irritated throats visited me monthly. Instead of an elongated recovery, complicated by the brain injury, this time my symptoms got worse. A few days later a physician diagnosed me with bronchitis (I'd forgotten to mention hitting my head) and prescribed antibiotics to battle the now acute illness.

After a week and a half of convalescence, by the afternoon of Christmas Eve, I was feeling better—good enough to attend my aunt's traditional Christmas Eve get-together. Over the phone I told her to expect my boyfriend and me (Rick's kids were celebrating the holiday with their mother). Since the depressing Thanksgiving weekend, Rick and I hadn't seen each other. The respite gave us a needed breather, although circumstance, rather than design, had separated us. Between his business travel, custody court dates and children's needs, and my doctor's appointments and illnesses, the best we could coordinate was talking every day on the phone. After weeks apart, Rick missed me dearly and his enthusiasm built as Christmas break approached. I'm sure if I'd possessed the ability to step outside of the "now" time zone and miss people, then I would have felt a building excitement too. Despite the previous holiday's disaster, love still shone through.

Our reunion wasn't as happy as Rick had anticipated. By the time he arrived to pick me up, I was running a high fever, about 104 degrees, and had broken out into cold sweats. Rick drove me to the hospital emergency room instead. Decked in holiday black velvet, I spent the evening on a gurney with Rick, in suit coat and tie, by my side. The junior staff observed me in a quiet ER until my fever broke out of the excessively high range. The intern released me with a couple of new prescriptions to fight a second flu bug that he said I had caught.

One would think that twenty-four hour drugstores and Chicago suburban hospitals would be in close vicinity to each other, but the closest such pharmacy open on Christmas Eve was an hour away. I was too weak to walk inside the drugstore, so Rick left the car running with the heat on while he purchased my pills. After a long time, Rick popped back to tell me that the pharmacist was mobbed, filling prescriptions for every infirm person in the county. The wait would be an hour. I drifted in and out while the radio played. In between Christmas songs, the DJ tracked Santa and his sleigh throughout Chicago's neighborhoods. "Saint Nick, with Rudolph in the lead, has just landed on a roof in Elgin." None too soon, my sleigh driver would deliver me back to my bed.

By New Year's Eve the illness was dying, but the medication caused me serious side effects: diarrhea, dehydration and cramping. I would not attend any holiday party thrown by friends or family, and would miss most of the seasonal cheer—a fitting summation of the year. So, on New Year's Eve, I went to bed early, never happier to end the year.

Two weeks later I was back at the doctor's office getting another prescription to treat a urinary tract infection. That evening I quickly fell ill with a high fever and chills and went to bed early. Around midnight, a pounding headache, a racing heart, and the need to pee woke me. When I lifted my upper body to sit up, the spinning in my head came on so strong that I gently lowered my body back down. Instead of up, I slunk down to get out of bed, and then crawled, plodding on all fours along a wavy line to the bathroom. Clutching the commode and bracing against the toilet, I pulled myself onto the seat and relieved my urge. After I'd rested, I grabbed the commode and slowly elevated my body to the mirror. Woozy and hanging on, I stared at my image in the dimness of the bare-bulbed night-light. *Who is this person in the mirror?* My bright red face, covered with bumps the size of quarters, appeared so swollen that I couldn't recognize myself. Frightened, I looked at my blood red eyes and thought I saw differently-sized pupils. In shock, I slumped to the floor.

I didn't understand what was happening to me. Using my fading energy, I snaked back to my bedroom and used the nightstand as a prop to help me inch up and onto the mattress. As I laid on my back and contemplated my predicament, I eventually realized that I should call an ambulance. My phone sat only ten paces away. But each time I tried to move to call 911, my eyes rolled back into my head and I could feel myself slipping away, on the verge of blacking out. Remaining as still as I could, I listened to my body. Compared to when I first awoke, my head pulsated stronger, my voodoo doll's skin had more deeply pricked pins and needles, and my heart behaved as if I'd sprinted a half mile farther. Quickly, I was taking a turn for the worse. Immobilized, I did the only thing that I could do. I laid in my home, alone, for hours, concentrating on remaining conscious lest death would claim me, hoping and praying that I would get to see another morning. *Another chance. Please God, give me another chance.*

Stay awake. Stay awake. Stay awake. Whatever you do, stay awake.

Breathe in. Stay awake. Stay awake. Stay awake. Breathe out. Stay awake. Stay awake. Stay awake.

Please, God, let me live. I want to live.

I didn't feel ready to die. *Thirty-six seems too young.* And so did thirty-seven, my real age that night. *Not now,* I pleaded. *Not now.* I don't think Death cared.

He had me in the grip of what I later realized as anaphylactic shock. Squeezing tighter and tighter, he tried to burst my heart. Using the only power I had left—ironically, my mind—I counterattacked with concentration and prayer.

Don't close eyes. Don't close eyes. Don't close eyes.

Please, God, surround me in light. Help me to fight.

Don't close eyes. Don't close eyes. Don't close eyes.

Through the darkness I continually bantered.

Keep alive. Keep alive. Keep alive.

Concentrate hard.

Keep alive. Keep alive. Keep alive.

Through the shadowiness I uninterruptedly chanted.

Hang on. Hang on. Hang on.

You've come this far. Don't let go.

Hang on. Hang on. Hang on.

When the dawn broke and light passed through the window, I recognized a reversal of my condition. My heart started to slow down its frantic beat. Death was succumbing to my meek brain, to the vigilance my neurons were keeping. Lying exhausted in a bed of soaked sheets, my mood lifted. *Oh, my precious, victorious brain.*

I don't know if I received a second head injury before the Christmas of 1996. I forgot to check if my brain injury symptoms worsened or if I'd acquired any new ones.

Shortly after my near-death experience, I determined that I'd experienced an allergic reaction to Septra. On the day of the attack, I had swallowed one antibiotic pill for my urinary tract infection. The month before the attack, during my bronchitis bout, I had ingested a week's worth of Septra pills until I landed in the ER on Christmas Eve. I had not contracted a second flu bug that Eve. Contrary to the intern's opinion, I now believe that I'd experienced an allergic reaction. (Later, via a letter, I informed the hospital of the misdiagnosis. They wrote back to inform me that I was mistaken, their doctors don't make diagnosis mistakes.)

Since when did I become allergic to antibiotics? Since when did I get serious side effects to antibiotics? Because these pills were the first antibiotics I took after the brain injury, my extrapolation was that the brain injury had somehow changed my chemistry.

Curiously, none of my doctors mentioned an allergy connection to BI. Years later, after reading hundreds of pages about brain injury, I still haven't found a documented allergy link. Even on a BI intake form for new patients which asks the patient to report BI-related symptoms, the form fails to include choices "new allergies" or "stronger allergic reactions" among its otherwise exhaustive array of selections. Ergo, I believe that doctors and brain researchers have not explored the allergy avenue yet.

In my own pre-BI, medication history, I had taken one full course of Septra and other antibiotics (including the powerful Cipro drug which is now given for inhalation anthrax) with no allergic reactions and no serious side effects. Sure, there had been a couple of medications (Erythromycin and Amoxicillin) from which I'd gotten minor side effects and I'd preferred not to take them, but that comprised the extent of my pre-BI prescription drug experience.

To this date, eight years later, every pharmaceutical I have consumed since BI has given me side effects. The least offensive antibiotic is Doxycycline. But another drug, Claritin, an anti-allergy medication, could kill me. From my first brush with death by prescription drugs, I developed a primal fear of medicine, called the bait-shy effect. Thus, in 2001 I wouldn't have taken Claritin had not my work supervisor exerted pressure on me to cure or mask my formaldehyde allergy, now a stronger response to perfume than before the BI. The bossy woman wouldn't accept my allergist's expertise, that no treatment existed for my particular problem. When I'd gone back to the doctor, he said I could try taking Claritin and see if my head aching, throat swelling and voice croaking ceased during a prolonged exposure. At least, he said, doing something would show my manager that I was trying. Reluctantly and fearfully, I'd started popping the pills—taking half doses over longer-than-recommended lengths of time to guard against a potentially brutal allergic reaction to the medication. When the Claritin hives came, covering every third inch of my body, but sparing my face and hands this time, and my heart started to race, I knew what was happening and got to the ER in time. Once there, the emergency doctors were afraid to give me an anti-allergy treatment, because, after all, I was obviously allergic to one type of anti-allergy dosage. (And in light of this incident, maybe *not* calling the paramedics during the Septra episode, assuming they could have broken into my home to get me, may have saved my life.) So, the ER nurses simply observed my vital signs. After every health care professional on the ER staff came in to see me, a most unusual case, and after my symptoms subsided, an ER physician sent me home with a note: *You must NEVER take Claritin again. Not even one pill.* (In the fall of

2001, my allergist told me that I was one of thirteen people in the country who were known to be allergic to Claritin.)

Yet January 1997 and some months afterward, I needed a memory jogger of how I should feel about taking medication. For six months, the Septra-activated, red, swollen hives covering my face became my indispensable reminder of how afraid I should feel.

19

Curtains to Act I

ANNIVERSARY
GRIEVING

When your memory is filled mainly with images and knowledge
pre-accident, loving yourself is loving a ghost.
—my haunting feeling whenever reality collided into my self-perception

I know I spent the beginning of 1997 quite ill for a while from the nearly fatal drug reaction. I kept coming down with high fevers. My journal writing trails off and so does my mention of Rick. Even on my 1997 calendar, Rick's name doesn't appear as often as it had in 1996. We still talked daily, but our lives drifted different directions He began going to church three days a week and focused even harder on winning his custody battle, which was heating up. In 1997, his kids were becoming more vocal in what they wanted to have happen and started siding with their mom. Quickly, his home life began spiraling out of control.

His problems were BIG and my problems were BIG. Neither of us had answers for ourselves or for each other. Mainly, we spent our energies protecting ourselves from a constancy of hits.

During this time period, he talked a lot about his faith, his possession of faith, and my lack of faith. He wanted me to sit with him before God. I didn't anticipate resolution through or comfort from his church for me—quite the opposite.

He was transforming into a deeply religious man and I was baby stepping toward reclaiming some of my independence. Initially so cognitively broken, I became dependent on Rick to plan my schedule, to drive me places, and to get me out of pickles. A rescuer-personality type, he'd enjoyed saving me and I, without awareness or choice, had settled into a subservient role. But as I began to heal,

I tugged back for some control. Surprisingly, he resisted my yanks. As a regular churchgoer, he took the evangelical Christian teachings to heart: be a better citizen and fill the leadership role in the romantic relationship. All of a sudden my autonomy became antithetical to his newfangled partnership definition. I interpreted his tight grip on the reins and overprotection to mean that he liked me better brain-injured. I couldn't fathom that a lover of mine, who knew me both ways—fully functioning and later, as a head case—would love the latter more. A thought so distasteful, a dynamic which kept surfacing, I continued unhitching emotionally from his wagon. I went more places and saw more people without him than the year before—not that I got out much.

But our tug-of-war over my freedom also sprouted from another place. When I'd been independent and low maintenance, Rick couldn't find enough to do for me. I could afford what I wanted. With the right tools, I could tile a floor, replace a kitchen sink, or wire a doorbell. And I thrived at my job. Telling me that I couldn't do something motivated me to learn how. In contrast, Rick relished stepping in to help people, such as career-counselling friends, lending his manpower for a home project, or offering self-improvement advice. Quite good at the aforementioned, I think giving of himself made him feel needed. So in one sense, he did have more to accomplish for an ailing me, which added to his feelings of fulfillment.

Throughout the year of my disablement, he also became accustomed to a more agreeable mate, mainly because I was unaware much of the time and had lost my ability to construct an argument. The result: he got his way more often than before.

On the other hand, the part of our new relationship that frustrated him most was my lessened ability to verbally communicate, my poor memory, and my lack of energy. He definitely wanted those traits back for me, and in general, he did want me to get better. I think my accompanying independence wouldn't have looked so frightening to him if I could have kept myself out of harm's way, if I could have embraced his new religion, and if I could have assured him I'd keep the good parts of my new personality: showing more of my vulnerable side, acting less willful, and leaving more for him to do for me.

So even though we disagreed on some principle matters, we continued to spend time together when we could. We had a date night on Valentine's Day and spent a Saturday at a flower show. We worked together on home maintenance projects, such as building an erosion control wall for Rick's yard and siding a section of my house (Rick did most of the work while I watched or handed him a tool). We talked to my new neighbors and Rick helped me to remember their names. The end was near, but neither of us wanted to say it. We'd been through so much together. On the surface, we continued on like we had since my brain's injury.

Three weeks prior to my one-year anniversary of the accident, Rick mentioned, "Easter is approaching."

"Easter? Already?" Instantly my brain sent me into something akin to a flashback. The accident became real again—as fresh and palpable as if the crash had happened minutes ago, except that this time I possessed the perspective of knowing the full consequences. My cells remembered a potent trauma that triggered incessant crying. Experiencing the entire impact all at once, the deaths of a million neuronal stars, the dimming of a glowing galaxy, I became unglued. I dreaded Easter. Intellectually, I had not known until this moment that my unconscious had paired the 1996 Easter with the two-days-later accident.

From Rick's simple statement and during the week leading up to the 1997 Easter, memories emotionally stabbed me. Yet, my mental collapse encapsulated more than traumatic recollections. The holiday represented one year with brain injury which, according to my neurologist, equated to the end of major improvements in my brain's functioning. I'd reached the end of the line. I should have had a ninety percent or better return of functionality. But, scrutinizing my mental self, I saw gaping flaws—a large-holed sieve memory, klutsy movement, emotional eruption. I hadn't made the ninety percent cut and this grade was final. With the rest of my life sprawled lucidly before my eyes, destiny settled solidly. Living meant managing a laundry list of disabilities. My capabilities set in concrete, my future appeared drab, bleak, funereal.

Easter, which was nine days before my anniversary date in 1997, came and went. Since I'd not made a recording of what transpired, I don't know how I felt—possibly cold as a stone in a mountain creek bed, frozen in place.

Astonishingly, I worked the week before Easter and the week afterward too. But a couple days before my one-year mark, I decided to take a day off, my anniversary, to have a funeral. I planned to symbolically bury aspects of myself that had died in the accident and were unlikely to return. At last I understood, piece by piece, most of the injury, having howled over the discovery and rediscovery of loss. I was hoping the ritual would put a stake in the ground, dam the loss, and move out the sorrow so I could move forward with my new restricted life.

My idea was to write a list of what I'd lost, put it in a shoe box, and bury the box in my garden. Because watching plants grow had helped to heal me and represented a place of joy, the garden, my sacred place after the accident, seemed like the right burial ground. Also, I wanted the grave close to me; I meant a lot to me and my original virtue would always occupy my heart. On the headstone, the only epitaph I liked thus far was *Rest in Peace*.

On my first anniversary day I awoke to a frigid temperature, like on the day of the accident. The chilliness brought back the memory of feeling icy to the bone during the wait for the police to arrive. While trying to shake off the image, the phone rang. The person identified himself as an agent from the other driver's insurance company. Insurance agents' calendars must contain accident anniversaries of unsettled claims. These are bad days to get vexing calls from adjustors. I should have directed the insensitive caller to my attorney, but I didn't remember to follow my lawyer's instructions.

From my journal's notes, I reconstruct our conversation.

Sounding administrative, he began, "It's been a year now since the car accident and we'd like to close out this case."

"Close out the case?" I felt confused. "B-u-u-u-t, you can't close out the case. I'm still seeing doctors for my injuries."

"What problems can you still have a full year later?" he asked, fishing for a reaction.

Annoyed with the question and his nasty tone, I stood my ground. "I have a lot of problems! My back, neck and shoulder still ache and don't move right. I have a full-blown brain injury."

"You're claiming a brain injury?"

"Y-e-e-e-s. You should know I'm claiming a brain injury!"

"Ma'am, you may have a brain injury, but I doubt that it was caused by this car accident."

I took a moment to let his statement sink in and then retorted, showing my snarly brain-injured lack of restraint, clawing, hurling defensive stances and venom. "W-w-h-h-a-at? You've got to be kidding me. Now, uh, listen here. My life has been turned upside down ever since that car accident. It's been a year of constant, CONSTANT confusion and pain. My short-term memory is shot. I never know what time it is. I can't even cook a meal properly! This all started right after the crash. I don't need you telling me that the car accident didn't cause my brain injury!"

That crash had pinned me to the ground for the last year and consequently, I had to plan a life strategy around my suite of limitations. No way was anyone going to tell me that the accident had not affected me, especially on the day I was burying myself.

"All I'm saying ma'am, is that it's very rare that car accidents cause brain injuries."

A lie, I realized later.

He continued, "You're not a medical professional, and you haven't proved your case yet."

His statement frightened me and I reacted, blaring a rarely-used swear word. "Why the *hell* are you calling me?" My whole body shaking, I stuttered, "And . . . and . . . This conversation is over!" Click.

In retrospect, I believe I was dealing with a company looking out for its bottom line on a claim that, statistically speaking, insurance adjustors knew would remain hard to prove.

Bristling from the call, I got to work on the private funeral as, surprise and no surprise, I had not done much pre-planning. Besides the shoe box list, which I now called my Lost Forever/Will Never Return list, I also thought I would create two more lists: What I've Gained and What I Can Work On (all lists are in Appendix C). After a couple hours of thoughtful writing, I had a list that acknowledged losses: "clear as a bell" feeling, mental energy and "big picture" vision. Another list recognized gains: here and now living, compassion and humility. On the final list I tagged areas for improvement: write more, develop more strategies to reduce embarrassing situations, and push more limits. Then, I set out by foot to buy two sets of flowers—a rose for the grave and a bright bouquet for the new me. Unfortunately, one florist was closed and the other one in town did not have the flowers I wanted. Disappointed, flowerless, I returned home.

Next, I needed a casket. In my basement I rummaged through empty cardboard containers and instead of a shoe box, I selected an old mixer box—a perfect choice since my brain had become "mixed" since the accident. I brought the "mix master" enclosure upstairs and set it down next to my three lists. *Am I ready to start my ceremony? Hmmmm. No. I want music. I know what to do. I'll look through my CD and cassette tapes for appropriate songs.* Thinking hard, I established three musical themes: Who I Was, Funeral and Who I Am. For a piece to make any of the lists, it had to have been an easy-listening favorite of mine with near-appropriate lyrics matching the theme. Additionally, I required the Funeral Play list to contain only somber music and the Who I Am tunes to have only uplifting melodies.

In the midst of my song search and slight lyric revision, I became aware that I was running out of time before my haircut appointment. The day was not happening as imagined. Instead of getting emotional, I talked myself calm. *Stop.*

Remember the meaning of this day. You are releasing your old ideas, like how to put together a funeral. Embrace your new self, new ways, new notions. Figuratively, I put my old super-planner-everything-in-place perspective in the coffin and relaxed with the fly-by-the-seat-of-my-pants method that the new me employed on a daily basis. Later, while in the kitchen making lunch, I accidentally started a small fire. The short blaze made me laugh—it was so new me.

After eating the burnt meal, I resumed organizing the ritual's musical portion. Minutes later I realized I had to stop planning or the day would pass without the burial. I set down a CD case and pen, and quickly began the ceremony. I read aloud the Lost Forever list. "Today I acknowledge loss and list parts of my old self that I will never regain. They are lost forever: my steel-trap memory . . . my 'real time' comprehension . . . smooth social interaction . . . the sound of silence . . . multi-tasking . . . my dedication to sports." After saying good-bye to thirty attributes, I placed the paper carcass inside the mixer coffin and turned on the cassette tape player. Song "I Used to be a King [queen in my mental rewrite]," a Crosby, Stills and Nash favorite, floated in the air. Sovereignty swirled around me and then was sucked into the makeshift casket. I'd played the only song I could find for the Who I Was theme.

John Hiatt, at the top of the Funeral Play list, monotonically and sparsely sang good-bye to me in "Friend of Mine." Next up, acappella church-like music rang through a Crosby and Nash introduction in "To the Last Whale: Critical Mass," bringing sanctity to the occasion. Then in "Ghost," the Indigo Girls' harmonic voices and acoustic guitars sang to my heart, particularly at the point in the song when a ghost passed through the singer's body. During the emotionally bleeding chorus, the music crescendoed and accentuated a wrenching loss after a loved one left. Scared to let go, I didn't want to say farewell.

During the middle of my year-long struggle, I'd developed great fear of being brain-injured. I didn't have fall-back people or a fall-back plan. Who would financially support me if I couldn't make it? My mother hadn't worked in decades and my father was nearing retirement. My boyfriend wasn't a husband and the illness strained our relationship. Would I end up on the street? I couldn't perform my job satisfactorily, yet the doctor had pronounced me fit to work. I lost friends each month. Soon, I'd be alone. My only choice was to rely on my brain-injured self to figure it all out. Too gigantic a job, my addled persona passed the load along to the pre-injury me. I depended heavily on the idea of "who I used to be" and "what I could do."

I must say good-bye. Leading up to my anniversary, I'd built up the new me to the confidence level of knowing I could survive as a single woman living alone, earning my keep. (Looking back, my tower of confidence stood on the sands of magical thinking and shortsightedness.) I was ready to push, PUSH, the old me out. Arriving at my neuropsychologist's ideology, new me needed room to blossom into a fuller habitual person. It was time to transfer title from the end of the first third of my life, a foundation with a high activity life-style, to the beginning of a new third, to focus on the important and to stay realistic. I replayed "Ghost" to force the transition to the other side and finished the set on a Chris Isaak blue note, "Nothing's [everything's] changed."

Judging from how emotional the year had been, my recent proclivity to emotionality, and what the day represented, I'd expected myself to act like an overwrought basket case at my funeral. Yet, even after playing meaningful music, I was still acting from my head. I was caught up in the arrangements, the doing. Frankly, I found it difficult to transform completely, head, heart and body, into the deathly mood, and continued on with the ritual.

The only pallbearer of a heavy soul, I proceeded to the burial site. I hadn't dug the grave and took time from the ceremony to do so. In the shallow indent I set the casket, covered it with dirt, and at the head of the grave planted a stone from the garden embossed with an angel playing a mandolin. I spoke softly, "I loved you and now I love your ghost. I'll miss that old gal. Rest in peace." Then I went inside, tracking mud on my floors, and my emotional dam burst. I cried for my ghost, my first life, for the good I'd tirelessly done and had to leave behind.

At the beauty salon, Elton John's "Candle in the Wind" piped in over the radio, which was close enough to the "Funeral for a Friend" that I'd wanted for my Funeral list but could not locate earlier. A half hour later I strode out with a new look for a new me.

At home, I bopped in my new 'do to the songs on my Who I Am list. The first tune made a positive statement: "I Will Be Here" by Steve Winwood. Next, the Indigo Girls introduced "Least Complicated" with a maxim about choosing to respond to your own blunders with laughter rather than tears. Then the group playfully sang about the difficulty of learning simple things, which seemed especially apt for my new life. In "Carry On," Crosby, Stills, Nash and Young embarked along a new path, one they didn't choose, and hope sprang from heartbreak. Then, with a strong finish of lyrics, Peter Himmelman on his *From Strength to Strength* CD told me that better days were on the horizon in "G-d Don't Have to Teach You This Way," and soothed my fatigued body and mind in "This Too Will Pass." I closed the meaningful day on a peaceful musical stream of lulling classical rhythms—new me top picks.

The strong, crippling, gushing feelings I'd experienced with the approach of Easter, I then expected on my anniversary day. Yet, apparently my body associated the accident with Easter, not the actual date it occurred. For the next couple of years I'd forget the timing, brace myself for the anniversary, only to have the Easter holiday blitz me.

"Intelligence" and "problem solving ability" failed to appear on the Lost Forever list. At all times I felt that these qualities still lived inside of me. Many days I couldn't reach solutions or I retrieved them too late or I couldn't communicate intelligent thoughts, but my faith never wavered that I still possessed "brains." More than anything in my mind, my certitude in my intellectual brand's existence accounted for my persistence in trying to connect to my buried wits. Because divinity let me keep my intellect, delivering concentration, will power, and short-term memory to the grave wasn't as big as a full power outage.

Over the second year of brain injury, my ghost visited me often like Fred Flintstone's dog Dino scratching at the door. Each time I heard the cries for re-entrance—when I'd thought about something my old self would have done—I brought my mind to the soul next to the garden with the serene angel headstone. Separate from me, I loved her dearly and honored her lessons. After a long while, a year or two, she began drifting away.

I couldn't let go of her until I could retain morsels of my new personality. Liberating my original self was not the same as forgetting her.

Epilogue

UP TO YEAR NINE
CONTENT

I didn't escape with my life, I escaped from my life.

Almost seven years since the smack of brain injury, I look in my rear view mirror and see a teenage driver talking on a cell phone. She seems too involved in her conversation and this thought pops into my head: *She is going to hit me.* Despite my experience with one particular cell phone driver on my back bumper, I do not go around thinking that all cell phone drivers might jolt me. This one is different. I straighten up in my seat and place my head against the headrest. I'll be ready this time.

At the next red light, we both stop in our places. At the one after that, however, her car taps mine. I spin my head around, glare at her, and in an exaggerated fashion, mouth, "Yooou hittt mmeeee!" She continues to jabber on her cell phone, her only acknowledgment a short nod.

Where is her guilt? I want to run out of my car, fling her car door open while she cackles to her wireless friend, and rip that cell phone from her hand, only to hurl the distraction to the ground and stomp, stomp, stomp on it until it breaks into jagged plastic splinters and flattened wires and unconnected metal parts.

I want to grab her by the shoulders and shake her and shout, "Hang up and drive!

I want to scream, "Do you know who you've hit?"

Then I'd tell her, "I'm an author writing about drivers who cause accidents because they are talking on cell phones. You're now Chapter 9!"

My self-shocking fury is directed toward what could have happened and what did happen years ago. Afraid of what I might actually do while in an unfamiliar, volatile state, I decide it's best to stay inside my car. When the light turns green, I drive forward, fixating my eyes on her image in the rear view mirror. She drifts one car length behind me, then two, then three. A car to my left pulls into the gap. I turn right at the next light, and leave the gabber in my dust.

I have and will probably always have a managed life. I require silent spaces to maintain a cooperative brain, note taking to remember, and yoga and therapeutic massage to stave off pain. Standards don't motivate me as they once had. A balanced, peaceful life is the important goal.

A year and a couple months after the accident, I broke up with Rick. I needed to shed the caregiver/dependent relationship we'd developed and cut myself free from the pressure to infuse his religion into my life. He wouldn't let go and I realized that he'd become a pious Christian. Despite all he'd done for me, I didn't get along with his religion and he needed someone who did (later he would marry another Christian devotee).

Of course, I overrepresented to myself how much I could handle life on my own and the rest of 1997 proved itself one disaster followed by another. I experienced panic attacks, massive disorientation, and deep sorrow. My schedule ran out of whack. My roof leaked and I didn't know what to do. Management moved my job down to Phoenix and I scrambled to find another position. Somehow, I survived. The next year went better than 1997, and in the summer, I began dating again. In the spring of 1999, I started seeing Dave—a bicycle store owner with an incredible sense of humor and creative side. He meshed with my new personality. I felt comfortable around him and my quirkiness seemed more adorable to him than "in the way." By year's end, he asked me to marry him and I said Yes. We've been together ever since. He still laughs when I do brain-injury-type things, like when I broiled the pizza last night and turned it jet black. He likes his food burnt (fortunately for me), but this charcoal disc went far beyond what he would eat. I have to say that the BI cuteness factor is definitely less than our first year together because he also remarked that I could have burnt our house down. He takes the lumps with me.

Over the healing years I've vacillated on whether to have children or not. Ultimately I settled on the severely disappointing answer. Because motherhood requires multi-tasking ability, long periods of attentiveness and in-the-moment solutions, and because kids can be chaotic and boisterous, and because my brain injury is not conducive to this or to providing a stable income base, I concluded that I am no longer mother material. I chose, instead, to look at this book as one of my children. It is my best creation with my DNA marker to date.

On work, I hung on for five years with brain injury at that high technology company. The first two years were gifts. But by the third year I'd changed jobs, and my productivity and work quality began to rise. During the fifth year of the injury I proved to myself that my work, which was task-oriented and not people-focused, had returned to top notch. Given enough time, I could persevere and produce it. I felt contributory and that I was earning and deserving. Yet, the fast pace, multiple projects and meeting pressures still leapt beyond my abilities.

Around this time, America's work climate changed. Companies were laying off workers in record numbers. When this happens, morale plummets and politics rise. At my company, they were rescinding everyone's telecommuting privileges. I knew my brain went haywire in a hectic and disruptive work environment and fought to retain my work-from-home privilege. Eventually the stress got to me; brain tremors started and my blood pressure soared. After months of battling for a position amidst company trimming, for my own health, I let go and resigned.

A month later, I began the path of a writer. I would write the book that had preoccupied my mind for the last years. I was bound by love of and duty to my kind who could not write their own memoirs.

For four years after I quit my paying job, I was plagued with monthly nightmares. The theme always ground in the same groove. I show up to a job site only for "real" employees to ignore me. I work on the fringe, knowing I'm trespassing, and wonder if I can still get paid. I feel society's negative message: You're too disabled to hold a job, not disabled enough to collect disability money, and we expect you to get worse, so we'll deny you health insurance. Not valued, I'm set up to die. Each restless dream ended suddenly. Thrown into sudden consciousness, the vision's significance pierced my heart, shook my nerves, and created fear which raced around in my head.

Lately, going on two months now, I do a job in my dreams and management doesn't send me home. People listen. I get paid. I awake believing that some employer will find me valuable again.

Life continues. Every day I bucket my behavior into BI and not-BI pails. I need to know how well I am doing and the impact of the ailment. I play with it, work through a scheduled break and see how I react. It's never as good as my expectation. Surprisingly, I am not better than I am. Each day my BI pail is full, although with less egregiousness. I don't walk out of a restaurant without paying, but I do forget to order my sandwich without tomatoes. I don't feel hopelessly lost, but I do take an extra hour to find a building for the first time. I don't forget what happened ten minutes ago but I do forget that I talked to a neighbor two weeks ago or that I went to a supposed memorable party with my fiancé a year ago. I can walk through doorways, but I clock myself in the eye when I reach for a pillow, pull and come up empty-handed. My black holes are gone, but I find myself with no thought too often. I can usually tell who is the first to go at a four-way stop sign, but at bridal shower bingo I fail to cover a square with a chip even though I heard its contents called. I missed my bingo and later wondered why. Was it too much activity? too many people? not enough sleep? Is this telling me I should pack it in and leave before I get too far gone and can't drive myself home? I plop it into my BI pail.

On a grander scale, I monitor myself for too many BI happenstances. The week that I punched myself in the eye, I also tripped myself, landing with a thud on the ground and scattering the contents from my hands. And I dropped a half of a bowl of soup down my stove. And while driving, I temporarily got lost just two blocks from my home. This told me that I did too much that week. My brain could not handle socializing both days of the weekend, writing full-time and cooking meals and treats after work.

Looking out through a film over my lens, I strain to keep up in social conversation. I miss dialogue in movies. I feel behind the general curve. But I can fake comprehension and fake well. In others' eyes, I don't seem that far behind them.

I am at peace with who I am. My new line of work brings joy, creativity and goodness to me, as does my partner-for-life. I can ride a bicycle again and have pedaled fifty miles in one day. Today, I am finishing this book. In a distant whisper, though, as a mom remembers a deceased child of her loin, I, too, will always remember the gift of my precious brain. *Baby, if you can't come home, then be Home. You will always occupy my heart.*

Appendix A

Faculties Returned Timeline

For nine years I have kept track of my brain injury symptoms—every day at first, then every month, then every few months, then whenever I noticed I could do something I haven't been able to do in years. Below is my unscientific chart of when certain faculties returned and any major setbacks along the way. As you can see, I have experienced major improvements far beyond the doctor's prediction that not much improvement would occur after my first anniversary of the accident. Also jumping out at me, I am more prone to thwack my head than before the accident. Note that minor head-hitting incidents, which happen about four times a year, are not included.

Time	Faculty Returned or Setbacks
week 4	hand uncurled, first dream since dreaming stopped
week 7	hearing returned—sounds no longer muffled
month 3	second night dream, would log only ten dreams for full year
month 4	headache pain inconsistent (was consistent)
month 6	some energy returning
month 6.5	first instance of planning/thinking ahead
month 8	possibly received another brain injury (whacked head on underside of car roof when getting out of car)
month 10	first time felt good enough to attend two meetings in same day (hours apart)
year 1	brain vibration is gone, believe epileptic "staring" seizures gone
year 1.5	whiplash pain breaking up, first instance of impatience, ringing in ears stopped, can listen to classical music and drive at the same time
year 1.75	first time remembered a new acquaintance's name

year 2	pain dull and manageable, movement freer, more energy, can jog some
year 2.25	able to ride bike short distance (rode slow since scenery rushed past), physical therapist thought I was 80% recovered, first time felt confident while conducting a meeting
year 2.5	met goal of riding 25 miles but physically drained, first time able to defend my view in a technical discussion at work
year 3	beginning to feel normal on the inside, light sensitivity waned enough to drive at night, noticeable memory improvements, dizziness sporadic and event-related
year 4.25	can switch tasks at work, but still not as well-versed as most; can listen to any type of music and drive at the same time
year 4.75	first instance of thinking about past, present and future on own without cues from environment, thoughts flowed one right after the other
year 5	brain tremors started, lasts a couple seconds, happens when falling asleep or waking up
year 5.25	first instance of missing a loved one (missed my cats on first couple days of a vacation)
year 5.5	received another brain injury (disoriented from making a complicated dinner, slammed head on bed's headboard when lying down to sleep): ringing in ears returned, minor setback in cognitive/memory functioning
year 6.25	met goal of riding bike 50 miles
year 6.5	speed of mental processing increased, first time wanted to drive fast and felt things were not moving fast enough (old feeling), feel ball of energy inside
year 7	first time figured out someone's hidden agenda while in conversation, first time seemed to know more detailed information off the top of my head than anyone else in the room, my number sense is returning: remembered a page number in a book (page 56) where a piece of information was stored, can now remember the phone number of my second line that I've had for four years, first time remembered a date (March 25) off the top of my head of something that will happen in the future (Spring Break), can now remember fiancé's date of birth
year 7.1	have moments where can type as fast as I used to; reruns no longer feel like brand new shows—although I don't remember much of them, I remember enough to know that they are reruns; feel a sense of social connectedness again

year 7.5	discovered I forgot my second line's phone number (must only stick in brain for a couple months or so)
year 7.75	possibly received another brain injury (banged head on underside of car roof when retrieving something from back seat): loud ringing in left ear, throbbing headache, woozy, fever, no noticeable cognitive malfunction
year 8	first time felt bored watching a rerun (remembered enough of it to feel bored)
year 8.1	hit head twice in one day, iced bumps, only aftereffect was a week-long headache
year 8.5	menopause starts in earnest—hot flashes, heart palpitations—and during times of high stress my mind also races
year 8.8	my sociability is coming back—I can think about others; people recognition has improved: I recognized a person I'd met a week before; she didn't exactly match my image of her, which was more like a sister of the person I'd met

APPENDIX B

Strategies and Rules

Below is the list of compensatory strategies and scheduling rules that, with the help of my therapist and boyfriend, I developed during the first two years of brain injury. These rules brought sanity to my brain-injured life.

Scheduling

- Keep one schedule for business and social events.
- Plan in days to do nothing and breaks. The light days should follow heavily scheduled days.
- Every week take two down days.
- Break at work every half hour.
- When brain is scrambled, work less hours and take more breaks.
- Take naps during the day.
- Minimize drive time.
- Do not drive at rush hour, especially going home.
- Plan alternate transportation for night meetings.
- Do not work two days in a row at the office.
- Work from home three days/week.
- Rarely eat lunch with others at work.
- Walk outside a half hour every day.
- No more than one meeting in a day and no longer than one hour. If break this rule, no back-to-back meetings.
- Schedule time to take notes after meetings.
- Avoid gatherings greater than six people and socialize for no more than three hours. Take breaks.
- Do physical therapy exercises and yoga for a half hour each day.
- Reschedule day(s) if one event is rescheduled.

Work

- When leave for work, the number is three. Remember to bring purse, briefcase and lunch.
- Set timer on Palm Pilot to remind myself to go to meetings, classes and appointments.
- Take copious notes in and after meetings at work.
- Tape record meetings.
- Write down anything that I want to remember.
- Agree to take on jobs that are self-contained and low stress, and have limited contact with others and flexible deadlines.
- Ask for help when a job is a two-person job, when I don't have the knowledge or skills to do the job, and when, for health reasons, I am unable to do the job.

Decision Making

- Don't make a major decision on same day as problem is posed.

Task Management

- When assigned a task, do it immediately or else immediately set up some type of clue to remind myself to do it.
- Don't put something away until it is done.

Managing Stress

- Only listen to classical music.
- Do not drink alcohol.
- Keep a journal.

Sleep

- Try to maintain regular sleeping hours.
- If brain is too hyped to sleep, get out of bed and write, listen to soothing music, or sit with a cat on lap.

Meals

- Keep freezer loaded with prepared meals for the many nights when I am too tired to cook.
- Prepare army portions of meals on Sunday.

- Set timer to indicate when food is done.
- Take vitamins B and E and ginkgo (ginkgo didn't help me).
- Take ginger for dizziness, especially before traveling.

Reminders

- Put post-it notes in prominent places.
- Leave empty laundry basket in living room to remind myself that I am washing laundry.
- Leave clues at back door for things I need to do, like leaving a receipt at back door to remind me to pick up the dry cleaning.

Phone

- Don't talk on phone after 8.
- Don't talk on phone longer than a half hour.

Setting Environment

- Dim the lights in the room.
- Change computer colors to muted colors and fonts to large.
- Adjust chair to proper settings.
- Use left-handed mouse.

APPENDIX C

Funeral Lists

Below are the lists from my "funeral": Lost Forever/Will Never Return, What I've Gained, and What I Can Work On. In parentheses, I have added more information from the vantage point of living with brain injury for eight years.

Lost Forever/Will Never Return

I have divided the original Lost Forever list into three sections: Never Returned—something I thought was lost forever at the one-year mark and seven years later can say that it has not returned, Improvement, But Still a Substantial Limitation—I've seen improvement in these "lost forever" capabilities, however, they still limit my life in some substantial way, and Improved—these "lost forever" functions, although not what they once were, have improved enough such that they no longer pose a mentionable restriction or else I have ceased caring about their return.

Never Returned

- sound of silence (ringing in ears actually went away, then returned for good the next time I hit my head)
- perfectionism (glad to see go except when editing this book)

Improvement, But Still a Substantial Limitation

- keen short-term memory/"clear as a bell" feeling/one time learning/steel trap memory (repetition still a major part of my life)
- smooth social interactions (limits number of friends)
- parallel processing in brain/multi-tasking/involvement in many activities (still need long blocks of uninterrupted time to complete task and must limit number of tasks per day)
- mental stamina (must pace day with lots of breaks to prevent fatigue)

- control of emotions/ability to handle stress (crumble too easily, must drop everything)
- "real time" comprehension (rely on repetition and replaying events to understand fully)
- sense of time (when something happened still foggy, but on any given day know month and day, and can judge short increments of passing time)
- normal use of right arm: pinched nerve in neck traveling down right arm causing neck, shoulder, elbow and wrist pain, and numb fingers—gets worse with activity including computer use (can't play sports involving right arm, must limit use of right arm each day)
- any form of travel including bicycling and ice skating without motion sickness (can bicycle and take local car rides now without sickness, but train, plane or long car trips can make me very ill)
- light tolerance (light sensitivity still an issue with night driving)

Improved

- interest in others—more egotistical in conversation/heat of moment since can't parallel process well, have memory loss, and it takes total concentration to remain aware of my body
- synchronicity with others—since interacting from blank slate, get out of synch with others' expectations
- sense of direction (still get lost)
- ability to concentrate
- initiation—now a procrastinator
- will power
- immunity to illness
- ability to visually scan lists, items in store, books on shelf
- decision making—jump to conclusions
- loud noise tolerance/enjoyment of music other than classical (can listen to other music, but not head banger variety)
- acute sense of smell and taste
- dedication to sports/maintaining my figure

What I've Gained

- how to live in the here and now
- easier for me to get along with others I've fought with since I don't remember the past at time of interaction
- more compassion
- more humility

- learned a lot about the brain/understand from deeper position of experience/gained new perspective on others
- another personality/coming back a different person after a long struggle
- grateful able to live two different lives
- changed my perspective
- a re-prioritization of work in my life
- learned a lot about disability—how the workplace/others treat you, how to manage it, got a lot of perspective!
- appreciation for all I've done prior to accident and for all I could do
- not in God's power to stop bad things from happening
- new perspectives on medical profession—many doctor's do not understand brain injury, medically could not cure me and even diagnostic tools were too rough to pick up fine damage
- working from home as an option
- spending more time with cats
- renewed interest in walking
- new interests: cooking, crosswords and classical music
- a new favorite shopping item: shoes

What I Can Work On

- nursing self back to health
- put together a work plan
- take a vacation by plan
- develop more habits/procedures to reduce embarrassing situations
- get into habit of saying "this seems okay now, but let me check notes to confirm"
- get into habit of keeping separate things separate
- get into habit of always preparing for every situation no matter how small
- get into habit of writing everything down and organizing
- push self to do things by writing them down and scheduling/rescheduling
- walking
- talking to more brain-injured people
- preparation to see if I can fly—take train ride and try motion sickness reduction pills
- purge music no longer listen to (glad I didn't give away my CD collection because years later I could listen to and did like the music again)
- push my limits—more social interaction; more assignments at work; once able, more local driving at night; more meetings (all of these were bad ideas at the one-year mark because they incapacitated me afterward)

Glossary

I have selected and defined key terms and spelled out acronyms applicable to mild traumatic brain injury (MTBI) cases. Where appropriate, I've provided information beyond what would be in a standard definition to point out the relevance of the term to MTBI.

ADD. Attention Deficit Disorder.

agnosia. Reduction in ability to interpret sensory input. See also **anosognosia; memory; prosopagnosia; topographagnosia.**

amnesia. Inability to recall past experiences. A person with an MTBI might experience amnesia because of: memory storage problems; degradation of memories; distractibility, inattentiveness or emotionality during retrieval; medications, alcohol or drugs. See also **anterograde/posttraumatic amnesia; memory; retrograde amnesia.**

anosognosia. Failure to recognize one's own illness.

anterograde/posttraumatic amnesia. Inability to recall the trauma itself or events which happen afterward. This type of amnesia impairs learning. See also **amnesia.**

aphasia. Difficulty using language to express oneself or to understand another. See also **conductive aphasia; expressive aphasia; receptive aphasia.**

BI. Brain Injury.

BIAI. Brain Injury Association of Illinois.

brain. An organ in the vertebrate central nervous system responsible for thought and neural coordination.

brain plasticity. The brain's ability to use working brain cells in novel ways to compensate for injured cells.

brain SPECT scan. Single Photon Emission Computed Tomography scan of the brain. A nurse injects the patient with a radioactive chemical which stays in the bloodstream while a photon detector array collects data on the brain's blood supply. The results, cross-sectional brain slices in multiple colors, can show if blood flow, and hence brain function, has been compromised. PET scan pictures, although fuzzy, are clearer than SPECT scan pictures, but the SPECT scan is less expensive and more readily available than the PET scan.

Patients of reproductive age must weigh the impacts of these radioactive tests with their doctors. See also **medical tests of brain damage; PET scan.**

Broca's aphasia. See **expressive aphasia.**

CAT scan. Computerized Axial Tomography scan, or CT scan. When performed as a medical test of brain damage, a series of x-rays capture cross-sectional pictures of the brain's surface. The pictures can show swelling or bleeding of the brain, or a mass in the brain. MTBI patients usually have normal CAT scan results. See also **medical tests of brain damage; MRI.**

CDC. Centers for Disease Control.

cognitive flexibility. Ability to switch from performing one task to performing a different task.

concussion. Blow to or jarring of the head which impairs brain functionality, possibly only for a short period of time. Loss of consciousness may or may not occur.

conductive aphasia. Word finding and word repetition problems while expressing oneself. See also **aphasia.**

coup/contrecoup injury. Trauma in which the forward moving head strikes an object or rapidly decelerates (coup) and recoils backward (contrecoup), causing brain damage at opposite ends of the brain.

diffuse axonal injury. Trauma in which powerful forces rotate the head, causing brain cells to stretch, twist and tear. This type of injury is not localized, but scattered throughout the brain.

EEG. ElectroEncephaloGram. Measures frequencies of brain waves, which can show brain seizures or abnormal cell growth. MTBI patients usually have normal EEG results. See also **medical tests of brain damage.**

ENG. ElectroNystagmoGraphy. Tracks movement of the eyes under varying conditions. Results can show if an inner ear problem is causing dizziness or imbalance.

epilepsy. Seizure disorder. MTBI patients with epilepsy typically experience staring, hyperactivity or loss of inhibition.

expressive aphasia or Broca's aphasia. Coherency or fluency problems while expressing oneself. See also **aphasia.**

figure-ground disturbance. Difficulty picking out relevant sounds, sights, tastes, and/or smells from extraneous ones.

headache. See **posttraumatic headache; tension headache.**

hypochondria. Persistent anxiety about imaginary ailments.

illness. An unhealthy condition of body or mind.

intracranial pressure. Excessive pressure on the skull from an excess of blood or water in the brain.

long-term/secondary memory. Information stored in the brain for longer than one minute. A person with an MTBI might not store short-term remembered information in long-term memory because of: inability to recognize emotional significance or importance of information, organization problems (such as, lack of rehearsal), attention/concentration problems, comprehension problems, pain, fatigue, medications, alcohol or drugs. See also **memory.**

medical tests of brain damage. A neurologist who suspects brain damage usually orders an EEG to check for brain seizures, neuropsychological testing to check cognitive performance, and one of the following tests: a CAT scan or MRI to check for tissue damage of the brain, or a brain SPECT scan or PET scan to check the brain's blood flow. In 2004 or 2005, the PET/CT fusion, a hybrid test, and the MRS, a check on the brain's chemical levels, may also become available. See also **brain SPECT scan; CAT scan; EEG; MRI; MRS; neuropsychological tests; PET/CT fusion; PET scan.**

medical test of ear damage. See **ENG.**

memory. Has three stages: *registration, storage* and *retrieval. Registration* is a sensory awareness of the environment and a person's perception of it. *Storage* involves how long a person can hold information: for a second, for up to a minute, and for longer than a minute. *Retrieval* is a person's ability to recall what is stored. A person with an MTBI might not *register* information because of: blackouts, impairments to any of the five senses, attention/concentration problems including distractibility and inability to focus on more than one item at a time, fatigue, medications, alcohol or drugs. See also **agnosia; amnesia; long-term/secondary memory; sensory/immediate memory; short-term/working memory.**

MRI. Magnetic Resonance Imaging. When performed as a medical test of brain damage, magnetic fields and radio waves capture cross-sectional pictures that can show damage to the brain's structure. The MRI, which depicts deeper sections of brain than the CAT scan, is more sensitive to brain contusions—bruising, swelling or hemorrhaging—than the CAT scan. MTBI patients usually have normal MRI results. See also **CAT scan; medical tests of brain damage.**

MRS. Magnetic Resonance Spectroscopy. In 2003, the MRS was a new research tool. Used in combination with the MRI, the MRS measures chemical levels in gross areas of the brain. See also **medical tests of brain damage; PET scan.**

MTBI. Mild Traumatic Brain Injury.

neurologist. Doctor trained in diagnosing and treating nervous system disorders. This physician also oversees the patient's case—recommending surgeons, neuropsychologists, physical therapists, rehabilitation specialists and other appropriate specialists.

neuro-ophthalmologist. Doctor who specializes in visual problems stemming from the nervous system.

neuropathic pain. Shooting or searing pain due to a dysfunctional nervous system. For brain injury patients, the problem may exist in the thalamus, is usually worsened by minor skin irritations, and may last for a year or more.

neuropsychological tests. A series of written, verbal and physical standardized exams. Results can indicate cognitive performance in areas such as, abstract reasoning, short-term and long-term memory, visual-motor coordination, planning ability and others.

neuropsychologist. A psychologist, trained in anatomy, physiology and pathology of the nervous system, specializing in brain-related behavioral problems.

PET/CT fusion. A new technology in late 2001 that combines the PET scan and the CT scan. The CT component brings picture clarity and the PET component captures more abnormalities than would have been discovered by the CT scan alone. See also **CAT scan; medical tests of brain damage; PET scan.**

PET scan. Positron Emission Tomography scan. When performed as a medical test of brain damage, a nurse injects the patient with a radioactive glucose solution which infiltrates the brain. Then the PET scan, a receiver, collects data on the brain's activity. The results, a snapshot of the brain in multiple colors, can point to regional abnormalities and blood flow problems and can detect some chemicals, such as dopamine and serotonin. See also **brain SPECT scan; medical tests of brain damage; MRS.**

phonophobia. Atypical noise sensitivity.

photophobia. Atypical light sensitivity.

posttraumatic headache. Caused by head injury, a type of headache which may last for a year or longer.

prosopagnosia. Face recognition difficulty. See also **agnosia.**

psychopharmacologist. Doctor trained in prescribing medication to treat neurological, psychological and behavioral problems.

receptive aphasia or Wernicke's aphasia. Language interpretation and comprehension problems. See also **aphasia.**

retrograde amnesia. Inability to recall information/events learned/remembered prior to brain damage, such as forgetting events from a specific period of time or unlearning certain types of information. See also **amnesia.**

sensory/immediate memory. Information stored in the brain for a second. See also **memory.**

short-term/working memory. Information stored in the brain for up to a minute. A person with an MTBI might not store registered information in short-term memory because of: attention/concentration problems, comprehension problems, rapidity of incoming information, sensory overload, pain, fatigue, medications, alcohol or drugs. See also **memory.**

SPECT scan. See brain **SPECT scan.**

TBI. Traumatic Brain Injury.

tension headache. Prevalent in whiplash cases, a head pressure caused by muscle tension.

tinnitus. Constant ringing in the ears.

topographagnosia. Difficulty reading maps/floor plans and finding places. See also **agnosia.**

Wernicke's aphasia. See **receptive aphasia.**

whiplash injury. Neck injury of muscles, tendons and ligaments, possibly pinching nerves and/or rippling the upper back, face and jaw muscles in spasm. Caused by a sudden jerking of the head.

Notes

Chapter 4: Diagnosed

1. Brain Injury Association of Illinois, "Traumatic Brain Injury Facts" (Posted Facts at the Annual Meeting of the Brain Injury Association of Illinois, Lisle, IL, 3 October 2003).
2. Merriam-Webster, Inc., *Webster's Collegiate® Dictionary*, 11th ed. (Springfield, Massachusetts: Merriam-Webster, Inc., 2005), http://www.Merriam-Webster.com (accessed November 10, 2005).

Chapter 6: The Evacuation Upstairs

1. Hansard Reporting and Interpretation Services, "Standing Committee on Justice and Social Policy," Legislative Assembly of Ontario, June 4, 2002, http://www.ontla.on.ca/hansard/committee_debates/37-parl/Session3/justice/J001.htm (accessed October 31, 2003).

Chapter 8: Brain Images and Waves

1. Departments of Neurology and Otolaryngology, "Dizziness and Imbalance" (Handout from Northwestern Memorial Hospital, Chicago, IL, 1996).
2. Brain Injury Association of America Poster, (Handout at the Annual Meeting of the Brain Injury Association of Illinois, Lisle, IL, 5 October 1996).

Chapter 12: The Winds of Autumn

1. Stoler and Hill, *Coping with Mild Traumatic Brain Injury*, 33.
2. Damasio, *Looking for Spinoza*, 270-271.

Chapter 14: Subtraction of Self

1. Damasio, *Looking for Spinoza*, 152, 153.

Chapter 16: Guidelines to Return to Work

1. Nancy Mairs, *Waist-High in the World: A Life Among the Nondisabled* (Boston: Beacon Press, 1996), 71.
2. U.S. Department of Labor, "The Americans with Disabilities Act of 1990," http://www.dol.gov/esa/regs/statutes/ofccp/ada.htm (accessed June 25, 2004).

Selected Bibliography

Because a full bibliography is too unwieldy, I list here only the main sources relied upon to research this book.

Brain Injury Association of America, *TBI Challenge!* 6 (2003).

Brain Injury Association of America. http://www.biausa.org/pages/home.html.

Centers for Disease Control and Prevention. http://www.cdc.gov.

Chudler, Eric H. "Neuroscience for Kids." University of Washington, http://faculty.washington.edu/chudler/neurok.html.

Colligan, Robert C., David Osborne, Wendall M. Swenson, and Kenneth P. Offord. *The MMPI: A Contemporary Normative Study.* New York: Praeger Publishers, 1983.

Damasio, Antonio. *Looking for Spinoza: Joy, Sorrow, and the Feeling Brain.* New York: Harcourt, 2003.

"'Hidden Danger' of Brain Damage," Health, *BBC News*, August 1, 1998, http://news.bbc.co.uk/1/hi/health/143416.stm.

Howard, Pierce J. *The Owner's Manual for the Brain: Everyday Applications from Mind-Brain Research.* Austin: Leornian Press, 1994.

Igou, Steven. "Traumatic Brain Injury Information Resource." http://www.braininjury.com.

Keller, Julia. "The Broken Brain." Three part series. Tempo, *Chicago Tribune*, sec. 5, December 17, 2003-December 19, 2003.

Letarte, Peter B., MD. "Improving the Lives of Persons with Brain Injury and Scanning the Spectrum of Care: A Neurosurgeon's Perspective." Presentation at the Annual Meeting of the Brain Injury Association of Illinois, Lisle, IL, 3 October 2003.

Lohrasbi, John, MD. "Neuropsychiatric Aspects and Treatment of Traumatic Brain Injury." Presentation at the Annual Meeting of the Brain Injury Association of Illinois, Lisle, IL, 3 October 2003.

Miranti, Vincent and Rachel S. Hitch, "Improving Interpersonal Skills and Conflict Resolution for TBI Survivors." Presentation at the Annual Meeting of the Brain Injury Association of Illinois, Lisle, IL, 4 October 1996.

National Institute of Neurological Disorders and Stroke. "Disorders." http://www.ninds.nih.gov/disorders/disorder_index.htm.

Prigatano, George P. "Disturbances in Self-Awareness After TBI: Importance for Diagnosis and Rehabilitation." Presentation at the Annual Meeting of the Brain Injury Association of Illinois, Lisle, IL, 5 October 1996.

Prigatano, George P. "Mechanisms of Recovery following TBI: A Neuropsychologist's Perspective." Presentation at the Annual Meeting of the Brain Injury Association of Illinois, Lisle, IL, 5 October 1996.

Ramachandran, V. S., MD, and Sandra Blakeslee. *Phantoms in the Brain: Probing the Mysteries of the Human Mind.* New York: William Morrow and Company, 1998.

South Carolina Department of Disabilities and Special Needs. *Head Injury: A Family Guide*, South Carolina State Government, http://www.state.sc.us/ddsn/pubs/hinjury/sec1.htm.

Stoler, Diane Roberts, and Barbara Albers Hill. *Coping with Mild Traumatic Brain Injury: A Guide to Living with the Problems Associated with Brain Trauma.* Illus. William Gonzalez. Garden City Park, New York: Avery Publishing Group, 1998.

Stone, Andy. "After the Accident." *Forbes*, August 16, 2004.

Time-Life Books. *Mind and Brain: Journey through the Mind and Brain.* Alexandria: Time-Life Books, 1993.

Winslade, Willaim J. *Confronting Traumatic Brain Injury: Devastation, Hope, and Healing.* New Haven: Yale University Press, 1998.

Young, James, MD. "Pharmacologic and Alternative Treatment in Brain Injury." Presentation at the Annual Meeting of the Brain Injury Association of Illinois, Lisle, IL, 3 October 2003.

978-0-595-38351-1
0-595-38351-3